T0203269

Software Architecture 2

# Software Architecture 2

Edited by
Mourad Chabane Oussalah

*Series Editor*
*Jean-Charles Pomerol*

WILEY

The rights of Mourad Chabane Oussalah to be identified as the author of this work have been asserted by him in accordance with the Copyright, Designs and Patents Act 1988.

Library of Congress Control Number: 2014934512

British Library Cataloguing-in-Publication Data
A CIP record for this book is available from the British Library
ISBN 978-1-84821-688-4

Printed and bound in Great Britain by CPI Group (UK) Ltd., Croydon, Surrey CR0 4YY

# Table of Contents

Chapter 1

# Metamodeling in Software Architectures

To manage the complexity of systems and enhance their understanding, different modeling techniques (e.g. object-oriented, component-based and services-oriented software architectures) often define two or more modeling levels using the definition of a metamodel, or even a meta-metamodel to explain, comment, document, simplify, create and compare models.

In this chapter, we intend to emphasize the importance of metamodeling in the context of software architecture compared to the metamodeling in the object paradigm. This concept helps to abstract architectural concepts (components, connectors and configurations) and facilitate handling, using and reusing, analyzing and developing software architectures.

## 1.1. Introduction

During the last two decades, several languages for describing software architectures have been proposed to promote the development of architecture-focused applications. These languages provide, in general, formal or semi-formal notations for describing and analyzing software systems. They are usually accompanied by tools to analyze, simulate and, sometimes, to generate the code of the modeled systems. The consensus on the fundamental concepts that architecture description languages (ADLs) must include was achieved relatively late; however, through the efforts of

Chapter written by Adel SMEDA and Mourad Chabane OUSSALAH.

standardization and interoperability, new ADLs (known as second generation ADLs) were introduced.

Moreover, it is proved that the specification of an architecture may go through several levels of modeling, thus reflecting different categories of users (application architects, application developers, builders of software infrastructure, etc., see Chapter 3). One of the most appropriate techniques to highlight these different levels of modeling is metamodeling and, more precisely, the software architecture modeling frame that implements the four levels of modeling proposed by the Object Management Group (OMG) [OMG 03]. The highest level is represented by the meta-object facility (MOF) meta-metamodel [MOF 02]. The goal of MOF is to define a single standard language for describing metamodels. It consists of a relatively small set (although not minimal) of "object" concepts for modeling this type of information. For example, unified modeling language (UML) is one of the metamodels described using MOF. Other notations for object metamodeling also exist, including KM3 [JOU 06], ECORE [BUD 08] and Kermeta [MUL 05].

In software architecture field, very few works have adopted the technique of metamodeling. Architecture Meta-Language (AML) [WIL 99] is the first attempt to offer a base that provides ADLs with a solid semantic base. AML only defines the statements of three basic constructions: components, types and relationships.

In this chapter, we propose an approach to model software architectures at different levels of abstraction using a meta-metamodel called Meta Architecture Description Language (MADL) [SME 05a].

In this context, MADL, like MOF, works as a unified solution for architectural representations. In addition, it allows easy handling, using, reusing and developing of software architectures. It reduces the complexity of software architectures and facilitates the transformation and transition of architectures from one to another. In addition, this meta-metamodel has a minimal core whose purpose is to define the concepts and basic relations, such as metacomponents, metaconnectors and metainterfaces. Based on this meta-metamodel, we describe a strategy for mapping of ADL concepts to UML concepts (particularly UML 2.0). We used UML as an example of mapping because of its popularity in the industrial world. This strategy is carried out in four steps: instantiating MADL by the selected ADL, mapping

MADL to MOF, instantiating MOF by UML and, finally, the selection of the most appropriate UML concepts for the selected ADL. This strategy reduces the number of concepts obtained. As an example, we will show how to map the ADL Acme [GAR 00] to UML 2.0.

## 1.2. Metamodeling, why?

An act of metamodeling has the same objective as an act of modeling with the only difference in the modeling purpose. In all cases, it involves supporting all or part of the lifecycle of a model: (formal or informal) specification, design and implementation. In the case of reflexive models, metamodeling makes it able for models to describe themselves.

We distinguish three different views of metamodeling [BOU 97]:

– Metamodeling as a reflexive technique: metamodeling is an act of modeling applied to a model. It can allow a model to self-represent itself: we refer to this as reflective models.

– Metamodeling as a technical dialogue: a picture is worth a thousand words. This technique is increasingly used to explain, comment upon, document and compare models (in particular semi-formal models used in design methods). It is concerned with describing a model by its conceptual concepts, the result of this is a specification step using a semi-formal (most of the time) metamodel. This mapping therefore constitutes an explanatory document and/or documentation of the model. It can also serve as a means of comparison and unification of models.

– Metamodeling as technical engineering: this is concerned with documenting, explaining and unifying "semi-formal" models. Natural languages, if not so ambiguous, could be used as a metamodel. This is not the case in an objective to support model engineering. It means applying our own engineering techniques to our models. We can model a model for the same reason as application systems are modeled.

## 1.3. Software architecture metamodeling

Metamodeling techniques have now reached maturity and have been widely used to address real problems in programming languages, databases, engineering models or distributed systems. In this chapter, we will show how these techniques can be applied to the field of software architecture. We will also highlight the need to propose mechanisms of reflexivity in the context of software architectures metamodeling.

In knowledge representation, we talk about meta-knowledge to evoke knowledge about knowledge, metamodel for a model representing a model, etc. [OUS 02]. In the context of software architectures, metamodeling is an act of modeling applied to the architecture. The result of an act of modeling, i.e. using an architecture to establish an abstraction of an application architecture, is called architecture (level A1 in Figure 1.1) the A0 application. Similarly, the meta-architecture of an architecture itself is an architecture that models an architecture. Since the act of modeling applies to software architectures, the process is called meta-architecting. A meta-architecture is therefore a formal or semi-formal ADL that allows the modeling of particular systems, namely architectures. The meta-architecture (level A2) is an architecture itself and therefore, in a more general way, a system can thus be modeled. We then obtain the architecture of the meta-architecture: meta-meta-architecture (level A3). As with any recurring modeling, this process should stop on a reflexive architecture, that is self-description. The number of levels makes little difference, but it seems that three levels of modeling are sufficient in an architecture engineering framework where level A3 will be used to self-model and model ADLs.

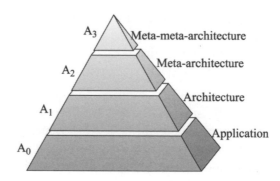

**Figure 1.1.** *Four levels of modeling in software architectures*

In the context of object-oriented models, this self-modeling is generally implemented by the concept of a metaclass that guarantees the uniformity of concepts and extensibility of the system. This involves designing an architecture by itself or using an architecture to describe or design another architecture.

Metamodeling can also be a means of formalizing semi-formal architectures. Formal ADLs based on mathematical forms ensure unambiguous specification. However, these formal ADLs may seem repulsive to application designers, and they are not easily understood by an untrained person. It is therefore useful to be capable of carrying out transcription of a semi-formal specification using a formal specification. The approach is to specify, once and for all, the concepts of semi-formal architecture in a formal specification. We then obtain a meta-architecture of the semi-formal architecture, which can be used directly. The formal architecture is used as a meta-architecture and produces the meta-architecture of the informal architecture.

To summarize, we can say that the meta-architecture is a good way to:

– Standardize: architectures that are based on well-defined semantics. These semantics are provided through meta-architectures. Each architecture must conform to a meta-architecture, which shows how to define architectures. The description of different architectures using the same meta-architecture gives the meta-architecture a standardization role.

– Use and reuse: the same meta-architecture can be used and reused several times to define new architectures.

– Compare: the meta-architecture is a good tool to compare several architectures. In fact, the description of several architectures with the same formalism facilitates comparison and analysis.

– Define and integrate multiple architectures: the meta-architecture facilitates and supports exchange of architectures between the ADLs.

## 1.4. MADL: a meta-architecture description language

### 1.4.1. *Four levels of modeling in software architectures*

The four levels of OMG metamodeling [MOF 02] (see Table 1.1) can be applied to software architecture. The result is a conceptual structure of four levels: meta-meta-architecture level, meta-architecture level, architecture level and application level, as shown in Table 1.1:

– The meta-meta-architecture level ($M^2A$, denoted as level A3): this provides the minimum components of modeling architecture. The basic concepts of an ADL are represented at this level (e.g. metacomponent and a metaconnector in Figure 1.2).

– The meta-architecture level (MA, denoted as level A2): this provides the basic modeling components for an ADL – component, connector, architecture, ports, roles, etc. These basic concepts are used to define different architectures. Meta-architectures conform to the meta-meta-architectures. As part of a conformity relation, each element of MA is associated with an element of $M^2A$. For example, in Figure 1.2, component is associated with metacomponent.

– The architecture level (known as level A or A1): at this level, several types of components, connectors and architectures are described. Architectures comply with meta-architectures (ADL); therefore, each element of A is associated with an element of MA. For example, in Figure 1.2, the client and server are components, the RPC is a connector and the client-server is a system.

– The application level ($A_0$): $A_0$ is the place where the executive bodies are located. An application is seen as a set of instances of types of components, connectors and architectures. Applications are consistent with an architecture. Each element $A_0$ is associated with an element of A. For example, in Figure 1.2, CL1 is an instance of client, S1 is an instance of server, RPC1 is an instance of RPC and C-S is an instance of client-server.

| | Modeling by objects | Modeling by components |
|---|---|---|
| The meta-metamodel at M3 level | MOF | MADL |
| The meta-metamodel at M2 level | UML, CWM, SPEM, etc. | Acme, COSA, UniCon, C2, Fractal, etc. |
| The model at M1 level | Models | Architectures |
| The instance at M0 level | Information | Applications |

**Table 1.1.** *The four conceptual levels in object-oriented modeling and component-oriented modeling*

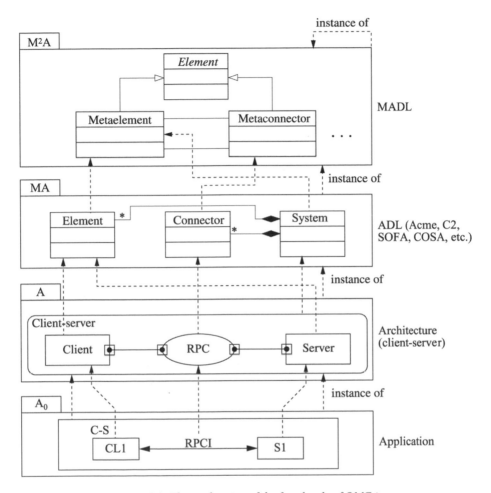

**Figure 1.2.** *The application of the four levels of OMG in software architecture*

### 1.4.2. *MADL: reflexive core dedicated to the meta-meta-architecture*

In this section, we describe the entities that are essential to precisely define a reflexive meta-meta-architecture dedicated to metamodeling. This meta-meta-architecture, like the MOF, functions as a unified solution of representing architectures. It also needs to define a minimum core whose purpose is to define the concepts and the following basic relations:

– meta-element to define components and compotation units;

– metaconnector to define connectors and associations;

– meta-architecture to define architectures and configurations;

– metainterface to define interfaces.

MADL is a "reflexive" model, i.e. it models itself. This provision is intended to end the "stacking" of architecture models, i.e. the use of an architectural model to model the considered architecture model. In theory, such a process can be infinite.

### 1.4.3. MADL structure

The meta-meta-architecture must be a minimum core whose purpose is to define the components of meta-meta-architecture, which in its part defines the element types for meta-architectures. It introduces the concepts of metacomponents, metaconnectors, metainterfaces and meta-architectures that are required to process and define the architectural concepts (structural and behavioral). These metaconcepts are organized in a meta-meta-architecture called MADL, shown in Figure 1.3 [SME 05a, SME 05b].

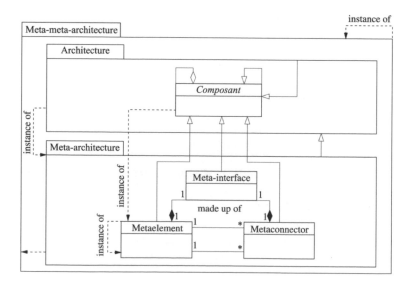

**Figure 1.3.** *MADL structure*

Some basic principles about the structure of MADL are the following:

– MADL is component oriented in the sense that everything is a component (all components are subtypes of the abstract class "Component"), as in the MOF where everything is subclass of the abstract class "modelElement". We consider that the component is the basic architectural entity of the model.

– Each architecture must be explicitly derived from a meta-architecture; thus, all components of an architecture component are derived from the meta-architecture.

– To remain compatible with the four conceptual levels of the OMG, each architecture is an instance of its superior architecture (its meta) including the meta-meta-architecture, which is an instance of itself.

– Dependencies between architectures and components are based on the dependencies used in the model of the OMG, including instantiation, inheritance and composition. Thus, we do not introduce new relationships.

MADL is organized into three packages:

– The meta-meta-architecture package: to define an architecture we need a meta-architecture, and to define a meta-architecture we need a meta-meta-architecture. Hence, the meta-meta-architecture package reflects the fact that any architecture is derived from a meta-architecture. The meta-meta-architecture package has all the concepts needed to define meta-architectures and architectures. Meta-meta-architecture is not consistent with another architecture, but it acts as its own meta-architecture. Similarly, each element of a meta-meta-architecture must be combined with another element of a meta-meta-architecture, to meet the self-consistent relationship, except the meta-meta-architecture package, which is an instance of itself.

– The meta-architecture package: to define architectures, we need a meta-architecture; thus, the meta-architecture package classifies and defines architectures. Architectures contain components and connectors. Therefore, meta-element and metaconnector are components of the meta-architecture package. Accordingly, each component and each connector at the MA level must be part of an architecture at the MA level. Meta-architecture itself is an architecture; therefore, meta-architecture inherits the architecture package. To allow architectures at the MA level to have interfaces, meta-architecture also includes metainterface within its components. Meta-architecture is consistent with the definition of meta-meta-architecture, that is, it is an instance of meta-meta-architecture. The meta-architecture package contains the following metacomponents:

- Meta-element: this is an architectural metaelement that classifies and defines constructors for the computing and support units at the MA level. Meta-element is a component, so it inherits from the component class of the architecture package. Meta-element is a part of the meta-architecture package. To respect the principle of reflexivity upon which the MADL is based, meta-element is an instance of itself;

- Metaconnector: this is an architectural meta-element that classifies and defines constructors for the interactions at the MA level. Metaconnector is part of the meta-architecture package;

- Metainterface: this is an architectural meta-element that classifies and defines interfaces. Meta-element, metaconnector and meta-architecture may have metainterfaces to allow the definition of interfaces for components, connectors and architectures at the MA level. We assign a metainterface to architecture for enabling architectures at the MA level to communicate with other architectures or components. Moreover, metainterface can be composed of another architecture and can inherit other architectures.

– The architecture package: software architecture components are part of architectures; also MADL components are part of the MADL architecture package. The principle on which the MADL is built, "everything is a component", is applied to the architecture package. Thus, the architecture package inherits components. Note that this relationship is a conceptual relationship. Therefore, architectures at the MA level behave like components, i.e. they can communicate and have a relationship of composition, and inheritance architecture is an instance of meta-architecture. Architecture consists of the abstract class component that classifies and defines all components of MADL. Therefore, all components of MADL are inherited, directly or indirectly (the principle of "everything is a component") from the component class. Components and connectors at the MA level may be generalizable and specializable, and they can also be composed of other components. This justifies the existence of the inheritance relationship and the relationship of the composition between the component class and itself, and thus allows components at the MA level to have these relationships. The component class is a part of the architecture package, and each element at the MA level must be part of an architecture.

### 1.4.4. *MADL instantiation: example of the ADL Acme*

The definition of a meta-architecture can be approached in two ways:

– In the first definition: "a meta-architecture is considered as an architecture whose instances are architectures". This definition fits well within the paradigm of object-oriented languages. According to this definition, MADL can be considered as a MADL allowing the creation of concepts of languages such as Acme and C2. Based on this definition, a meta-architecture can help create architectures by instantiation like in object-oriented languages.

– In the second definition: "a meta-architecture is a representation of an architecture made with an architecture model". This definition is applied to designate the representation of an Acme architecture made with an extension of a MADL meta-architecture. Thus, for example, the "Meta-element" Acme modeled with MADL represents all components that can be created with Acme such as client components and servers. Based on this definition, a meta-architecture is derived from an architecture by representation operation.

The above two definitions of a meta-architecture are based on two operations:

– instantiation: operation that helps create architectures from a meta-architecture;

– representation of an architecture: operation that helps create a meta-architecture from an architecture.

To define a new meta-architecture (new ADL), MADL is instantiated, and a new model consistent with the definition of MADL is obtained. Each element of the meta-architecture is an instance of an element MADL. For example, the components and notations related to computation are instances of meta-element; components and notations related to interaction and communication are instances of metaconnector. Thus, for example, components, properties and constraints are instances of meta-element, while connectors, bindings and attachments are instances of metaconnector.

Figure 1.4 shows how MADL can be instantiated to obtain Acme. As shown in this figure, each Acme element must conform to an element of MADL. Components and systems are instances of meta-element; connectors

are instances of metaconnector; ports and roles are instances of
metainterface; attachments (which connect a port to a role) and bindings
(which connect two ports or two roles) are instances of metaconnector.
Similarly, styles (which define families of systems) are instances of meta-
architecture.

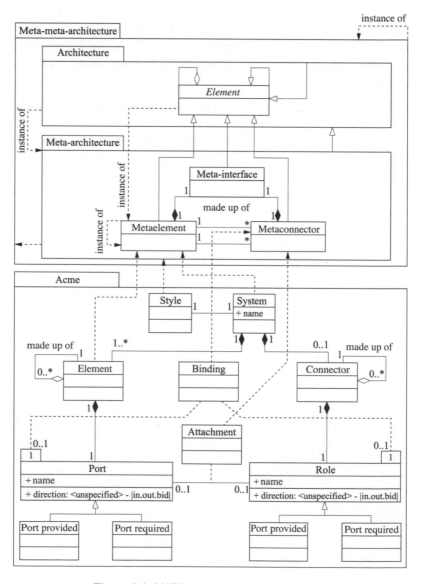

**Figure 1.4.** *MADL instantiation to obtain Acme*

### 1.4.5. *Comparison of MADL and MDA/MOF*

In this section, we will try to position MADL compared to the MDA (model-driven architecture [FRA 03]) approach and to MOF.

#### 1.4.5.1. *Model-driven architecture (MDA) approach*

The MDA approach was proposed by the OMG. It is presented as a product in line with the OMG's concerns of integration and interoperability ("ensure that you can incorporate what you've built, with what you are building, with what you will build" [FRA 03]).

MDA provides a response to the complexity of middleware. These middleware can be "standard" such as CORBA, DCOM or "somewhere in between" (JMI or HTTP/XML/SOAP) [TRA 05]. The idea of MDA is to provide a "stable", independent model for middleware, from which it is possible to derive different tools. The objective is to build the model and use/reuse it instead of constantly migrating one middleware to another. The MDA is based on the OMG modeling standards: UML, CWM and MOF.

In fact, MDA offers several core models, corresponding to the M2 level of the four levels of metamodeling architecture. According to the terminology of the OMG, these models are also called "UML Profiles". They are dedicated to a class of problems, such as Enterprise computing or Real-Time computing. These models are independent of any platform. Their number is expected to grow to cover other needs. However, it is intended to be relatively unimportant because everyone wants to be "general" and includes features common to all problems in its category.

The UML profile is the foundation of the MDA approach, which explains the use of the equivalent term "core model". Below, we give an overview of the concept of the UML profile. At present, there is no standard definition of the UML profile. However, it is widely accepted that a UML profile is a specification consistent with one or more of the following points:

– Identification of a subset of the UML metamodel: this subset can be the entire UML metamodel;

– Definition of well-formalized rules, in addition to those contained in the subset of the UML metamodel: a *well-formalized rule* is a term used in the standardized specification of the UML metamodel. Such rules help describe a set of constraints in natural language (or using the Object Constraint Language (OCL)) to define an element of the metamodel;

– Definition of standard components (standard components) in addition to those contained in the subset of the UML metamodel: a *standard element* is a term used in the specification of the UML metamodel to describe a standard instance of a UML stereotype or a constraint;

– Definition of new semantics expressed in natural languages, in addition to those contained in the subset of the UML metamodel;

– Definition of common components of the model, i.e. instances of UML components, expressed in terms of a profile.

Whatever the target platform (component corba model (CCM), entreprise java bean (EJB), etc.), the first step in developing an MDA-based application is the creation of a Platform Independent Model (PIM) by instantiating the metamodel.

Second, specialists of the target platform are responsible for the conversion of this general application model to CCM, EJB or another platform. Standard mappings, based on the "core model", help consider a partial automation of the conversion.

Not only artifacts specific to the platform are generated (in interface description langage (IDL) and other languages), but also a specific model (Platform-Specific Model (PSM)) is generated in this way. This model is also described using a UML profile. This is called "jargon". Due to the mapping, UML reveals components related to the implementation on the target platform. This gives a richer sense to the semantics of the solution than with IDL or XML.

The next step is the generation of the code itself. The higher the UML of the PSM reflects the target platform, the better the semantics and behavior of the application can be integrated into the PSM, and the code can be generated.

Among the advantages of the MDA approach described by the OMG, we can report the simplicity of managing interoperability between developed applications using the same "core model".

Although the MDA approach is very often associated with profiles, the OMG describes the MDA as a general framework for metamodeling in which the model is considered a first-class entity. Applicable operations to these models (mainly PIM and PSM) are of two kinds:

– Manipulation: this term covers various operations such as storage, exchange, display, derivation, fusion and alignment;

– Mapping (between models): conventionally, we count "PIM2PIM", "PIM2PSM", "PSM2PSM" mappings, etc.

### 1.4.5.2. *Positioning MADL/MDA/MOF*

The MDA approach has a number of advantages. From the general point of view, it combines the advantages of metamodeling and standardization implemented by the OMG. If the number of basic models available is low, it is, however, not fixed. The MDA device is "extensible" through new models, as much as the MDA approach leaves open many challenges. Strictly speaking, the integration activity, the consideration of legacy applications of previous developments and the management of interoperability between middleware are points frequently mentioned by the OMG as a number of avenues to be explored. In addition:

– If the maximum automation of the mapping is a goal, we must consider the use of the "manual" procedure, in the absence of MDA tools.

– At present, the degree of automatic code generation is relatively low.

– The OMG recommends completing the middleware-centered approach by a model-centered approach.

As a result, it is possible to position the MADL as a new MDA base model. More specifically, it involves proposing a new UML profile (PIM) dedicated to software architecture whose originality, besides the fact that it deals with a meta-architecture problem understudied in the ADL, lies in the nature of its specialization. In fact, existing UML profiles are dedicated to an application type (distributed systems, real time, etc.); thus, MADL would be "orthogonal", specialized in a particular activity of modeling ADLs. Being able to represent meta-architectures with MADL with UML notation provides a natural reuse of the graphical UML modeling tools associated with it.

More specifically, the "UML Profile" approach is aimed to extend the UML metamodel by adding new concepts of ADL. This operation is based on the use of stereotypes, tagged values and OCL constraints [WAR 98]. The recognized advantage of this approach is the use of UML tools. The major drawback lies in the difficulty to understand the separation between the meta-meta-architecture ($M^2A$ level), the meta-architecture (MA level) and architecture (level A). The term "dialect UML" is also used to describe this situation.

The OMG proposes another metamodeling approach, which overcomes this problem. This approach is called the "MOF". It involves building a new metamodel binding metaclasses by meta-associations and specifying OCL constraints. It is an alternative to positioning the MADL. This approach is tantamount to depriving de facto the UML tools and in any event has no ADL concepts equipped with independent semantic loads from object-oriented support concepts.

This is usually shown as the main drawback of this approach. At present, the MOF approach is less "popular" than the UML Profile approach. The latter is clearly implemented more frequently.

Currently, some research conducted by the ADL community focuses on the development of "second generation" generic languages. The ADL approach arising from academic circles has not been imposed. It is often criticized for using difficult to implement formal notations and for providing tools that are difficult to process.

Research is thus taking a new direction toward the work of the OMG. These two communities have worked in parallel in recent years; the UML semantics poverty in terms of software architecture concepts probably being the cause (at least partially). Nowadays, the integration of the component concept in UML 2.0 can also be interpreted as a sign of this development and suggests the possibility of defining architectures (based on components) whose passage to the adapted platforms of execution will be facilitated.

We place the MADL in this latest trend. It combines the advantages of the ADL approach and of the MDA/MOF of the OMG approach. From the ADL approach, it retains the concepts and mechanisms inherent to components, connectors and architectures. As for the MDA/MOF approach based on the metamodeling, it has the advantage of being able to consider the models (in our case, architectures, meta-architectures and meta-meta-architectures) as first-class entities, and being able to apply various operations, in particular, mappings enabling the implementation of the system on different execution platforms [ALT 07].

Standardization of architectural concepts around the MADL allows the provision of common functionalities for handling different architectures arising from these different meta-architectures. MADL has therefore been defined as an expression language of meta-architectures. This is its main function, but it can also be used so as to be independent of a particular ADL and to manipulate the architecture of these ADLs.

Concerning the technical point of view of the MADL, we have opted for a MOF-type approach, but one which explicitly responds to the following shortcomings:

– the absence of meta-entities representing meta-architectures;

– the absence of meta-entities representing architectures;

– the absence of meta-entities representing components;

– the absence of meta-entities representing connectors;

– the lack of an explicit relationship between an architecture and its meta-architecture;

– the lack of an explicit relationship between an element and its meta-element, a connector and its metaconnector.

In summary, we can consider MADL as a "new" MOF intended for modeling ADLs and, more importantly, it can be part of the MDA approach.

## 1.5. Mapping of ADLs to UML

Some studies have tried to establish a mapping of an ADL to UML such as Acme to UML and C2 to UML. In this section, we show an approach enabling the mapping of a given ADL to UML 2.0. This method is based on the instantiation of the MADL by ADL, then mapping MADL to MOF and, finally, the instantiation of the MOF by the UML.

### 1.5.1. *Why to map an ADL to UML?*

After the introduction of UML as a unified language for all notations and object-oriented modeling techniques, object-oriented modeling has become a *de facto* standard in the development process of software systems. In fact, UML has become a standard language for specifying, visualizing, constructing and documenting the objects of software systems [BOO 98]. However, UML lacks the semantic support for capturing and exploiting certain architectural aspects whose importance has been demonstrated by software architecture research and practice. In particular, UML lacks direct support for modeling and exploiting connectors, interfaces and architectural styles. However, with the introduction of UML 2.0 [OMG 03], new notations have been proposed and existing ones were modified to meet the needs of software architecture, including:

– the definition of components as a kind of classifier, thus the components may have instances and have access to some mechanisms, such as subtyping by the generalization relationship, behavioral description, internal structure, interfaces and ports;

– the redefinition of interfaces that can include not only interfaces but also the required interfaces;

– the introduction of ports as points of interaction for classifiers;

– the introduction of structured classifiers to represent the internal structure (decomposition) of classifiers;

– the introduction of connectors to represent a connection between two or more instances. However, connectors in UML 2.0 are defined by a simple relationship between two components and thus cannot be associated with a behavioral description or attributes that characterize the connection.

The idea of mapping ADL concepts to UML concepts enables UML to include semantics related to ADLs and also to get the benefit of:

– the variety of advantages of UML such as multiple views, a semiformal semantics expressed in a metamodel, a powerful associated language to express constraints (e.g. OCL [WAR 98]) and a code generation rules;

– a variety of tools that are implemented for UML, such as Rational Rose, Microsoft Visual Studio, Poseidon for UML. Most of these tools provide code generation services in different languages such as C++, Java and C#;

– the widespread presence of UML in the field of modeling and the description of software systems, where UML is a dominant standard for the analysis and design of software systems;

– the MDA approach, which aims to provide an accurate and efficient framework for the production and maintenance of software [FRA 03].

### 1.5.2. *ADL mapping to UML*

Mapping an ADL to UML can be done in two ways: either manually by examining all UML notations and then selecting the appropriate concepts, or semi-automatically by defining a connection between their respective metamodels. In the second strategy, we map the notations of the meta ADL to MOF and, by instantiation, we obtain the correspondence of their respective instances. Figure 1.5 shows the two mapping strategies.

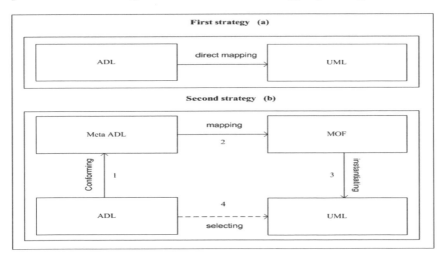

**Figure 1.5.** *The two strategies for mapping an ADL to UML*

### 1.5.2.1. *First mapping strategy (at the meta level)*

This strategy should be considered first because it has the merit of having paved the way to work regarding mapping of ADL to UML. It is based on the review of all connections between the notations and semantics of UML and a given ADL. If appropriate notations are not found, the UML extension mechanisms (stereotypes, tagged values, constraints, etc.) are used (see Figure 1.5(a)). However, this strategy has a number of disadvantages:

– The mapping is done manually. A well-established methodology that guides the process does not currently exist, but some researchers have proposed a number of criteria in order to justify their choices [GAR 02].

– This strategy requires that the entire UML metamodel should be considered for each ADL notation.

– The same long research process takes place every time a new ADL is considered for mapping to UML.

This strategy has been used in several studies. In [MED 02], the authors presented two approaches to support components and architectural notations in UML 1.4. The first approach uses UML notations without changes, "UML as is", while the second approach uses the UML extension mechanisms (stereotypes, tagged values, constraints, etc.) to incorporate the concepts of three ADLs (C2, Wright Fast). The mapping of C2 is shown in Table 1.2 and the mapping of Wright is given in Table 1.3.

In [GAR 02], the authors have tried to select a number of UML 1.4 notations that best represent architectural notations. They stressed the advantages and limitations of each notation and showed aspects of architectural description that are intrinsically difficult to model by UML 1.4. However, UML 1.4 and earlier versions are not adequate enough to represent architectural concepts such as connectors, configurations, interfaces (ports and roles), styles or even components as components in UML 1.4 are representations of a deployable and replaceable system part which encapsulates execution.

UML 2.0 [OMG 03] has been enriched by new architecture concepts such as connectors, ports and structural classifiers and has redefined the concept of components to be a subtype of classes in UML metamodel. Thus, components have an expressive power similar to the classes as they may have interfaces, they can contain other components or classes, etc.

In [GOU 03], the authors considered connectors as stereotyped components without other interfaces than those defined by their roles and properties. However, describing the connectors as components can clutter the design and make it difficult to understand its overall structure and the roles of connector and component ports difficult to distinguish. Mapping Acme to UML 2.0 using this strategy is summarized in Table 1.4.

In [IVE 04], Ivers *et al.* studied the relevance of these new notations to describe the view of components and connectors (C&C) of software architecture, in particular for the Acme language. They examined the mapping of Acme notations that are related to the C&C view (i.e. components, connectors, ports, roles and attachments) to UML 2.0. They chose the semantic connection, visual clarity and support by tools as basic criteria for selecting UML notations, which may represent the architectural description. They offered two choices for each notation (except for attachments that have not been considered) as shown in Table 1.5. They concluded that even if the new notations have improved the description of software architecture using UML, they still have major drawbacks. Moreover, some aspects of architectural description continue to be problematic, for example, the lack of ability of UML 2.0 to associate semantic information with a connector to describe its behavior. Also, UML 2.0 does not distinguish the roles, which are interface connectors, and ports, which are component interfaces.

| C2 | UML 1.4 | OCL/Tagged values |
|---|---|---|
| Component (Type) | <<C2 Component>> (Class metaclass instances) | C2 Component must implement exactly two interfaces. |
| Connector (Type) | <<C2 Connector>> (Class metaclass instances) <br> <<C2 Attach Over Comp>> (Association metaclass instances) <br> <<C2 Attach Under Comp>> (Association metaclass instances) <br> <<C2 Attach Conn Conn>> (Association metaclass instances) | C2 Connector must implement exactly two interfaces. <br> C2 Attachments are binary associations, one end of attachment must be a C2 Component and the other end must be a C2 Connector. |
| Port | <<C2 Interface>> (Interface metaclass instances) | |
| Role | <<C2 Interface>>(Interface metaclass instances) | |
| System | <<C2 Architecture>> (Model metaclass instances <br> <<C2 Attach>> | Architecture is a network of C2 concepts. |
| Message | <<C2 Operation>> (Operation metaclass instances) | C2 Operations are labeled as notifications or requests and as incoming or outgoing. |
| Interface | <<C2 Interface>> | |

**Table 1.2.** *Mapping C2 to UML 1.4 [MED 02]*

| Wright | UML 1.4 | OCL/Tagged values |
|---|---|---|
| Component (Type) | <<WrightComponent>> (Class metaclass instances) | WrightComponent must implement at least one WrightInterface. |
| Connector (Type) | <<WrightConnector>> (Class metaclass instances) <<WrightGlue>> (Operation metaclass instances) | WrightComponent must implement at least one WrightInterface. WrightGlue contains a WrightStateMachine. |
| Port | <<WrightInterface>> (Interface metaclass instances) | |
| Role | <<WrightInterface>> (Interface metaclass instances) | |
| System (Architecture) | <<WrightArchitecture>> (Modelmetaclass instances) <<WrightAttachment>> (Association metaclass instances) <<WrightComponentInstance>> (WrightComponent instances) <<WrightConnectorInstance>> (WrighConnector instances) | Architecture is composed of instances of components and connectors. |
| CSP protocol (state machine) | <<WSMTransition>> (Transitionmetaclass instances) <<WrightState>> (Statemetaclass instances) <<WrightStateMachine>> (StateMachinemetaclass instances) | WSMTransition is labeled as an event or action. All transitions made in a WrightState must be WSMTransitions. |
| Operation | <<WrightOperation>> (Operation metaclass instances) | WrightOperations have no parameters. All operations in a WrightInterface are WrightOperations. |
| Interface | <<WrightInterface>> (Interface metaclass instances) | WrightInterface is labeled as ports or roles. |

**Table 1.3.** *Mapping Wright to UML 1.4 [MED 02]*

| Acme | UML 2.0 | OCL/Tagged values |
|---|---|---|
| Component (Type) | <<AcmeComponent>> | Components only have interfaces known as ports or properties. |
| Connector (Type) | <<AcmeConnector>> | Connectors have no other interfaces than those defined by their roles. |
| Port | Port | Ports can only be used with Acme components and they have a provided interface and a required interface. |
| Role | <<AcmeRole>> | Roles are related to Acme connectors and have a provided interface and a required interface. |
| System | <<AcmeSystem>> | Systems represent a graph of components that communicate with each other. |
| Rep-maps | Delegation connector | All delegation connectors binding ports and roles |
| Properties | <<AcmeProperties>> | <<AcmeProperty>> port has a provided interface that must provide the *get* and *set* operations for the value and the type of property. |
| Constraints | <<AcmeConstraints>> | This stereotype must have an enumerated attribute with two allowed values: invariant and heuristic. |
| Style (Family) | Package | All connectors used in a pipe filter system must comply with PipeT. |

**Table 1.4.** *Mapping Acme to UML 2.0 [GOU 03]*

| Acme | Choice 1 | Choice 2 |
|---|---|---|
| Element (Type) | Object (Class) | Element instance (Element) |
| Connector (Type) | Object binding (Association class) | Object (Class) |
| Port | Port | Port |
| Role | Port | Port |
| Attachment | – | Assembly connector |

**Table 1.5.** *Mapping Acme to UML 2.0 [IVE 04]*

### 1.5.2.2. *Second mapping strategy (at the meta-meta level)*

We believe that the best way to benefit from UML in the field of software architecture is to map the concepts of architectural description to the UML metamodel (certainly without changing the metamodel itself and taking advantage of all its tools and environment). To do this, we propose to establish the connection of architectural concepts and objects at the meta level (MOF) to reduce the number of concepts to be translated and help improve the readability and visibility of different notations at stake. Therefore, we rely on the MADL as meta ADL for software architecture and then map the MADL components to the MOF. In this strategy, the mapping is carried out in four steps [SME 05a]:

– instantiating MADL to obtain the desired ADL (i.e. we want to map to UML);

– mapping each MADL element to an MOF element;

– instantiating each element of the MOF for one or more UML components. At the end of this step, we can obtain more than one choice for each ADL component, but the number of choices is very limited;

– reviewing and selecting the UML concept, which is the most suitable for our ADL, by using appropriate criteria.

The advantages of this strategy are:

– Instead of working with the UML metamodel, we work with the UML meta-metamodel (MOF); therefore, the number of notations and elements that we deal with is considerably less.

– The passage from an ADL to the meta-ADL is natural and inherent, hence quite easy, where the two use coherent architectural elements.

– The passage from MOF to UML already exists and is well defined.

– The selection of the corresponding UML concept is easier when the number of choices is reduced.

However, this strategy requires the definition of a higher level of abstraction for the software architecture, i.e. the metacomponents, the metaconnectors and the metaconfigurations. That is why we use the MADL meta-metamodel.

In the following sections, we will describe the process of mapping an ADL to UML (Figure 1.5(b)).

### 1.5.2.2.1. Instantiating MADL by an ADL

The first step (Figure 1.5(b)) is instantiating MADL by an ADL; each component of the ADL must comply with a component of the MADL. For example, we will try to map Acme to UML 2.0. Figure 1.4 shows how the MADL was instantiated by Acme. Components and systems (which represent configurations of components and connectors), connectors, attachments (which connect a port and role), connections (which connect two ports or two roles), ports and roles (which are the interfaces of components and connectors), styles (which define families of systems) are obtained through successive instantiations of the meta-element, metaconnector, metainterface and meta-architecture. Table 1.6 summarizes the instantiation relationship of the MADL by Acme.

| Acme | MADL |
|---|---|
| Element | Meta-element |
| Connector | Metaconnector |
| System | Meta-element |
| Attachment | Metaconnector |
| Binding (Rep-Map) | Metaconnector |
| Port | Metainterface |
| Role | Metainterface |
| Architectural style | Meta-architecture |

**Table 1.6.** *MADL instantiation by Acme*

### 1.5.2.2.2. Mapping of MADL concepts to MOF

MOF is a meta-metamodel, which is used to define metamodels (e.g. UML). In principle, MOF can be used to define a metamodel for software architecture. However, as we noted earlier, MOF has a number of limitations on the architectural description.

In fact, MOF contains basic concepts to define meta-entities (MOF Class), the metarelations (MOF Association) and packages acting as containers for these meta-entities and metarelations. A meta-architecture described with the MOF for example, will consist of a main package that contains all the MOF definition of the meta-architecture. Therefore, although there is no concept for representing the MOF meta-architectures, a package can be used for this purpose.

A package can therefore be used and generalized to represent a meta-architecture, but nothing can be used to represent an architecture. Therefore, the MOF relationship, which enables binding of an architecture to its meta-architecture, does not exist. In addition, although the concept of the MOF Class may represent the concept of meta element, no concept can be used to represent a component or connector. Therefore, no MOF relationship can be defined between a component and its meta-element or a connector and its metaconnector.

It may be noted that no relationship in the MOF enables the specification that an architecture is defined by a meta-architecture (i.e. all the architectural components of an architecture cannot find their type in that meta-architecture).

For all these reasons, we turned to the definition of MADL, which is equivalent to the MOF for software architecture. In fact, MADL, by construction, includes the concepts and mechanisms of ADLs.

When considering integration strategies, it is important to define a number of criteria to select a notation from several notations. These criteria help determine whether a particular notation is likely to be appropriate or not. The criteria that we selected for our study are:

– the semantic connection: the interpretation chosen by the MOF notations must comply with the homogeneous interpretation of the original description of the MADL;

– expressiveness: all architectural concepts that are defined in the MADL must have the capacity to be represented by the MOF;

– structural connection: mapping (of the topology) of the MADL on the MOF must comply not only to the MADL but also to the MOF;

– compliance with the MOF specification: mapping of the MADL must correspond to specific components of the MOF complying with their definitions.

Each component of the MADL is represented as a subclass component of the MOF, which has a similar semantic. The reason for which we define MADL notations as subclasses of MOF notations is that we do not want to violate the semantic of the MOF by changing its structure with new associations and new notations.

However, if no semantic connection is found, a new component is introduced by stereotyping a subclass. In the following, we map each component of the MADL to its connection in the MOF (see Figure 1.6):

– A component of the MADL is mapped to ModelElement MOF. In MOF, ModelElement is an abstract class that classifies the basic manufacturer's models. It is the root element in the MOF model. Thus, all components of MOF are subclasses of ModelElement. The same principle is applied to the MADL. Component classifies and defines all components and entities of the MADL (MADL is based on the principle that "everything is a component").

– The MADL Architecture is mapped to Namespace MOF. In MOF, Namespace is a subclass of ModelElement. It classifies and characterizes ModelComponents, which may contain other ModelComponents. Namespace contains ModelComponents. Note that in the MADL, the Architecture contains one or more components.

– The meta-element of the MADL can be represented by the MOF class. A class in the MOF defines a classification for a set of instances defining the state and behavior. It is a subclass of class Namespace. A class can be associated with another class. In MADL, meta-element classifies and defines the components that may associate themselves.

– The MOF association is the metaconnector of the MADL. The Association in the MOF defines a classification for a set of bindings through classes. Each binding, which is an instance of the association, denotes a connection between instances of Class. In the MADL, the metaconnector defines connectors that handle relationships between components. The Association is redefined by the composition relationship with the Feature class in order to have connectors with interfaces.

– The metainterface of the MADL is mapped to the MOF Feature class. In the MOF, Feature defines static and dynamic characteristics of ModelElement. Thus, it defines the services offered by ModelElement. The metainterface in the MADL classifies and defines interfaces for components and connectors. These interfaces represent services provided or required by a component or connector.

– The package of the MOF represents the MOF meta-architecture. In the MOF, a package is a container for a collection of ModelComponents that forms a logical metamodel. Packages may consist of and inherit other packages. The meta-architecture classifies and defines the architectures, which are containers of components and connectors, and can compose and inherit other architectures. The definition of the package is redefined; we then have architectures with interfaces and therefore they may be combined with other architectures.

The MADL meta-meta-architecture as a meta-architecture is stereotyped with the following constraints:

– A meta-meta-architecture only contains meta-architectures and architectures.

– A meta-meta-architecture cannot inherit from other meta-meta-architectures.

The relationship of composition between the meta-meta-architecture and Namespace and Package is defined to allow the meta-meta-architecture to contain meta-architectures and architectures.

Figure 1.6 shows the mapping of the MADL concepts and those of the MOF. Even with the introduction of new relationships, the criteria mentioned above are taken into account and respected. Table 1.7 summarizes this mapping.

In this model, only a stereotype and three relationships (relationship of composition between Feature and Class, Feature and Association, Feature and Package) are added to the original model. Note that other studies have stereotyped almost all concepts (see [GOU 03, MED 02]).

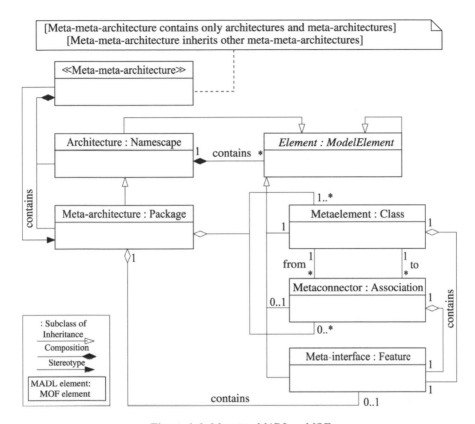

**Figure 1.6.** *Mapping MADL to MOF*

| MADL | MOF |
|---|---|
| Element | ModelElement |
| Meta element | Class |
| Metaconnector | Association |
| Metainterface | Feature |
| Architecture | Namespace |
| Meta-architecture | Package |
| Meta-meta-architecture | Stereotype package |

**Table 1.7.** *Mapping MADL to MOF*

1.5.2.2.3. Instantiation of MOF by UML

The instantiation of the MOF by UML is done automatically using the specifications of the OMG [OMG 03], which describe the instantiation of the MOF by UML. Each element of a UML is an instance of the MOF component including the UML itself. Table 1.8 shows the possible UML instances for each element of MOF. We deduce the following comments regarding the instantiation of the MOF by UML:

– Components and systems can be represented as UML classes, or UML components or stereotyped UML classes.

– Connectors are mapped to UML classes, UML associations, UM association classes or UML communication paths.

| MOF | UML 2.0 |
|---|---|
| Class | Class, Component, Stereotype |
| Association | Class, Association, AssociationClass, CommunicationPath |
| Feature | Interface, Port, Operation, Property, Connector UML |
| Package | Package |

**Table 1.8.** *MOF instantiation*

Associations can be used for connectors defined implicitly (as in Darwin, Fractal, etc.) and classes or association classes, which are statements of semantic relationships, for connectors defined explicitly (as in Wright, Acme, etc.). However, UML communication paths cannot represent ADL connectors because a UML communication path is a physical association that can only be defined between nodes. Therefore, the choice of ADL connectors as UML communication paths is discarded.

ADL interfaces are mapped to UML interfaces, ports, operations, properties or connectors. However, only interfaces, ports and operations may represent the interfaces of software architecture. Other concepts cannot represent interfaces insofar as properties are values denoting a characteristic of a component and the connectors are bindings that allow communication between two or more instances; therefore, this choice is discarded. In addition, ports may represent points of interaction and operations may represent services for the ADLs which separate the services of points of interaction; architectural styles can be represented as UML packages.

### 1.5.2.2.4. Selection of UML 2.0 concepts

The last stage of mapping is the selection of the final concepts. At the end of the instantiation step of the MOF by UML, we obtain a reduced number of choices for each ADL concept and we must choose the concept which is the most representative and which is semantically closest to the concept of the ADL mapped. To do this, the user can define and apply some criteria that will help and guide him in his choices.

### 1.6. A mapping example: the case of the Acme language

Let us take Acme as an example and try to map its concepts to UML 2.0. This example has been studied by Ivers *et al.* [IVE 04] (Table 1.5). Table 1.6 summarizes the mapping of Acme to MADAL. From the table, we can see that Acme components and Acme systems are instances of the MADL meta-element, Acme connectors, bindings and attachments are instances of the MADL metaconnector, Acme ports and roles are instances of the MADL metainterface, and Acme styles are instances of the MADL meta-architecture. Table 1.7 shows that the MADL meta-element is mapped to the MOF class, the MADL metaconnector is mapped to the MOF association, the MADL metainterface is mapped to the MOF Feature class and the MADL meta-architecture is mapped to the MOF package. From Table 1.8, we find that UML classes, components and stereotypes are instances of the MOF class, associations and UML association classes are instances of the MOF association, UML packages are instances of the MOF package and UML ports, operations, properties and connectors are instances of the MOF Feature class.

Therefore, we can deduce that the Acme concepts can be mapped as follows: components and systems to classes, UML components or stereotypes; connectors, bindings and attachments to associations or to UML association classes; Acme styles to UML packages and roles and ports to UML ports or operations. Table 1.9 summarizes the mapping of Acme concepts to UML 2.0.

| Acme | UML 2.0 | Comment |
|---|---|---|
| Element and systems | Class, component, stereotype | The UML components are the most appropriate components to represent the components and systems of Acme. However, stereotyped classes may also represent the Acme components. |
| Connector | Class, Association, AssociationClass | The association classes (AssociationClasses) are the most appropriate components to represent the Acme connectors. Using AssociationClasses, we can define the behavior of connectors and interfaces. |
| Style | Package | Systems and styles can be considered as packages. |
| Port | Interface, Port, Operation | As Acme does not separate the points of interaction of services, UML ports are the most appropriate components to represent the ports and roles of Acme. |
| Role | Interface, Port, Operation | |
| Attachment | Association, AssociationClass | The UML associations represent bindings between classes; they represent the most appropriate components to describe attachments and bindings. |
| Binding (Rep-Map) | Association, AssociationClass | |

**Table 1.9.** *Final mapping step of Acme to UML 2.0*

## 1.7. Some remarks on the mapping of ADL concepts to UML

The mapping of Acme concepts to UML has raised a number of comments and issues concerning the use of UML to describe software architecture.

### 1.7.1. *UML 2.0 as an ADL*

UML 2.0 cannot be considered as an ADL even with new notations and redefinitions. For example, the introduction of connectors to represent a binding between two instances is not sufficient to represent connectors of software architecture. A connector in UML 2.0 remains a simple binding between two components and, therefore, cannot be associated with a behavioral description or attributes that characterize the connection. In general, some software architecture notations are absent in UML 2.0. For example, we can note the absence of entities to represent architectures (configurations) and architectural styles.

### 1.7.2. *Mapping strategies*

The first strategy:

– This strategy has served as a starting point for the mapping of the ADLs to UML. It is based on an evaluation of the entire UML metamodel for each component of the ADL. Also a long research process takes place, every time a new ADL needs to be mapped.

– The mapping is done manually.

The second strategy:

– This strategy can be seen as a mapping methodology dedicated to software architecture.

– Although this strategy leads to a finite number and reduces choices for each component, it has the merit of systematizing the connection and providing better readability and, therefore, a better understanding of concepts. In fact, the first strategy uses the entire UML metamodel, which has a significant number of notations and definitions. In addition, some of these are not related to software architecture.

This strategy proposes a semi-automatic method for mapping any ADL to UML. All components and notations of software architecture are considered in the meta-meta-architecture. Therefore, the model is reusable and can be applied to most existing ADLs. In fact, steps 2 and 3 of this strategy are completely reusable for other ADLs.

The fact that the largest part of the process is carried out at the meta-meta level allows us to work with a reduced number of notations (more than 100 notations for the meta level and 10 notations for the meta-meta level).

In contrast to existing work [IVE 04] on the mapping of ADLs to UML, the second strategy has the advantage of being reusable on different ADLs and of automatically justifying the selected connections.

The process can be used for any version of the UML as it is based on the same version of the MOF.

## 1.8. Conclusion

In this chapter, we have discussed the meta-architecture concept. The meta-architecture of an architecture is an architecture that models an architecture. The meta-architecture being itself an architecture can therefore be modeled. We then obtain the architecture of the meta-architecture, i.e. the meta-meta-architecture. We have also presented a meta-metamodel for software architecture called MADL. This meta-metamodel works as a unified solution for representing software architectures. It makes it possible to structure these architectures, reduces their complexity, facilitates the mapping of architectures and, finally, promotes the passage from one to another.

By using this meta-metamodel, we described a strategy to map ADL concepts to UML 2.0. The mapping of architectural notations to UML is strongly encouraged due to the extensive use of UML in the industrial world. This strategy consists of four steps: instantiating MADL by ADL, mapping MADL to MOF, instantiating MOF by UML and, finally, the selection of the most appropriate UML concepts for the ADL concerned. This strategy reduces the number of concepts obtained. To illustrate this strategy, we have shown how to map the concepts of Acme to UML 2.0.

## 1.9. Bibliography

[ALL 04] ALLOUI I., OQUENDO F., "Describing software-intensive process architectures using a UML-based ADL", *Proceedings of the 6th International Conference on Enterprise Information Systems (ICEIS '04)*, Porto, Portugal, April 2004.

[ALT 07] ALTI A., KHAMMACI T., SMEDA A., "Integer notation software architecture concepts into the MDA platform with UML profile", *Journal of Computer Science*, vol. 3, no. 10, pp. 793–802, 2007.

[BOO 98] BOOCH G., RUMBAUGH J., JACOBSON I., *The Unified Modeling Language User Guide*, Addison-Wesley Publishing, Reading, 1998.

[BOU 97] BOUNAAS F., CHABRE-PECCOUD M., CUNIN P.Y., *et al.*, "Objets et méta-modélisation", in OUSSALAH M. (ed.), *Ingénierie objet – Concepts et techniques*, Interéditions, Paris, 1997.

[BUD 08] BUDINSKY F., MERKS E., STEINBERG D., *Eclipse Modeling Framework*, Addison-Wesley Professional, Reading, 2008.

[FRA 03] FRANKEL D., *Model Driven Architecture Applying MDA to Enterprise Computing*, Wiley, Indianapolis, 2003.

[GAR 00] GARLAN D., MONROE R., WILE D., "Acme: architectural description of component-based systems", in LEAVENS T., SITARAMAN M. (eds), *Foundations of Component-Based Systems*, Cambridge University Press, Camridge, 2008.

[GAR 02] GARLAN D., CHENG S., KOMPANEK J., "Reconciling the needs of architectural description with object-modeling notations", *Science of Computer Programming Journal*, Special UML, no. 44, pp. 23–49, 2002.

[GOU 03] GOULÃO M., ABREU F., Bridging the gap between Acme and UML 2.0 for CBD, Specification and Verification of Component-Based Systems Workshop, Lapland, Finland, 2003.

[IVE 04] IVERS J., CLEMENTS P., GARLAN D., *et al.*, Documenting component and connector views with UML 2.0, Technical Report CMU/SEI-TR-008, School of Computer Science, Carnegie Mellon University, April 2004.

[JOU 06] JOUAULT F., BÉZIVIN J., "KM3: a DSL for metamodel specification", *8th IFIP International Conference on Formal Methods for Open Object-Based Distributed Systems*, Bologna, Italy, 14–16 June 2006.

[MED 00] MEDVIDOVIC N., TAYLOR R., "A classification and comparison framework for software architecture description languages", *IEEE Transactions on Software Engineering*, vol. 26, no. 1, pp. 70–93, 2000.

[MED 02] MEDVIDOVIC N., ROSENBLUM D.S., ROBBINS J.E., *et al.*, "Modeling software architecture in the unified modeling language", *ACM Transactions on Software Engineering and Methodology*, vol. 11, no. 1, pp. 2–57, 2002.

[MOF 02] META-OBJECT FACILITY – MOF, version 1.4., Object Management Group, Document Formal/2002-04-03, April 2002.

[MUL 05] MULLER P.A., FLEUREY F., JÉZÉQUEL J.M., "Weaving executability into object-oriented meta-languages", *Model Driven Engineering Languages and Systems*, pp. 264278, 2005.

[OMG 03] OBJECT MANAGEMENT GROUP, UML 2.0 Superstructure specification: final adopted specification, available at www.omg.org/docs/ptc/03-08-02.pdf, August 2003.

[OQU 06] OQUENDO F., "Formally modelling software architectures with the UML 2.0 profile for π-ADL", *ACM SIGSOFT Engineering Notes*, vol. 31, no. 1, January 2006.

[OUS 02] OUSSALAH M., "Component-oriented KBS", *14th International Conference on Software Engineering and Knowledge Engineering (SEKE'02)*, Ischia, Italy, 2002.

[SME 05a] SMEDA A., OUSSALAH M., KHAMMACI T., "MADL: Meta Architecture Description Language", *Third ACIS International Conference on Software Engineering, Research, Management and Applications (SERA '05)*, Pleasant, MI, 2005.

[SME 05b] SMEDA A., KHAMMACI T., OUSSALAH M., "Meta architecting: towards a new generation of architecture description languages", *Journal of Computer Science*, vol. 1, no. 4, pp. 454–460, 2005.

[SME 05c] SMEDA A., OUSSALAH M., KHAMMACI T., "Mapping ADLs into UML 2.0 using a meta ADL", *5th Working IEEE/IFIP Conference on Software Architecture (WICSA '05)*, Pittsburg, PA, 2005.

[TRA 05] TRAVERSON B., "Les Modèles de Composants Industriels", in OUSSALAH M. (ed.), *Ingénierie des Composants: Concepts, Techniques et Outils*, Vuibert Informatique, Paris, 2005.

[WAR 98] WARMER J., KLEPPE A., *The Object Constraint Language: Precise Modeling with UML*, Addison-Wesley Publishing, Reading, 1998.

[WIL 99] WILE D., "AML: an architecture meta language", *14th International Conference on Automated Software Engineering*, Cocoa Beach, FL, October 1999.

Chapter 2

# Architecture Constraints

In this chapter, we introduce an additional, yet essential, concept for describing software architectures: architecture constraints. We explain the precise role of these entities and their importance in object-oriented, component-based or service-oriented software engineering. We then describe the way in which they are specified and interpreted. An architect can define architecture constraints and then associate them with architectural descriptions to limit their structure, and ultimately make a certain level of quality persistent. These constraints enable us to enforce adherence to a particular architecture pattern or style so as to ensure a certain level of maintainability. By interpreting these constraints, we are able to check whether these patterns/styles are respected, after the evolution of architecture descriptions. We present a state of the art on the current techniques and languages for expressing these constraints. We then introduce our recent research, where we have developed languages for expressing these constraints on architectures of object-oriented, component-based and service-oriented applications. We will use different examples of architecture constraints representing known patterns and styles, like the *Pipe and Filter* architecture style and the *Service Facade* or *Model-View-Controller* architecture patterns, to illustrate these works. We conclude this chapter with a summary of some of

Chapter written by Chouki TIBERMACINE.

the open questions which have given rise to ongoing research about this concept of architecture constraints.

## 2.1. Introduction

Over the past few years, software systems have been ceaselessly evolving, growing in size and complexity[1]. Software architectures therefore play a leading role and have become a central artifact in the lifecycle of computer systems because they provide various players with an overview of the organization of those systems. Software architecture is defined in [BAS 12] as the set of structures of a software system, necessary for reasoning about it. It is constituted of software entities, the relations between them as well as properties of these entities and relations. This definition brings to the forefront the fact that this artifact makes the components of a software system explicit, as well as the dependencies between these components[2]. This enables us to give a general overview of the organization of this system and reason on it to verify certain properties, such as quality attributes.

The activities surrounding software architecture are many and varied. They include documentation [CLE 10], evaluation [CLE 02] and reasoning [TAN 09], among others. Of these, the activity that has held the attention of software engineering practitioners considerably over these past few years is architecture documentation. Indeed, in the literature and in practice, a plethora of models, languages and tools have been proposed to document software architecture. This documentation may concern the architecture itself, and in this case we speak of *architecture description*, as it may concern architecture decisions [HAR 07, JAN 05, KRU 09, TYR 05] or the *rationale* behind these decisions [TAN 05].

Documenting architecture decisions is an important activity in the software development process [KRU 09]. Indeed, this type of documentation allows us to limit the evaporation [BOS 04] of architectural knowledge [BOE 08], among other things. A multitude of models for defining this type

---

1 See, for example, the development of JUnit: http://edmundkirwan.com/general/junit.html.
2 The term "component" is used in the broadest sense, i.e. an element in the architecture which constitutes a system. They are not components in the sense of component-based software engineering (CBSE).

of documentation exist [FAL 11]. These models include both textual and (more or less) formal specifications (which can be automatically interpreted by programs). These models include, among other things, the description of the decision itself, its state and its alternative decisions. Among the most important descriptions encountered in the documentation of an architecture decision, we find the architecture constraints.

An architecture constraint represents the specification of a condition that an architecture description must adhere to in order to satisfy an architecture decision. This specification must be defined using a language that facilitates its automated interpretation. For example, an architect may make the decision to use the *Model-View-Controller* (MVC) pattern [REE 79]. An architecture constraint allowing the verification of the adherence to this pattern in an architecture description would then consist of checking, among other things, that there are no dependencies between the components representing the model and those representing the view.

This type of constraint does not necessarily have to be expressed in the design phase, accompanying, for example, UML class diagrams. It is quite possible to define them in the implementation phase. Indeed, we can envisage writing and verifying this type of constraint in code, in which we can easily identify the architecture descriptions, as in some object- or service-oriented applications, or in component-based applications. Specification of constraints in the implementation phase allows them to be dynamically interpreted, beyond their static verification. It then becomes possible to verify whether they are violated, if the applications architecture evolves during runtime.

If we consider the architecture constraint verifying a part of the MVC pattern and which is expressed on an object-oriented application, for example, we can specify a condition stipulating that the objects marked (the classes of which would have been stereotyped if we were in UML in the design phase, or annotated if we were in Java in the implementation phase, for example) as entities of the model must not contain references to the objects marked as entities of the view.

Various languages have been developed to specify this type of constraint. They are mainly used in the design phase and are often associated with architecture description languages [MED 00]. There are, however, some languages that are used in the implementation phase. A state of the art on these different languages is given in the next section.

In sections 2.3–2.5, we present a language, called *Architecture Constraint Language* (ACL) [TIB 10], which was developed by us. We explore the use of this language in contexts different from that for which it was originally developed, which is that of component-based applications[3]. We show how this language could be used for writing architecture constraints on object-oriented applications, described in UML in the design phase and then in Java in the implementation phase. We also explain the use of this language with service-oriented applications, described in the implementation phase with *Business Process Execution Language* (BPEL). All of this is presented in sections 2.3–2.5.

We conclude this chapter with a summary of the contribution of this work to the field of software engineering. We then close the discussion with a presentation of our ongoing research study about this concept of architecture constraints.

## 2.2. State of the art

In this state of the art, we distinguish two kinds of languages: languages used to specify architecture constraints in the design phase, and which have been jointly proposed with, or directly integrated into, architecture description languages (ADLs), and languages used in the implementation phase.

### 2.2.1. *Expression of architecture constraints in the design phase*

We present architecture constraint expression in the design phase in two steps. First, we present the languages and methods to express these constraints in ADLs. Second, we show different uses of the *Object Constraint Language* (OCL) language for specifying this particular constraint type.

#### 2.2.1.1. *Expression of architecture constraints in ADLs*

In [MED 00], Medvidovic and Taylor proposed a classification *framework* of the ADLs developed till 1998–2000. In this article, the authors discuss

---

3 Here, the meaning of the term "component" is that used in component-based software engineering (CBSE).

architecture constraints, which are introduced in this chapter, as "programmable invariants" specified during architecture configuration modeling. Only certain languages offer this option. These languages are Aesop [GAR 94], SADL [MOR 95, MOR 97] and Wright [ALL 97].

Aesop allows the writing of "style" or "topology" constraints (also called "configuration rules" by these authors) to force a particular organization of the architecture so as to adhere to an architecture style [SHA 96], such as *Pipe and Filter* or "client/server". These constraints are specified in the form of implementations of methods in C++ abstract classes[4] displaying the architecture types (*Filter, Server,* etc.).

These classes all inherit a programming interface (set of functions), called *Fable Abstract Machine* (FAM). This makes it possible to add or remove ports from the components, or to put connectors in place, among other things. These classes must be specialized (by subtyping) to create components, connectors or configurations adhering to the style introduced by these classes. Every new description of architecture (components, ports, connectors, etc., added) adhering to a style verifies that these constraints are met by invoking the methods that implement them. An example of a constraint in Aesop, taken from [GAR 94], is given in the listing below:

```
1  fam_bool pf_source :: attach (fam_port p) {
2    if (! fam_is_subtype (p.fam_type () ,PF_WRITE_TYPE))
3    {
4      return false ;
5    }
6    else
7    {
8      return fam_port :: attach (p) ;
9    }
10 }
```

In this constraint, the port received as a parameter of the `attach` function is verified. If its type is a subtype of a specific type introduced by the *Pipe and Filter* style, then the attachment is established.

---

4 Even if an architect writes code in this ADL, it is not considered in the implementation phase. As the architect only writes architecture specifications, it is still considered in the design phase. The implementation of functionalities offered by architecture components is thus not defined with this language.

SADL is an ADL which allows the specification of constraints (called *Well-formedness Rules* by its authors) enabling adherence to architecture styles. It introduces a syntax for expressing predicates in the first-order logic restricting the types of elements constituting an architecture description or style (component, connector, port, etc.). As in Aesop, in SADL, basic types are defined for displaying the architecture elements without any constraint. Every new architecture description or architecture style will have to introduce subtypes (by inheritance) with possible constraints. These are verified during interpretation of the instantiation primitives of components and connectors or of their interconnection. A constraint concerning the connectors of the *Dataflow* style, taken from [MOR 97], is presented below:

```
1  connects_argtype_1 : CONSTRAINT =
2     (/\ x)(/\ y)(/\ z) [ Connects(x, y, z) => Dataflow_Channel(x) ]
3  connects\_argtype_2 : CONSTRAINT =
4     (/\ x)(/\ y)(/\ z) [ Connects(x, y, z) => Outport(y) ]
5  connects\_argtype_3 : CONSTRAINT =
6     (/\ x)(/\ y)(/\ z) [ Connects(x, y, z) => Inport(z) ]
```

This constraint stipulates that a connection between components in this architecture style involves three architecture elements: a channel (x), which must be of the type `Dataflow_Channel`, a port (y) of the type `Outport` and another port (z) of the type `Inport`.

Wright follows on from the Aesop language, which was developed by the same research team. It enables the formal description of architectures, especially the connectors between components in these architecture descriptions. It relies on a process algebra notation, a variant of CSP [HOA 78], for modeling the behavior of ports and connectors. This language enables the specification of constraints for formalizing architecture styles. The following constraint, for example, stipulates that the configuration must have a star-shaped topology:

$\exists center : Components \bullet$

$\quad \forall c : Connectors \bullet \exists r : Role; p : Port \mid ((center, p), (c, r)) \in Attachments$

$\wedge \forall c : Components \bullet \exists cn : Connectors; r : Role; p : Port$

$\quad \mid ((c, p), (cn, r)) \in Attachments$

The first predicate indicates that there is a component ("center") among all the components of the architecture description (the keyword `Components`) which is attached to all connectors of the description. The second predicate indicates that all the components must be attached to a connector. Hence, this constraint guarantees that every component is connected to the component representing the center of the star.

Besides these languages, the ADL Acme [GAR 00] offers a separate constraint language (not cited alongside the others in the Medvidovic and Taylor classification [MED 00]) named Armani [MON 01]. This language allows the expression of what the authors call "design rules", which correspond to architecture constraints. Armani is a language that allows the writing of predicates in first-order logic. It also introduces, among others, a number of functions for the verification of the type of an architecture element (satisfiesType(e:Element,t:Type):boolean), or for testing the properties of graphs (for example, attached(con:Connector,comp: Component): boolean). It enables two types of predicates to be defined: "heuristics" and "invariants". These two entities are defined in the same way, except that heuristics are not intended for type verifications. The example below shows an invariant and a heuristic specified in Armani:

```
1  Invariant  Forall  c1,c2  :  component  in  sys.Components  |
2               Exists  conn  :  connector  in  sys.Connectors  |
3               Attached(c1,conn)  and  Attached(c2,conn);
4  Heuristic  Size(Ports)  <=  5;
```

The invariant specifies that all the system components must be connected to each other. The configuration thus forms a strongly connected graph. The heuristic indicates that the total number of ports must be less than or equal to 5.

FScript[5] is a scripting language for the reconfiguration of architectures based on Fractal components [BRU 04]. Its syntax is similar to programming languages. It is based on a navigation language in Fractal architecture descriptions, called FPath. This has a syntax inspired by the xPath language, a navigation language for XML documents. This language enables parameterizable architecture constraints to be expressed. An example taken from the tutorial for this language is given below:

---

5 A tutorial for this language is available at the following SVN repository: svn://forge.objectweb.org/svnroot/fractal/tags/fscript-2.0.

```
1 — Tests whether the client interface $itf is bound to
2 — (an interface of) component $comp.
3 function bound-to(itf , comp) {
4   servers = $itf/binding::*/component::*;
5   return size($servers & $comp) > 0;
6 }
```

The constraint takes the form of a function, i.e. in FScript, the script has no side effects on the architecture description; the script uses only introspection[6]. This function accepts two parameters: a required interface (client in the terminology of the Fractal component model) and a component. The constraint makes it possible to test whether the required interface received in the first parameter ($itf) is connected to the component received in the second parameter ($comp).

The expression in line 4 makes it possible to get the set of components (stored in variable servers) which have provided an interface (server in the Fractal terminology) connected to the required interface $itf. The expression in the following line makes the intersection (operator &) between this set of components (servers) and the component $comp received in the parameter. If the intersection is not empty, the function returns the value "true". Otherwise, it returns "false".

More generally, this language relies on an FPath navigation language to achieve introspection. It provides a number of set operators: intersection (&), union (|), size (size), etc. The richness of this language lies in the use of a syntax similar to xPath for writing complex requests, and the possibility of calling functions already previously specified within these requests.

The *Architecture Analysis and Design Language* (AADL) [FEI 12]) is an ADL which enables the description of (software and hardware) component-based architectures for embedded and real-time systems. A language named *Requirements and Enforcements Analysis Language* (REAL) [GIL 10] was suggested as a constraint language for AADL. REAL makes it possible to express constraints in the form of theorems applying to a collection of architecture elements (for example, components or connections).

---

6 There is another version of the scripts in FScript called "Action", which allows modification of the architecture description (realization of the intercession), FScript being an architectural reconfiguration language rather than a constraint language.

In the following listing [GIL 10], the constraint applies to instances of Thread-type components and verifies their periodicity. Their property, named Dispatch_Protocol, must have periodic or sporadic as a value.

```
1  theorem task_periodicity
2  foreach t in Thread_Set do
3    check ((Get_Property_Value(t,"Dispatch_Protocol") = "periodic")
4         or
5            (Get_Property_Value(t,"Dispatch_Protocol") = "sporadic"));
6  end task_periodicity
```

The constraints in this language use an introspection mechanism to obtain the set of Thread-type component instances (Data, etc.), to obtain the values of their properties and to test access or the connections between instances of components (Is_Accessing_To(...), Is_Bound_To(...), Is_Subcomponent_Of(...), etc.), among others. This language proposes iterators (foreach) and set operations (Cardinal, Max, etc.) and Boolean and comparison operators.

### 2.2.1.2. *Expression of architecture constraints with OCL*

The OCL language [OMG 12] is the Object Management Group (OMG) standard for expressing constraints on UML models. The objective of this language is to provide developers with a means of specifying conditions for refining the semantics of their models. This constraint language was initially suggested for specifying conditions on functional, not architectural, aspects. For example, in a class diagram, where we find a class Employee, having an attribute age of type integer, an OCL constraint representing an invariant on this class can force the values of this attribute so that they always fall in the interval 16–70. This constraint will be verified on all instances of the UML model, and therefore on all instances of the class Employee.

There are, however, other uses of the OCL language, which are at the metamodel level and not at the model one. This allows the expression of architectural constraints like those discussed in this chapter. Below, we list some examples of specifications in which the OCL language is used to express architecture constraints.

1) Specification of the UML language [OMG 11]: in this specification, the metamodel of the UML language is introduced, and OCL constraints are associated with it, in order to refine the semantics of this metamodel. These

constraints navigate through this metamodel and impose their conditions on metaclasses in the metamodel, the values of their attributes, the number of their instances, their interconnections, etc. In Figure 2.1, taken from [OMG 11], we show a small excerpt from the UML metamodel in which the associations between classes are partially specified.

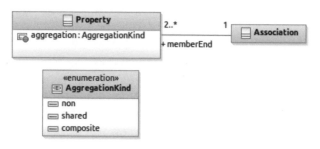

**Figure 2.1.** *Extract from the UML metamodel*

This figure shows that an association has two or several ends, which are instances of the `Property` metaclass. Each of these instances has an attribute `aggregation`, which can take the following three values: `none` (no aggregation), `shared` (aggregation in UML) and `composite` (composite in the sense of UML). Here is an example of a constraint [OMG 11] written in OCL on this fragment of the metamodel.

```
1 — Only  binary  associations  can  be  aggregations
2 context  Association  inv:
3 self.memberEnd—>exists(aggregation  <>  Aggregation::none)
4 implies  self.memberEnd—>size() = 2
```

The first line is a comment specifying the role of the constraint. Line 2 denotes the constraint context. This represents the metaclass in the metamodel which the constraint is applied to. Hence, the constraint will be evaluated on all instances of this metaclass. In our example, we are looking at the `Association` metaclass shown in Figure 2.1. In line 3, the constraint navigates across the association between the `Association` and `Property` metaclasses in the metamodel to obtain the `Property` instances linked to the `Association` instance on which the constraint is evaluated. The constraint then checks if there is at least one instance among these `Property` instances whose `aggregation` attribute value differs from `none` (to check if there is at least one association which is an aggregation or composition). In the next line, the constraint checks that, in this case, the number of ends of the association is equal to 2 (binary association).

2) UML profiles:  a UML profile is a standard extension to the UML language for handling a particular domain – real-time systems, telecommunications, systems on a chip, system tests, etc.[7].

Let us take the example of the UML profile for CORBA and the CORBA components (CCCMP [OMG 08]). An excerpt from the metamodel implemented by this profile is given in Figure 2.2.

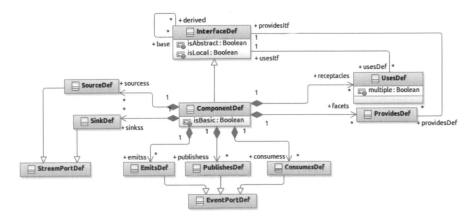

**Figure 2.2.** *Excerpt from the metamodel of the UML profile for CORBA and CCM*

In this metamodel, it is specified that a component definition declares a certain number of ports, which can be *receptacles* (required ports of type UsesDef), *facets* (provided ports of type ProvidesDef), event ports (EmitsDef, PublishesDef and ConsumesDef) or flow ports (SourceDef and SinkDef).

The following constraint stipulates that a basic component definition does not have to declare ports or inherit other component definitions:

---

7 See a complete list of UML profiles adopted by the OMG on the following website: www.omg.org/technology/documents/profile_catalog.htm.

```
1 context ComponentDef inv:
2 self.isBasic implies
3 facets −>isEmpty and receptacles −>isEmpty and
4 emitss −>isEmpty and publishess −>isEmpty and consumess−>isEmpty and
5 sinkss −>isEmpty and sourcess −>isEmpty and
6 base −>isEmpty
```

Lines 3 to 5 indicate that ports should not have as a type one of the types cited above. The last line specifies that the component definition does not have to be derived from another component definition (the base role being inherited from the InterfaceDef metaclass). In this case, the basic CORBA component definition can only have a HomeDef interface being able to declare operations of type FactoryDef or FinderDef (which are not shown in the metamodel in Figure 2.2 for the sake of simplicity).

3) Software architecture description in UML is proposed by Medvidovic *et al.* in [MED 02]: the authors introduce three different methods for using UML as an ADL in this article. The first method consists of using UML as it is. The second recommends the establishment of architecture constraints in OCL on UML metaclasses. The third method suggests extending the UML language. The second method seems the most interesting for us to present here. The authors present a set of OCL constraints applicable on the UML metamodel, to adhere to the restrictions imposed by some ADLs in component-based architecture definition. The authors have chosen three ADLs that they have deemed suitably representative, which are C2 [MED 96], Rapide [LUC 95] and Wright. More specifically, they have presented the UML profiles of these ADLs, because they have simultaneously introduced the constraints, stereotypes and tagged values which correspond to these ADLs. For the C2 language, for example, the authors introduce a stereotype named C2Component as an extension of the Class metaclass. An architecture constraint attached to this stereotype indicates that the C2 components must implement exactly two interfaces, which must be stereotyped C2Interface, one of them positioned above the component and the other positioned below. This constraint is expressed in OCL as follows: [MED 02]:

```
1 self.interface −>size = 2 and
2 self.interface −>forAll(i | i.stereotype = C2Interface) and
3 self.interface −>exists(i | i.c2pos = top) and
4 self.interface −>exists(i | i.c2pos = bottom)
```

The authors introduced an enumeration beforehand (used in lines 3 and 4) for the position of interfaces (top and bottom), and the stereotypes

C2Component, which is the context of this constraint, and C2Interface used in line 2.

It should be noted here that the constraints defined in this way, at the metamodel level, apply to all instances of that metamodel, and therefore on all models (architecture descriptions) defined using this metamodel. These constraints thus display quite strong conditions, being a part of the architecture description specification of the language. They will apply to every architecture description defined with this language. Therefore, these are not architecture constraints that will be verified on a particular architecture description (that of an X application).

### 2.2.2. *Expression of architecture constraints in the implementation phase*

In the implementation phase, the developer faces two scenarios: (1) manually writing the code (programs) corresponding to the architecture described in the design phase or (2) automatically generating code skeletons from the architecture descriptions and then filling in the missing parts. Everything depends on the language used in the design phase and the tools associated therewith. In an ideal scenario, the constraints accompanying the architecture description are themselves transformed into code, or into constraints that can be verified on the code. Unfortunately, to the best of our knowledge, no work in the literature has been developed on this subject. Recently, we were inclined to answer this question (see the conclusion in section 2.6), but the work that we undertook does not fall within the subject matter of this chapter and therefore will not be detailed here.

In this section, we focus on the works which have suggested languages and tools for expressing constraints on programs. It should be noted here that architecture constraints sometimes involve quite a fine granularity in the architecture description, like attribute access modifiers or method parameters. This is linked to the architecture style underlying the programming language. For example, object-oriented programming languages offer an architecture style for applications constituted of concepts such as classes, prototypes, attributes, methods, etc. Architecture constraints on object-oriented applications must therefore necessarily involve this level of granularity (on these concepts and their properties). These constraints do not arise at the functional level (constraints on attribute values, for example). They arise rather at the structural, and therefore architectural, level of these applications.

Boris Bokowski in [BOK 99] suggested a *framework* called *CoffeeStrainer*. This *framework* facilitates constraints specification in Java and their static verification in Java programs. It enables condition expression in programs in order to implement good design practices, such as encapsulation or systematic invocation of a superclass method when this method is redefined in a subclass. These constraints are defined in the form of particular comments (surrounded by the set of symbols /*/) which can be placed anywhere in a class. Within these comments, methods are defined for implementing the constraint using a reflexive layer (of metaprogramming) provided by CoffeeStrainer. These methods are invoked while analyzing the syntactic tree displaying the class in which the constraint has been defined, and therefore on which it is going to be verified. For example, the following constraint enables us to check that all the attributes of a class are private (data encapsulation principle in object-oriented programming).

```
1  interface PrivateFields {
2    /*/ public void checkField(Field f) {
3      if(!f.isPrivate()) {
4        reportError(f, "field is not declared private");
5      }
6    }
7  /*/
8  }
```

If a class implements this interface, the checkField(Field f)(line 2) method will be invoked as many times as there are attributes in the class, by passing it as an argument each time the object Field represents the attribute. This constraint reports an error by calling an inherited method known as reportError(...) if one of the attributes is not private.

CoffeeStrainer can allow quite a fine level of detail to be considered when expressing constraints, e.g. in checking the type of instructions which are in methods (is it a method invocation, an assignment, etc.?). This level of detail is not useful for expressing architecture constraints which involve aspects of a coarser granularity (declared attributes and methods, extended classes, implemented interfaces, etc.). To achieve this, java.reflect is quite sufficient. However, this library can only be exploited at the execution of programs, whereas architecture constraints can sometimes be statically evaluated. We will return to this point later in this chapter.

An older language, called *C++ Constraint Expression Language* (CCEL), is suggested in [CHO 93] for constraint specification involving the structure of C++ programs. Constraints expressible with this language only involve declarations in programs (declarations of classes, functions and variables) corresponding to the type of constraints that we would like to express. This language, however, introduces a new syntax inspired by C++ that requires specific learning.

In [KLA 96], the authors suggest a language called *Category Description Language* (CDL), which enables us to express architecture constraints in first-order logic as formulas involving trees representing program syntax (*parse trees*). This language allows constraint specification independently of all languages. However, in order to integrate this language into a concrete programming language, this language must be extended to enable the annotation, with the names of constraints, of the programs written with the target language on which the constraints must be verified.

*Dependency Constraint Language* (DCL) [TER 09] is an architecture constraint specification language for object-oriented applications. This language enables the expression of constraints which are statically verified, i.e. checked, on the source code of object-oriented applications, before their execution. *dclchek* is the tool provided by the authors of this language for checking DCL constraints on Java code.

First, this language allows us to indicate the parts of the object-oriented application which represent modules (a module = a set of classes and of interfaces). Next, the constraints specify conditions that these modules must adhere to. The authors of this language indicate that two categories of constraints can be specified: "divergences" and "absences". By "divergence", the authors mean that the source code of an object-oriented application contains a dependency which does not adhere to the constraint. By "absence", the authors mean that the source code does not contain a dependency. "Divergences" can be of two kinds:

1) constraints such as: "Only classes in module A can depend on the types in module B". By the word "depend", the authors mean access (a class of module A can access the public members of a class of module B), declare, create, implement, inherit, etc.;

2) constraints such as: "Classes of module A cannot depend on the types in module B".

Some examples of constraints are given below:

```
1  only A can−access B
2  only A can−declare B
3  only A can−useannotation B
4  A cannot−create B
5  A cannot−implement B
6  A cannot−throw B
```

The constraint in line 2 indicates that only classes in module A can declare variables of types defined in module B. By contrast, the constraint in line 6 stipulates that the classes in module A cannot throw exceptions of the types defined in module B.

"Absences" are constraints such as: "Classes declared in module A must depend on types declared in module B". Some examples of this category of constraints are given below:

```
1  A must−extend B
2  A must−throw B
3  A must−useannotation B
```

The first constraint shows that classes declared in module A must extend a class declared in module B. The second constraint specifies that all the methods of the classes in module A must throw exceptions, the types of which are declared in module B. The last constraint imposes the use of at least one annotation declared in module B in all classes in module A.

Expressing architecture constraints is quite limited in DCL. Indeed, with this language we can impose conditions on the dependencies between types, but it is, for example, impossible to write constraints limiting the number of architecture elements (e.g. number of instances, attributes or operations). This necessitates complex logical compositions or even requires a dynamic program analysis (e.g. to check if the value of an attribute does not correspond to a reference to an object of a certain "forbidden" type).

A number of works in the literature refer to architecture constraints as conditions on the structural dependencies between program elements. *Structural Constraint Language* (SCL) [DAQ 06] is a constraint language for predicate specification in first-order logic. This language enables the analysis of the syntax of programs, which is represented as a graph, through a number of operations. For example, the operation subclasses(class("X")) returns the set of subclasses of class "A". The following example, taken from [DAQ 06], introduces a constraint checking that the equals methods in Java classes have a correct signature:

```
1  def Object as class("java.lang.Object")
2    for p: packages, c: classes(p), m: methods(c)
3    (
4      (name(m)="equals" & isPublic(m) & sizeof(params(m))=1)
5      ->
6      (returnType(m) = boolean & type(ith(params(m),0))=Object)
7    )
```

This constraint iterates on all packages, and for each of the methods in the classes of these packages (the for loop in line 2), if the method is public, is called equals(...) and accepts an argument (line 4), it must have boolean as the return type and its parameter must be of type Object (line 6).

The designers of this language suggested a type of simplification of the OCL language, but presented as a new language with its own syntax. For example, the for loop in line 2 of the above listing is written more verbosely in OCL by nesting forAll operations. They also suggested a direct adaptation of this language to the procedural and statically typed object-oriented programming languages. To analyze the source code of programs, operations are directly integrated into the language, like isPublic(...) or methods(...). These operations could have been introduced as navigation in the metamodel of the programming language that the analysis concerns, as we introduced them in the previous section on OCL language, or as will be introduced in the next section. This has the benefit of rendering the constraint language independent of a particular programming language, and parameterizable by the latter. The OCL language provides this possibility and has the benefit of being a standardized language, well-known, with a strong tool support and easy to learn and to use [BRI 05].

Other languages proposed in the literature can be grouped together into one family, that of the languages stemming from Prolog. For example, *Logical Ensembles* (LogEn) [EIC 08]) is a language for expressing ensembles of elements, components of programs and constraints on the dependencies between these sets. This language is based on a formalism *a la* Prolog, called

DataLog [CER 89], allowing programs to be represented in the form of relations as follows:

```
1  type(t1 , 'bat.type.ObjectType')
2  type(t2 , 'bat.type.IType')
3  interface(t1 , t2)
```

In line 1, we have a type declaration whose identifier is t1 and which is called bat.type.ObjectType. In line 3, the relation shows that t1 declares to implement the interface whose identifier is t2 (declared in the line above).

Typically, constraints imposed by design patterns [GAM 95] are expressible using this language. This is done first by indicating the different roles in a patter by sets, then specifying the constraints of belonging (or not) to these sets, relying on logic operators of conjunction or disjunction. For example, for the pattern *Factory*, the authors specify three sets representing:

– all the program elements of a certain application;

– the Factory class (this set has the following identifier in the listing below: TypesFlyweightFactory);

– the class constructors whose objects will have to be created with the Factory class (this set has the following identifier: TypesFlyweightCreation).

This is done by using part_of(...)relations, as shown above. Next, the *Factory* pattern constraint imposes the creation of objects of a certain type, defined as follows through the Factory class:

```
1  violations(S, T, 'TypesFlyweight'): −
2    part_of(T, 'TypesFlyweightCreation'),
3    tnot(part_of(S, 'TypesFlyweightFactory')).
```

This constraint checks that all the S and T pairs are in uses(S,T) relation (i.e. dependent on one another), T belongs to the constructor set and S is not the Factory class. In other words, T (a constructor) must be used exclusively through T (the Factory class).

An interpreter of this language has been integrated into the incremental compilation/build process in Eclipse, to permanently check the constraints whenever the developers modify the source code of their programs.

The main benefits of this work are the interesting performances obtained during constraint interpretation (efficiency of set creation and verification of dependencies) and the incremental nature of the approach (its easy and efficient integration into Eclipse, the incremental compilation/build process). On the other hand, the authors focus exclusively on the structural dependencies between program elements (methods, attributes, super-classes, etc.). Constraints focus on the verification of the presence or absence of a dependency between these program elements. Nonetheless, this language suffers from a lack of expressiveness. Indeed, complex constraints involving complex navigations are expressed with difficulty in LogEn. *Law Governed Architecture* [MIN 96, MIN 97] is a similar approach, based on Prolog, for expressing and checking constraints of dependencies between programs written in Eiffel.

In [BLE 05], the authors present an approach that proposes a separate language based on Prolog, called Spine, for writing design patterns in the form of constraints. As in LogEn, a constraint is expressed using relations like `constructorsOf(...)` or `isStatic(...)`. The following example [BLE 05] shows the design pattern *Public Singleton*:

```
 1  realizes('PublicSingleton' , [C]) :-
 2    exists(constructorsOf(C),true),
 3    forAll(constructorsOf(C),
 4      Cn.isPrivate(Cn)),
 5    exists(fieldsOf(C),F.and([
 6      isStatic(F),
 7      isPublic(F),
 8      isFinal(F),
 9      typeOf(F,C),
10      nonNull(F)
11    ]))
```

In this constraint, we check that the C class has at least one constructor (line 2), that all its constructors are private (lines 3 and 4), and that it has at least one `final` attribute which is static and public whose type is class C, and its value is not null (lines 5 to 10).

This language is exclusively focused on design patterns. Based on a formalism in Prolog, it has the same limitations as the LogEn language.

In practice, there are several static code analysis tools that enable the verification of architecture constraints. A non-exhaustive list of these tools includes Sonar, Checkstyle, Lattix, Macker, Classycle, Architexa and JArchitect. These tools vary considerably in the functionalities that they implement. Some provide developers with the means to write constraints representing architecture styles or design patterns, by relying on a syntactic tree of programs (like Checkstyle). Others are limited to the specification of restrictions of dependencies between modules (like Lattix). They propose different notations, from program writing (as in Checkstyle) to the definition of specifications in a declarative (in XML, as in Macker) and/or graphic (as in Sonar) fashion. These tools allow constraints to be checked at different levels of the development process, e.g. during programming (and therefore relying on just-in-time compilation in Eclipse among others), during *commit* in SVN-type version management systems (like Checkstyle), or during the construction of projects with tools such as Ant and Maven (like Macker).

The last, but not least, of the language families is composed of languages that offer the possibility of writing metaprograms (also called reflexive languages). In these metaprograms, the developer has the possibility to access (introspection or intercession) the structure of programs which are reified in the form of objects (in reflexive object-oriented languages or component-based languages, like Compo [SPA 12]). Java is an example of an object-oriented programming language that mainly offers the capability of introspection, and Smalltalk is an example of an object-oriented programming language that offers introspection and intercession. For architecture constraint specification, we only need introspection, as architecture constraints analyze only the structure of programs, and have no side effects. However, by using this introspection mechanism, architecture constraints are dynamically evaluated, i.e. at the execution of programs on which the constraints are verified. This is unnecessary for some categories of architecture constraints in which a static analysis of the architecture is sufficient. In some cases (e.g. the MVC pattern, shown in the next section), the constraint must verify the instance types created at execution and their interconnections. Therefore, it must be dynamically evaluated.

In the following sections we will present some studies that we have conducted in the past few years on architecture constraint specification. We will show how we are able to exploit current languages that are well known by developers (such as OCL and Java) to express this type of constraint on applications written in various paradigms. We have chosen three paradigms that are the most well known in the software industry: the object, component and service paradigms.

## 2.3. Architecture constraints on object-oriented applications

Architecture constraints expressed on object-oriented applications enable (among other things) conditions imposed by architecture styles, design patterns, dependencies between types or any kind of invariant involving the checking of the architecture of an application and not its state. In the remainder of this section, we first show the specification of these architecture constraints on object-oriented applications in the design phase, and then in the implementation phase.

### 2.3.1. *Architecture constraints in the design phase*

Here we have chosen to show constraints expressed using the ACL language [TIB 10] on design models of object-oriented applications written in UML. ACL is a simplification of the OCL language. In ACL, only invariants can be expressed, i.e. it is not possible to define constraints of type pre, post-conditions, init, derive or body, which are possible in OCL. Moreover, in the context of the constraint, the identifier used represents the architecture description on which the constraint is applied. The element type identified is a metaclass in a metamodel. The navigation starts from this metaclass to analyze an architecture description in order to specify the constraint. We give some examples below to better illustrate our discussion.

Figure 2.3 shows an excerpt from the UML metamodel, obtained from the UML language superstructure specification, version 2.4.1 [OMG 11].

This metamodel focuses on describing classes, especially packages, attributes, dependencies and profiles. A package is composed of a number of types (see in the center of Figure 2.3). By means of the PackageableElement and NamedElement metaclasses, classes inherit the ability to participate in dependencies (top-right of the figure). On the bottom-right of the figure, it is shown that a class can declare attributes that are Property instances. A class also inherits from Classifier the fact that it can have inherited or imported attributes (association between Classifier and `Property`). The leftmost part of the figure illustrates the fact that we can apply a profile to a package, and that a profile is constituted of a number of stereotypes.

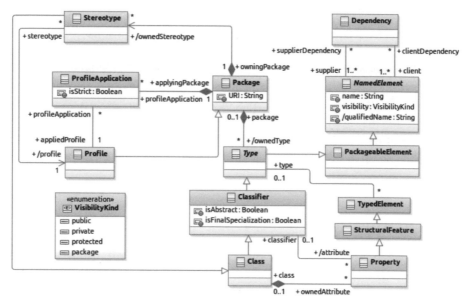

**Figure 2.3.** *(Package, property, dependency and profile)*
*from the UML metamodel*

We take the example of a constraint representing the MVC pattern. The dependencies between the different entities composing this pattern are illustrated in the diagram in Figure 2.4. To simplify, we have used UML packages to represent groups of classes that play three roles in this pattern (the model, the view and the controller). However, this does not necessarily have to reflect the application design (the classes of the view and those of the controller can be grouped in one package). Thus, we assume that we have three stereotypes, which allow us to mark the classes in an application which represent the view (*View*), the model (*Model*) and the controller (*Controller*).

This constraint is composed of three subconstraints, which will check the following:

– The classes stereotyped *Model* do not have to declare dependencies with the classes stereotyped *View*. This makes it possible to have, among other things, several views for the same model, and thus to uncouple them. In most

MVC implementations, the model classes do not depend directly on the view classes, but rather declare an attribute having as a value a collection of objects that listen to model changes. The view can perform the role of listener for modifications which have been performed on the model so that it can update itself (be refreshed).

– The classes stereotyped *Model* should not have dependencies with the classes stereotyped *Controller*. This makes it possible to have several possible controllers for the model.

– The classes stereotyped *View* should not have dependencies with the classes stereotyped *Model*. The controllers will play the role of "intermediate" between the view and the model.

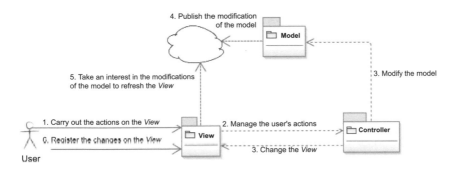

**Figure 2.4.** *MVC pattern illustration*

Using ACL, we obtain the following constraints:

```
 1  context MonApplication:Package inv:
 2  let model:Set(Type) = self.ownedType—>select(t:Type |
 3    t.getAppliedStereotypes()—>exists(name='Model'))
 4  in
 5  let view:Set(Type) = self.ownedType—>select(t:Type |
 6    t.getAppliedStereotypes()—>exists(name='View'))
 7  in
 8  let controller:Set(Type) = self.ownedType—>select(t:Type |
 9    t.getAppliedStereotypes()—>exists(name='Controller'))
10  in
11  self.ownedType—>forAll(t : Type |
12    (model—>includes(t)
13    implies
14    t.clientDependency.supplier—>forAll(tt |
15      view—>excludes(tt) and controller—>excludes(tt)
16    ))
17    and
```

```
18  ( view ->includes ( t )
19  implies
20  t . clientDependency . supplier ->forAll ( tt |
21    model ->excludes ( tt )
22  ) )
23  )
```

The first line in the listing declares the context of the constraint. It indicates that the constraint is applied to the whole application package; the metaclass Package (see Figure 2.3) is then the starting point for all navigations in the rest of the constraint. Lines 2 to 9 serve to collect together the sets of classes displaying the model, the view and the controller[8]. For example, in lines 2 and 3, we move on from the package to look for the types defined in it. Next, we select only those which have Model as an applied stereotype, due to the operation getAppliedStereotypes() (not specified in UML/OCL, but implemented in IBMs *Rational Software Architect* (RSA)).

Subconstraints 1 and 2, textually specified in the previous enumeration, are formalized using ACL in the previous listing, between lines 11 and 16. In these constraints, we ensure that if a class is stereotyped as Model, then it must not have dependencies (by navigating to the Dependency metaclass) with classes stereotyped View or Controller. To test if a class is stereotyped as Model, we simply check its presence, due to the includes(...)) operation at line 12 in the set of objects of type Class, named model, defined in lines 2 and 3 of the listing. The last subconstraint is formalized in lines 18–22.

Often, a dependency between two classes is translated as the declaration in the first class of at least one attribute having as a type the second class. We can also find some parameters in operations of the first class, which have as a type the second class. Furthermore, this can be translated in an operation of the first class, where the return type is the second class. To simplify, we will take into account the first case: "at least one attribute in the first class has as a type the second class". It is, moreover, most often the case during realization of an application in accordance with the MVC pattern. The constraint previously

---

8 We simplify the constraint here by assuming that the classes are found in one single package. If the classes are defined in subpackages or sub-subpackages, it will then be necessary to navigate recursively in these sub- or sub-subpackages.

given can be refined as follows, by supposing that the part from line 1 to 10 in the previous listing does not change:

```
1  ...
2  self.ownedType->forAll(t : Type |
3     (model->includes(t)
4     implies
5     if t.oclIsKindOf(Classifier)
6     then
7        t.oclAsType(Classifier).attribute ->forAll(a |
8           view->excludes(a.type) and controller ->excludes(a.type))
9     else true
10    endif
11    )
12    and
13    (view->includes(t)
14    implies
15    if t.oclIsKindOf(Classifier)
16    then
17       t.oclAsType(Classifier).attribute ->forAll(a |
18       model->excludes(a.type))
19    else true
20    endif
21    )
22 )
```

In this constraint, the dependency is verified on all attributes defined in classes. Note the use of the `oclAsType(Classifier)` operation in this constraint to allow navigation by going through specialization relations between `Type` and `Classifier` (static type conversion of `Type` objects for then navigating to `Property`).

We have not yet finished with the MVC pattern, which can only be partially verified in the design phase. Indeed, other checks will have to be run at execution. These are explained in the next section.

### 2.3.2. Architecture constraints in the implementation phase

In order to be able to check the previous architecture constraints in the implementation phase, and thus to check that the code produced in this phase always conforms to the constraints defined before, we will explain how to express these constraints in Java.

First, we will show these constraints expressed in ACL, but this time on the Java metamodel to ensure a smooth transition from the previous section.

Next, we show how to specify these same constraints by using the introspection mechanism provided by Java.

Figure 2.5 shows a simplified metamodel of the Java language. By simplified, we mean to say that this metamodel only shows entities in the Java language serving to write architecture constraints. We thus find classes that have attributes (Field in Java terminology), methods and constructors. A class belongs to a package. This meta-association is navigable in only one sense: that is to say that from one package, we cannot know which types are defined there. All these elements can be annotated (a property inherited among others from the metaclass AccessibleObject). With the exception of packages, the other metaclasses have modifiers, which can have different values listed in the enumeration Modifier. An attribute can have a reference toward another object as its value for a particular object. It should be noted that the semantics of the metamodel are not precise enough on this point. Indeed, the association between Field and ObjectReference only has to be navigable when we go, in a constraint, from an object (instance of the metaclass Object) toward its class (instance of Class), and finally toward the attribute (instance of Field). If the navigation starts from Class, then access to Field must not consequently allow access to ObjectReference. This metamodel was constructed on the basis of classes defined in the API java.reflect, whose methods allow introspection to be carried out. The lack of semantics raised above is linked to the fact that, on the one hand, in Java there is no equivalent of UML's Slot. On the other hand, the get(...) method of the Field class returns the value of the attribute, but we have to pass, as an argument, the object for which the value of the "attribute" (slot) must be returned. In reality, this is a more general problem. It is due to the fact that in Java, there is no true coupling between the objects and their metaobjects (instances of Class). Once we have done getClass() on an object, we obtain the metaobject, but in this metaobject there is no reference back to the object (we therefore lose access to the values of its "attributes").

The subconstraints of the MVC pattern introduced in the previous section can be expressed on this metamodel in the following manner:

```
1  context Class inv:
2  self.annotation−>exists(a:Annotation | a.type.name='Model')
3  implies
4  self.field−>forAll(f : Field |
5    not (f.type.annotation−>exists(type.name='View')
```

```
 6    or f.type.annotation —>exists(type.name='Controller')))
 7  and
 8  self.annotation —>exists(type.name='View')
 9  implies
10  self.field —>forAll(not (type.annotation
11    —>exists(type.name='Model')))
```

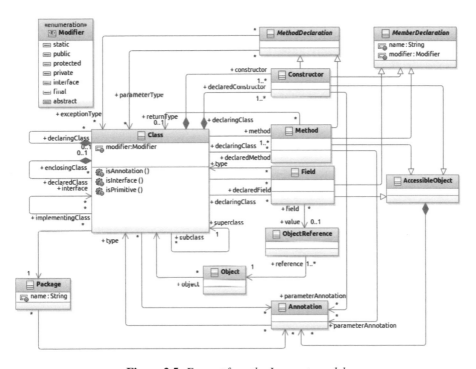

**Figure 2.5.** *Excerpt from the Java metamodel*

Here, we assume the existence of three annotations, applicable on types (classes) and present at execution (@Retention (RetentionPolicy.RUNTIME)), corresponding to the three stereotypes previously presented. The context of the constraint cannot be the package of the entire application. As we specified previously, we unfortunately cannot navigate to the types which are defined in a package. We have therefore specified every sort of class as the context of the constraint. The constraint must therefore be verified on all classes of the application. The navigation in the Java metamodel, shown in Figure 2.5, is quite simple. We analyze the attributes of the class here (objects of type Field), then their types and the annotations applied to them.

The constraint expressed in ACL above can be implemented in Java as follows:

```
 1  // We assume here that the classes of the application
 2  // have been already loaded in a certain manner
 3  public boolean invariant(Class<?>[] classesMyApplication) {
 4    for(Class<?> aClass : classesMyApplication) {
 5      if(aClass.isAnnotationPresent(Model.class)) {
 6        Field[] attributes = aClass.getDeclaredFields();
 7        for(Field anAttribute : attributes) {
 8          if(anAttribute.getType().isAnnotationPresent(View.class) ||
 9          anAttribute.getType().isAnnotationPresent(Controller.class)
              )
10            return false;
11        }
12      }
13      if(aClass.isAnnotationPresent(View.class)) {
14        Field[] attributes = aClass.getDeclaredFields();
15        for(Field aAttribute : attributes) {
16          if(anAttribute.getType().isAnnotationPresent(Model.class))
17            return false;
18        }
19      }
20    }
21    return true;
22  }
```

The method invariant(...) accepts as parameters objects of type Class, representing each of the application classes[9]. Unfortunately, we will be unable to start navigation from the Package object representing the application package, because in java.reflect, this object does not enable us to obtain references to the classes which are declared inside it. The Package object relates to a simple object containing information about the package (e.g. its name).

Unlike approaches for static code analysis, constraint verification and thus execution of this method necessitate the loading of the entire application by the class loader, in order to obtain the Class objects representing the different application classes, before putting them into an array that is passed as an argument during the invocation. In this chapter, we focus on architecture constraint specification, but not on constraint verification.

---

9 By "application classes", we mean the classes that compose the applications business domain. This excludes classes of the libraries used by the application.

Let us now return to a point raised during the introduction of the different subconstraints, which formalize the restrictions on dependencies imposed by the MVC pattern. In the first subconstraint, we have shown that the model classes do not have to declare dependencies with the view classes, which makes it a constraint on the static types. However, according to the implementations of this pattern, we may find ourselves with a reference to a view object in a model object at execution. Indeed, what was illustrated by a cloud in Figure 2.4 can be implemented by the Observer pattern. In this case, a model object stores a collection of objects listening changes on the model (the collection can be statically typed by an interface named, for example, ModelModificationListener). At execution, however, this collection will include view objects, whose classes implement ListenerModificationModel, the previous interface. Therefore, dynamically we find ourselves with dependencies between the model classes and the view classes, whereas statically this dependency is not noticeable. This only needs to be accepted for the first subconstraint. On the other hand, it does not need to be true for the other two subconstraints, which do not have to declare dependencies, statically and dynamically. This is translated by the following Java code, which comes to complement the previous constraint:

```
1  // We assume here the reception as an argument of an array
2  // constituted of different objects which compose the application
3  public boolean invariant(Object[] objectsMyApplication) {
4    for(Object anObject : objectsMyApplication) {
5      Class<?> aClass = anObject.getClass();
6      Field[] attributes = aClass.getDeclaredFields();
7      for(Field anAttribute : attributes) {
8        // Verification of the previous listing ...
9        boolean accessAttrModify = false;
10       if(! anAttribute.getType().isPrimitive()) {
11         try {
12           if(! anAttribute.isAccessible()) {
13             anAttribute.setAccessible(true);
14             accessAttrModify = true;
15           }
16           Class<?> cl = anAttribute.get(anObject).getClass();
17           if(cl.isAnnotationPresent(Controller.class)) return false;
18         }
19         catch(IllegalAccessException e) {
20           e.printStackTrace();
21         }
22         finally {
23           if(accessAttrModify) anAttribute.setAccessible(false);
24         }
25       }
26    }
```

```
27    }
28    return true;
29 }
```

This time, in this constraint, we rely on the objects that compose the application and not on Class objects that represent the application classes. Here, we go further in the execution to obtain the objects making up the application and to seek the values of their *slots* (defined by the attributes declared in the classes of these objects), because we are assuming that the application has been loaded as well as launched. Obtaining these object slot values occurs in line 16. This is preceded by several checks to ensure that the object class attribute is not of a primitive type and is accessible (it has a public accessibility). It is the slot value type in question which is checked, to ensure that it does not relate to an annotated Controller class. The last subconstraint formalizing the MVC pattern can be refined in the same way. This is not shown in the previous listing for reasons of simplicity and brevity.

The specification of this constraint at the design level is also possible, assuming that we have a model representing the instances making up the application. This constraint expressed in ACL will relate to the UML instances metamodel. An excerpt from this is given in Figure 2.6. In this metamodel, an instance specification has a Classifier which defines it and includes a number of slots. The latter have a StructuralFeature (e.g. a Property), which defines them. They have values designated by ValueSpecification. These can be of different types: InstanceValue (a reference to an instance), LiteralSpecification (an integer, real number, etc.), etc. The metaclass that interests us is InstanceValue (shown in the metamodel in Figure 2.6). This is linked to InstanceSpecification to designate the instance specification referenced in the slot.

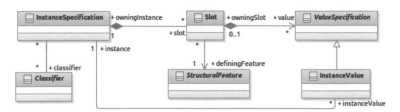

**Figure 2.6.** *Excerpt from the UML metamodel (instances)*

The ACL constraint applied on this UML metamodel could be defined as follows:

```
 1  context InstanceSpecification inv:
 2  — We assume here that we have already recovered
 3  — the model, view and controller sets of classes
 4  — as this had been done previously
 5  if model–>includes(self.classifier)
 6  then
 7    self.slot –>forAll(s : Slot |
 8      — Same verifications as previously
 9      — using s.definingFeature to access
10      — the attribute (StructuralFeature) which defines the slot
11      if s.value.isOclKindOf(InstanceValue)
12      then
13        controller –>excludes(s.value.oclAsType(InstanceValue)
14          .instance.classifier)
15      else true
16      endif
17    )
18  else true
19  endif
```

In this constraint, `InstanceSpecification` is the constraint context. We therefore assume that the constraint must be verified on all instance specifications making up the application. In the constraint, we specified the fact that if the classifier of the instance specification is a stereotyped `Model`, then we test if one of its slots contains a reference to an instance (line 11), i.e. the slot does not contain a primitive type value. In this case, we access the `Classifier` of the value stored in the slot. This does not have to be stereotyped `Controller`.

Here also, for reasons of simplicity and brevity, the last subconstraint formalizing the MVC pattern is not refined.

The same constraint on the Java metamodel can be defined as follows:

```
 1  context Object inv:
 2  if self.class.annotation –>exists(name='Model')
 3  then
 4    self.class.field –>forAll(f:Field |
 5      — Same verifications as previously
 6      — using f.type to access
 7      — the attribute type
 8      if f.value <> null
 9      then f.value.object.class.annotation = 'Controller'
```

```
10|      else true
11|      endif
12|   )
13| else true
14| endif
```

In this constraint, the context is an object (Object instance) making up the application. We next navigate to its class, then to its attribute values (see lines 8 and 9). This ACL expression does not formalize the last MVC pattern subconstraint.

In this section, we have shown how architecture constraints can be written simply in Java during the implementation phase, without any extension of the language (apart from annotations, which must be defined, if necessary, for the formalized architecture patterns or styles, but we can define them also as standard Java code). However, we have not explained how, and at what moment, these constraints are evaluated. Different solutions are possible, e.g. the automatic injection of verification code for these constraints at the end of the concerned class constructors. This is a work to which we will be turning our attention in the future. Moreover, we are in the process of developing a method, and a tool, for Java code generation (as in the listings above), from the architecture constraints expressed in ACL on the UML metamodel (such as those given previously).

## 2.4. Architecture constraints on component-based applications

After having explored how architecture constraints can be specified on object-oriented applications, in this section, we are going to show how to express these constraints in component-based applications. Components are considered here as an evolution of the concept of object (or class – we will go into more detail later) to bring greater modularity to the architecture of these applications. Indeed, in component-based development, it is recommended that the provided, as well as the required, functionalities of an application should be explicitly declared. This allows an application's components to be uncoupled and gives their connection more flexibility. To construct a new application, instances of components will have to be created and their required functionalities need to be satisfied by connecting them to other instances that provide these functionalities.

We will proceed in two stages, as in the preceding section. We will first present architecture constraint specification in the design phase and then show how this can be done in the implementation phase.

### 2.4.1. *Architecture constraints in the design phase*

We have chosen the UML standard as our modeling language in the design phase. We will explain how architecture constraints can be specified on component-based applications modeled with this language, which is widely used in academia, but also in the military sector.

Figure 2.7 shows an excerpt from the UML metamodel, specifying the modeling elements around software components. The UML component model shown encompasses the specification of both components and composite structures in UML [OMG 11]. The `Component` metaclass is a specialization of `Class`. This gives it all the abilities of a class (participating in an inheritance relation, for example). Moreover, the `Class` metaclass henceforth inherits from `EncapsulatedClassifier` and `StructuredClassifier`. In other words, a component (specialization of `EncapsulatedClassifier`) may have ports that can declare provided interfaces and required interfaces (see the bottom-left of Figure 2.7). This permits components to encapsulate (and thus hide from their environment) the elements they are made up of. They show their functionalities via these ports, which are communication points with the environment (other components). A component (specialization of `StructuredClassifier`) can declare `parts`, which are properties that reference instances constituting its internal structure (we would then say that the component has a composite structure). These instances can play `roles` in connections (being attached to connector ends). A component can have connectors which link "connectable" elements (`ConnectableElement` instances). That may be the port of a "part" in a component composite structure (association between `ConnectorEnd` and `Property` in the metamodel in Figure 2.7), or the encapsulating component port[10] (with the composite structure). Finally, a component can have one or several `Classifiers` (classes, for example) that "realize" it. By *Realization* of a component, the UML specification designates the set of classifiers that

---

10 These characteristics do not relate exclusively to components. Classes can also have ports and composite structures.

implement this components behavior. These may be other components (`Component` is a specialization of `Classifier`). This makes the UML component model hierarchical.

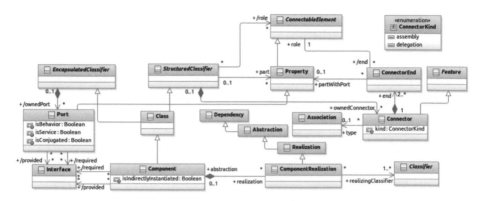

**Figure 2.7.** *Excerpt from the UML meta-model*
*(components and composite structures)*

We introduce now informally (textually) the constraint that we would like to specify in this section. It relates to a constraint which formalizes the structural conditions imposed by the `Pipe & Filter` architecture style [SHA 96]. In this style, the following conditions must be formalized:

– There is only one component which defines one or more input port (declaring provided interfaces only) connected to the encompassing component or these ports are not connected at all (this is the leftmost component in Figure 2.8). This same component must have at least one connected output port (declaring required interfaces only). The output ports of this component must all be connected to other components of the same hierarchical level as this component or else not connected at all.

– There is only one component which defines one or more output ports connected to the encompassing component or not connected at all (this is the right-hand component in Figure 2.8). This component must have at least one connected input port. The input ports of this component must all be connected to other components of the same hierarchical level as this component or else not connected at all.

– The other components define input and output ports, of which at least one input and one output port are connected.

– The connectors between each pair of components must go in the same direction. This means that there is no connector linking the input port of the first component to the output port of the second one, and another connector which links the output port of the first component to the input port of the second one.

– Connectors between all the components must go in the same direction. This means that for each pair of connected components, there is no third component connected by its input ports to the first component and by its output ports to the second component.

These constraints are illustrated in Figure 2.8. The components in this style are named filters and connectors are considered as pipes. In this chapter, we simplify the application architecture by considering the fact that it has been designed exclusively according to this style. Real-world applications are often constructed by combining various styles. In this case, the constraint will have a different formalization, which could, for example, rely on Pipe and Filter stereotypes applied on the components. The constraint must check that the conditions enumerated above are applied only to the stereotyped components, which participate thus in the implementation of the architecture style. Due to lack of space, we are unfortunately unable to develop this case here.

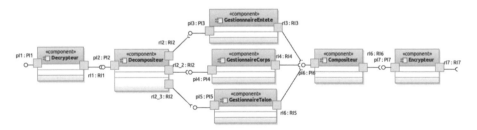

**Figure 2.8.** *Pipe and filter architecture style illustration*

We will be able to write the different subconstraints using ACL and relying on the metamodel in Figure 2.7. The first subconstraint can be specified as follows:

```
1  — We assume here that the components forming the application
2  — are encapsulated in a component with a composite structure.
3  — This is now shown in the figure illustrating the
4  — Pipe and Filter style
5  context MyApplication : Component inv:
```

```
 6 let internalComps : Set(Component) =
 7 self . realization . realizingClassifier ->select(c: Classifier |
 8   c. oclIsKindOf(Component))->oclAsType(Component)
 9 in
10 internalComps ->one(c : Component |
11   self . ownedConnector ->exists(con: Connector |
12     con . end . role ->exists(r1 ,r2 | r1 . oclIsKindOf(Port)
13       and (r1 . oclAsType(Port) = c . ownedPort)
14       and r1 . oclAsType(Port) . provided ->notEmpty()
15       and r1 . oclAsType(Port) . required ->isEmpty()
16       and r2 . oclIsKindOf(Port)
17       and self . ownedPort ->includes(r2 . oclAsType(Port))
18     )
19   )
20   and
21   self . ownedConnector ->exists(con: Connector |
22     con . end . role ->exists(r1 ,r2 | r1 . oclIsKindOf(Port)
23       and (r1 . oclAsType(Port) = c . ownedPort)
24       and r1 . oclAsType(Port) . required ->notEmpty()
25       and r2 . oclIsKindOf(Port)
26       and self . ownedPort ->excludes(r2 . oclAsType(Port))
27     )
28   )
29 )
```

In this constraint, we first create a set constituted of components (internalComps) forming the internal structure of the component representing the application. We will recall that the latter has an architecture organized according to the *Pipe and Filter* style. Next, we check that there is only one component in this set, which has at least one connector linking it with the encompassing component, through a port with only provided (and not required) interfaces. It should be noted here that the verification of the presence of connectors between components undergoes the analysis of the application connector set (self.ownedConnector). Indeed, we cannot obtain the connectors attached to the port of a component by going from this component. This corresponds clearly to the uncoupling between components recommended in component-based development: a component does not recognize other components which it is connected to; all it does is invoke operations on its required port; it does not depend on a particular component. In the second part of the constraint (from line 20 onward), we check that this single component is connected to the other application components through its output ports (declaring required interfaces).

The second subconstraint previously enumerated can be formalized in the same way by inverting the required and provided interfaces.

The third subconstraint is specified in ACL in the following listing:

```
 1  ...
 2  and
 3  internalComps ->select ( c  |
 4    not self . ownedConnector ->exists ( con : Connector  |
 5      con . end . role ->exists ( r1 , r2  |  r1 . oclIsKindOf ( Port )
 6        and ( r1 . oclAsType ( Port ) = c . ownedPort )
 7        and r2 . oclIsKindOf ( Port )
 8        and self . ownedPort ->excludes ( r2 . oclAsType ( Port ) )
 9      )
10    )
11    and c . ownedPort ->select ( provided ->notEmpty ()
12      and required ->notEmpty () ) )
13  ->size () = internalComps ->size () - 2
```

In this constraint, we count the number of components that participate in connections, but are not connected to the encompassing component. This number must be equal to the total number of application components minus the two components in the extremities.

Now, we see how the fourth subconstraint can be defined in ACL:

```
 1  ...
 2  and
 3  internalComps ->forAll ( c1 , c2  :  Component  |
 4    self . ownedConnector >select ( con : Connector  |
 5      con . end . role ->oclIsKindOf ( Port ) and
 6      con . end . role ->oclAsType ( Port )->one ( c1 . ownedPort ) and
 7      con . end . role ->oclAsType ( Port )->one ( c2 . ownedPort ) )
 8      ->forAll ( con  :  Connector  |  con . end . role ->select ( oclIsKindOf ( Port )
          )
 9      ->oclAsType ( Port )->exists ( p1 , p2 : Port  |
10        ( c1 . provided ->includesAll ( p1 . provided )
11          and c2 . required ->includesAll ( p2 . required ) )
12        xor  ( c2 . provided ->includesAll ( p1 . provided )
13          and c1 . required ->includesAll ( p2 . required ) ) ) )
14  )
```

Here, we check that in the connector set of the application, if a connector links two components c1 and c2, all other connectors between c1 and c2 must always link input ports (declaring required interfaces) from c1 to output ports (declaring provided interfaces) from c2, or inversely. There should not be connectors oriented from c1 to c2 and from c2 to c1.

The last, and undoubtedly the most complex, subconstraint is defined below:

```
 1  ...
 2  and
 3  internalComps ->forAll(c1,c2:Component |
 4    let conns : Set(Connector) =
 5    self.ownedConnector->select(con:Connector |
 6      con.end.role ->oclIsKindOf(Port) and
 7      con.end.role ->oclAsType(Port)->one(c1.ownedPort) and
 8      con.end.role ->oclAsType(Port)->one(c2.ownedPort))
 9    in — conns = {connectors between c1 and c2}
10    conns->notEmpty()
11    and
12    internalComps ->excludes(c3 : Component |
13      c3 <> c1 and c3 <> c2 and
14      if conns.end.role ->oclAsType(Port)
15        ->exists(p | c1.ownedPort.required ->includesAll(p.required))
16      then —Connector(s) c1 to c2
17        not (
18          self.ownedConnector.end.role ->select(oclIsKindOf(Port))
19          ->oclAsType(Port)->exists(p1,p2 |
20            c3.ownedPort.required ->includesAll(p1.required) and
21            c2.ownedPort.provided ->includesAll(p2.provided))
22        or
23          self.ownedConnector.end.role ->select(oclIsKindOf(Port))
24          ->oclAsType(Port)->exists(p1,p2 |
25            c1.ownedPort.required ->includesAll(p1.required) and
26            c3.ownedPort.provided ->includesAll(p2.provided))
27        )
28      else — Connector(s) c2 to c1
29        not (
30          self.ownedConnector.end.role ->select(oclIsKindOf(Port))
31          ->oclAsType(Port)->exists(p1,p2 |
32            c2.ownedPort.required ->includesAll(p1.required) and
33            c3.ownedPort.provided ->includesAll(p2.provided))
34        or
35          self.ownedConnector.end.role ->select(oclIsKindOf(Port))
36          ->oclAsType(Port)->exists(p1,p2 |
37            c3.ownedPort.required ->includesAll(p1.required) and
38            c1.ownedPort.provided ->includesAll(p2.provided))
39        )
40      endif
41    )
42  )
```

In this last part of the constraint, we check that for every pair of components (c1, c2) connected in the set of internal components, there is no third (c3) component connected via its input ports to c1, and *via* its output ports to c2, if the connectors go from c1 to c2, and inversely if the connectors go from c2 to c1. This guarantees that all connectors in the application are oriented in the same direction.

We have simplified the use of the UML components model in this formalization. We are assuming that the developer has not defined a port declaring required and provided interfaces that are attached to several connectors (input and output) at the same time.

### 2.4.2. *Architecture constraints in the implementation phase*

In the literature there are several component-based programming languages (such as ArchJava [ALD 02], ComponentJ [SEC 08] or SCL [FAB 08]), or *frameworks* (like Spring, OSGi or Fractal/Julia [BRU 04]). To write constraints we would need a language or *framework* offering the ability to realize introspection. Here too, we have several languages at our disposal. We have chosen a language developed in Petr Spacek's thesis. This language is called Compo [SPA 12]. It was developed as part of a larger context than architecture constraint specification; however, the choice of this language was made because:

1) it explicitly provides support for architecture constraint specification;

2) it is reflexive, at almost all levels (everything is reified, except the service implementations);

3) entity reification of this language is realized using components, and not by objects, unlike in other component-based programming languages.

Due to this last point, we propose a homogeneous environment for developers where they only define component descriptors; they will never have to choose between objects or components to define this or that business domain entity in their applications.

An excerpt from the Compo metamodel is given in Figure 2.9. In this metamodel, there is a clear distinction between a component descriptor and a component instance (simply called: Component). In UML, Component inherits from Class, making it a component descriptor. The fact of inheriting from the Class metaclass gives it the ability to be instantiated (see the meta-association between Classifier and InstanceSpecification in the metamodel in Figure 2.6). In UML, a component instance is nothing special composed with a class instance.

In Compo, there is a generalized dichotomy between descriptors and their instances: component descriptor and component, port descriptor and port, etc. In a Compo component descriptor (metaclass `Descriptor`), the programmer can declare a number of port descriptors. The latter must show the list of service signatures (a service is equivalent to an operation in UML), which can be grouped in a named or anonymous interface (`ServiceSignatureList`). These services have a signature. A (`BindDescription`)) connector links a source port descriptor to a destination port descriptor. A port realizes a port descriptor, and may be a Collection or simple type (*Single*). A port can, moreover, be provided or required. It can be internal or external. For example, an internal required port serves to connect component instances to their encompassing component. Lastly, we have integrated the inheritance in this language. A component descriptor can inherit from another descriptor (its *super-descriptor*[11]).

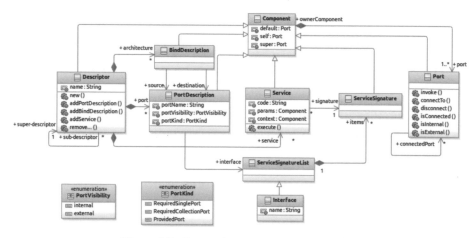

**Figure 2.9.** *Excerpt from the Compo metamodel*

Constraints imposed by the *Pipe and Filter* style can be programmed in Compo as follows:

---

11 This inheritance mechanism between component descriptors extends the classic inheritance between classes, especially by offering the option to extend the required ports [SPA 12].

```
 1  Descriptor PipeAndFilter extends Constraint
 2  {
 3      internally requires {
 4          scOne  <:  SubConstraintOne ;
 5          scTwo  <:  SubConstraintTwo ;
 6          scThree  <:  SubConstraintThree ;
 7          scFour  <:  SubConstraintFour ;
 8          scFive  <:  SubConstraintFive ;
 9      }
10      architecture {
11          delegate  contextscOne to context self ;
12          delegate  contextscTwo to context self ;
13          delegate  contextscThree oneDelegReq to context self ;
14          delegate  contextscFour to context self ;
15          delegate  contextscFive to context self ;
16      }
17      service  verify () {
18          |c1  c2  c3  c4  c5 |
19          c1  :=  scOne . verify () ;
20          c2  :=  scTwo . verify () ;
21          c3  :=  scThree . verify () ;
22          c4  :=  scFour . verify () ;
23          c5  :=  scFive . verify () ;
24
25          return  ((( c1 . and ([ c2 ])) . and ([ c3 ])) . and ([ c4 ])) . and ([ c5 ]) ;
26      }
27  }
```

In this listing, we rely on an architecture constraint specification model in the form of components initially introduced in [TIB 11]. Different sub-constraints imposed by the *Pipe and Filter* style are then defined by several component descriptors. In this listing, we declare the component descriptor, called PipeAndFilter, which contains the set of component instances verifying the five sub-constraints (declared in lines 4 to 8). These components are connected to their encompassing component (lines 11 to 15). Next, we start checks by invoking the verify() service on each port of the different internal components in the PipeAndFilter component verify service. The final result must correspond to the conjunction (in the Boolean logic sense) of different (Boolean) results returned by the internal component services (line 25).

For the sake of simplicity, we give the listings of two component descriptors here. They involve the descriptors formalizing the first and fourth subconstraints:

```
1  Descriptor SubConstraintOne extends Constraint
2  {
3      service verify () {
4          | retval |
5          retval := true;
6          intComps := context.getPorts ().select ([:p |
7              &p.isRequired ().and([&p.isInternal ()]);
8          ]);
9          intComps.each ([:ic |
10             ic.getPorts ().each ([:x |
11                 if (&x.isProvided ().and([&p.isExternal ()])) {
12                     | count |
13                     &x.getConnectedPorts ().each ([:cp |
14                         if (&cp.isProvided ().and([&p.isExternal ()]))
                             {
15                             if (&cp.getOwner () == context.yourself ()
                                 )
16                             { retVal := retVal.and([true]); }
17                             else
18                             { retVal := retVal.and([false]); }
19                         }
20                     ]);
21
22                 }
23                 if (&x.isRequired ().and([&p.isExternal ()])) {
24                     &x.getConnectedPorts ().each ([:cp |
25                         if (&cp.isProvided ().and([&p.isExternal ()]))
                             {
26                             if (&cp.getOwner ().getOwner () == context.
                                 yourself ())
27                             { retVal := retVal.and([true]); }
28                             else
29                             { retVal := retVal.and([false]); }
30                         }
31                     ]);
32                 }
33             ]);
34         ]);
35         return retVal;
36     }
37 }
```

In this listing, we have a component descriptor implementing the verify() service, which tests the first *Pipe and Filter* style subconstraint. This service first identifies references to the internal components (rather than their ports) by relying on the internal required ports of the composite. Access to the metalevel is gained using the "&" operator (see line 7, for example). This makes it possible to know if a port is required or provided, or if it is internal or external. This also allows access to the connectors linking one port to the port of another component (line 13). The rest of the constraint corresponds to the ACL constraint defined in the first listing in this section, where we verify the presence of a single component connected to its encompassing component (providing the context port in the listing above) *via* its provided port(s); the other required ports of this internal component must be connected to the other internal components.

```
1  Descriptor SubConstraintFour extends Constraint
2  {
3      service verify () {
4          conns := context.getDescriptor().getDescribedConnections();
5          conns.each ([: conn |
6              |dest source |
7              source := conn.getSourcePortComponent();
8              dest := conn.getDestinationPortComponent();
9              conns.each ([: conn2 |
10                 if ((conn2.getSourcePortComponent() == dest).and ([
11                     conn2.getDestinationPortComponent() == source ])
                       )
12                     { return false; }
13             ]);
14         ]);
15         return true;
16     }
17 }
```

The fourth subconstraint programmed in Compo above checks the absence of the following scenario: if we have conn and conn2 connectors between components, if conn has as its destination a component identical to the component representing the conn2 source (see line 10), then conn has as its source the destination of conn2 (line 11). This reflects the presence of connectors between a pair of components going in different directions, which is forbidden by the *Pipe and Filter* style.

We note here that architecture constraints expressed in Compo as components aim at improving reuse. These different "constraint-components" can be assembled to form a single constraint-component formalizing the *Pipe & Filter* style. Some among these constraint-components can be reused in the formalization of other styles, such as *Pipeline* or layered styles. These enable architects to avoid having to rewrite parts of subconstraints.

## 2.5. Architecture constraints on service-oriented applications

A service is a grouping of operations into one single "black box" entity, implemented in any language and deployed on any platform. This entity does not maintain a state between the invocations of these different operations, coming from a client program. When a service is accessible via the HTTP protocol (with SOAP or not), we have a *web* service.

There is a profile with a number of standard stereotypes in the UML specification. Among these stereotypes, we find an extension of the Component metaclass, called service, which designates "functional stateless components" [OMG 11]. This corresponds to the notion of service discussed in this section.

Among architecture constraints expressible on service-oriented applications, we find the SOA patterns [ERL 09]. These patterns, such as *Service Façade*, impose restrictions at the structural level of an application. These restrictions must be formalized, in order to guarantee the maintenance of quality attributes associated with the pattern during development.

In this section, we will show how we express architecture constraints on service-oriented applications, designed and implemented using only one language, called BPEL (standardized by Oasis under the name WSBPEL: *Web Services Business Process Execution Language* [OAS 07]). Our choice of BPEL is driven by the fact that it is a standardized language, widely used by information systems developers to model and execute their business processes based on *web* services. Thus, in this chapter, a service-oriented application is assimilated into a BPEL process with several *web* service partners.

Figure 2.10 shows an excerpt from the metamodels of BPEL (upper part of the figure) and WSDL[12] (lower part). A process is composed of various ordered activities (ordered qualifier on the role activity in the association between Process and Activity in the figure). These activities can be of different kinds. We have listed only three of them in the metamodel (for the purposes of the constraints defined above): Invoke to invoke the partner *web* service operations (providers), Receive to receive their responses or else to receive the requests of the partner *web* services (clients), and Sequence which is a composite activity (see composition with Activity in the metamodel). The latter serves to implement sequences of activities. A process

---

12 WSDL (*Web Service Description Language*) is the W3C standard for Web service interface description : www.w3.org/TR/wsdl20/.

can define a number of variables, which can contain request or response messages from *web* services. It declares links toward partner *web* services, (PartnerLink) which indicate the client or provider *web* services used by the process. Each *PartnerLink* designates roles for the process (myRole) and for the partner service (partner role). A role indicates a PortType (Interface, since WSDL 2.0) which represents the WSDL structure in which the provided or required operations are described, as well as the exchanged messages.

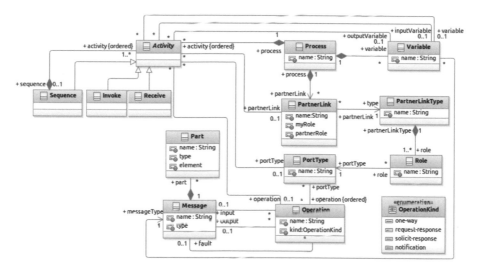

**Figure 2.10.** *Excerpt from the BPEL and WSDL (Process, Activity, PartnerLink and PortType) metamodels*

There is a plethora of architecture patterns for service-oriented applications in the literature and in practice, known as *Service-Oriented Architecture* (SOA) patterns [ERL 09]). Of these patterns, we have chosen the *Service Façade* pattern [ERL 09]. This pattern recommends defining a single service for publishing/providing operations, realized by a BPEL process. The main objective of this pattern is to set aside the (sometimes complex) details of the services presented by a number of suppliers, by proposing a single service. A "toy" example of the BPEL process designed with this pattern is given in Figure 2.11.

In this figure, the service facade is realized using the *partner link* attached to the first activity in the process (the Receive activity) and its corresponding

`Reply` activity, which is found at the end of the process. In the middle of the process, we find a number of `Invoke` activities[13] to invoke service operations provided by third parties.

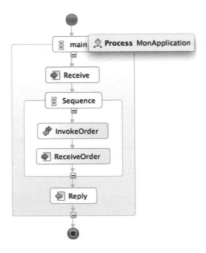

**Figure 2.11.** *Basic service façade pattern illustration*

The architecture constraint imposed by this pattern consists of several subconstraints:

– the process has as its first activity a `Receive` activity, linked to a *partner link* representing the client (of the process);

– the process has as its last activity a `Reply` activity, with the same `partner link`, the same `port type` and the same operation as the *Receive* activity of the previous subconstraint;

– the only `Receive` activities accepted in the middle of the process must be preceded by corresponding `Invoke` activities. These are used to invoke partner service operations provided by third parties. The `Receive` activities, authorized here, will then serve to receive messages returned by the invoked service operations.

Due to lack of space, we have deliberately simplified the constraint on the BPEL process. Indeed, if we want to be complete in the constraint

---

13 For the sake of simplicity, a single `Invoke` is shown in Figure 2.11.

specification imposed by the service facade pattern, we would have to add other types of activities, which could interact with a process client, such as `Pick` and `OnEvent` activities. Here, we have only dealt with `Receive`-type activities.

This constraint is formalized in ACL on the metamodel in Figure 2.10 in the listings below. The first subconstraint is specified as follows:

```
 1  context MyApplication : Process inv :
 2  let fst : Activity =
 3  if self.activity −>first().activity = null  — is not a composite
        activity
 4  then self.activity −>first()
 5  else if self.activity −>first().oclIsTypeOf(Sequence)
 6    then self.activity −>first().oclAsType(Sequence).activity −>first()
 7    else null
 8    endif
 9  endif
10  in
11  if fst <> null
12  then fst.oclIsTypeOf(Receive)
13  else false
14  endif
```

In this first sub-constraint, we firstly identify what the first activity declared in the process is[14]. The different (`if`) tests enable cases where the first activity is a composite (`Sequences` for example), rather than a simple activity, to be handled. In this case, the first activity within this sequence will have to be identified. The check undertaken in line 12 allows us to ensure that this is a `Receive` activity.

Here also, we simplify the constraint specification by considering only `Sequences` as possible composite activities within the process. In practice, other composite activities are possible. In this case, it suffices simply to add tests in the constraint, in order to take them into account (in the `else` in line 7). In this constraint, we consider only one level of depth in composite services. If we want to take several levels of depth into account (for the first activity in the process, which is rare), a recursive navigation should be performed (see below for an example).

---

14 Given that the activities in the process are ordered (see the metamodel), navigation to `Activity` from `Process` returns an `OrderedSet`, which allows operations like `first()` to be used to access the first activity in the process.

With the second subconstraint, as with the first, it is sufficient to replace first() with last() to access the last activity and check that the activity type corresponds to Reply. What follows must be added to this, to check that the properties of this activity and the first activity (Receive) have identical names:

```
 1 ...
 2 if  lst  <>  null  —  In  assuming  that  lst  contains  the  last  activity
 3 then  lst . oclIsTypeOf ( Reply )
 4    and  lst . oclAsType ( Reply ) . partnerLink . name
 5      =  fst . oclAsType ( Receive ) . partnerLink . name
 6    and  lst . oclAsType ( Reply ) . portType . name
 7      =  fst . oclAsType ( Receive ) . portType . name
 8    and  lst . oclAsType ( Reply ) . operation . name
 9      =  fst . oclAsType ( Receive ) . operation . name
10 else  false
11 endif
```

The third subconstraint can be written in ACL as follows:

```
 1 ...
 2 and
 3 let  activities  :  OrderedSet ( Activity ) =
 4 self . activity –>excluding ( fst )–>excluding ( lst )–>closure ( activity )
 5 in
 6 activities –>forAll ( a  :  Activity  |
 7 if  a . oclIsTypeOf ( Receive )
 8 then
 9    activities –>exists ( aa  :  Activity  |
10      activities –>indexOf ( aa )  <  activities –>indexOf ( a )
11      and  aa . oclIsTypeOf ( Invoke )
12      and  aa . oclAsType ( Invoke ) . partnerLink . name
13        =  a . oclAsType ( Receive ) . partnerLink . name
14      —  and  ...  ( same  thing  for  the  portType  and  operation )
15    )
16 else  true
17 endif )
```

A BPEL process can consist of composite activities, which in their turn contain other composite activities, and so on, up to a certain depth. In the subconstraint defined above, we thus recursively identify all activities in the process, by excluding the first (fst) and last (lst) activities. This recursivity is undertaken due to the OCL closure(...) operation in line 4. Next, we ensure that if there is a Receive activity among these activities, it is preceded by an Invoke activity corresponding to it, i.e. with the same partner link, port type and operation (lines 10 to 14).

We have shown in this section that simply combining OCL and a metamodel of BPEL and WSDL languages has allowed us to formalize architecture constraints imposed by an SOA pattern. We have done the same exercise on other patterns (results are in the process of being published), and we suspect that every difficulty resides in identifying the correct subconstraints (before their formalization), which represent a given pattern. It relates to a classic problem in formal specification languages. It is necessary to check that the set of these subconstraints is complete and that each of these is rigorously defined. This guarantees that we know, as a result of their simple verification, whether a service-oriented application conforms to an SOA pattern.

## 2.6. Conclusion

A software architecture defines the "coarse-grained" organization of a software system. These software systems have been growing in complexity which, for many decades, has driven the proposal of a multitude of works about software architecture documentation. This documentation has involved not only architects' product (the what: architecture description), but also the decisions taken during development of this product and the reasons for these decisions (the how and the why). We have focused on this second aspect in this chapter, where we have argued that architecture descriptions should be accompanied by a "formal" specification (formal, in the sense of being able to be automatically interpreted and verified), which describes the constraints imposed by architectural decisions. We have illustrated our remarks with a number of constraints formalizing some architecture styles and patterns (as examples of architectural decisions). We have shown how these constraints can be expressed using simple languages, which are even sometimes used to describe the architecture itself (in the case of Java and Compo). The objective of these architecture constraints is twofold. On the one hand, as supplementary documentation, they help in our understanding of the architecture of an application. On the other hand, as specifications able to be automatically verified, they allow reliable evolutions. This means that we can know, among other things, whether the new architecture (after evolution) consistently adheres to decisions previously taken (work that we have conducted on component-based applications [TIB 06a]).

Moreover, we have shown that the specification of these constraints is not limited to the architectures of component-based applications (work undertaken some years ago [TIB 10]). They have a use both in object- and service-oriented applications. Furthermore, we have shown their use not only in the design phase, but also in the implementation phase (accompanying code).

We have developed several interpreters for the different languages presented in this chapter. All these interpreters perform static analysis of architecture descriptions (written in most cases in XML dialects). Moreover, we have previously been interested in the conversion of constraints written in ACL from one metamodel to another for component-based applications [TIB 06b]. We have shown, for example, how we will be able to automatically convert architecture constraints written with ACL on applications modeled with UML components into constraints written with ACL on applications implemented with Fractal/Julia.

We can formulate the following ideas as future perspectives for this concept of architecture constraints:

– constraint specification independent of a given paradigm, by using a metamodel of graphs (an architecture description being considered as a graph with nodes and edges), then their conversion to different paradigms;

– proposal of a high-level language for the reuse of constraints by specialization (e.g. *Pipeline* style constraints are a specialization of *Pipe and Filter* style constraints);

– code generation from architecture constraints;

– application of these constraints in an integrated development environment.

## 2.7. Bibliography

[ALD 02] ALDRICH J., CHAMBERS C., NOTKIN D., "ArchJava: connecting software architecture to implementation", *Proceedings of the 24th International Conference on Software Engineering (ICSE '02)*, ACM, pp. 187–197, 2002.

[ALL 97] ALLEN R., A formal approach to software architecture, PhD Thesis, Carnegie Mellon University, Pittsburgh, PA, May 1997.

[BAS 12] BASS L., CLEMENTS P., KAZMAN R., *Software Architecture in Practice,* 3rd ed., Addison-Wesley, 2012.

[BLE 05] BLEWITT A., BUNDY A., STARK I., "Automatic verification of design patterns in Java", *Proceedings of the 20th IEEE/ACM International Conference on Automated Software Engineering (ASE '05)*, ACM, pp. 224–232, 2005.

[BOE 08] DE BOER R.C., FARENHORST R., "In search of 'architectural knowledge'", *Proceedings of the 3rd International Workshop on Sharing and Reusing Architectural Knowledge (SHARK '08)*, ACM, pp. 71–78, 2008.

[BOK 99] BOKOWSKY B., "CoffeeStrainer: statically-checked constraints on the definition and use of types in Java", *Proceedings of the 7th European Software Engineering Conference held jointly with the 7th ACM SIGSOFT International Symposium on Foundations of Software Engineering (ESEC/FSE)*, Springer-Verlag, Toulouse, France, pp. 355–374, 1999.

[BOS 04] BOSCH J., "Software architecture: the next step", *Proceedings of the 1st European Workshop on Software Architecture (EWSA '04)*, vol. 3047 of Lecture Notes in Computer Science, Springer, pp. 194–199, 2004.

[BRI 05] BRIAND L.C., LABICHE Y., DI PENTA M., *et al.*, "An experimental investigation of formality in UML-based development", *IEEE Transactions on Software Engineering*, vol. 31, no. 10, pp. 833–849, October 2005.

[BRU 04] BRUNETON E., THIERRY C., LECLERCQ M., *et al.*, "An open component model and its support in Java", *Proceedings of the ACM SIGSOFT International Symposium on Component-based Software Engineering (CBSE '04)*, held in conjunction with ICSE '04, Edinburgh, Scotland, May 2004.

[CER 89] CERI S., GOTTLOB G., TANCA L., "What you always wanted to know about datalog (and never dared to ask)", *IEEE Transactions on Knowledge and Data Engineering*, vol. 1, no. 1, pp. 146–166, March 1989.

[CHO 93] CHOWDHURY A., MEYERS S., "Facilitating software maintenance by automated detection of constraint violations", *Proceedings of the International Conference on Software Maintenance (ICSM '93)*, IEEE, pp. 262–271, 1993.

[CLE 02] CLEMENTS P., KAZMAN R., KLEIN M., *Evaluating Software Architectures, Methods and Case Studies*, Addison-Wesley, 2002.

[CLE 10] CLEMENTS P., BACHMANN F., BASS L., *et al.*, *Documenting Software Architectures, Views and Beyond,* 2nd ed., Addison-Wesley, 2010.

[DAQ 06] DAQING HOU, HOOVER H.J., "Using SCL to specify and check design intent in source code," *IEEE Transactions on Software Engineering*, IEEE Computer Society, vol. 32 no. 6, pp. 404–423, 2006.

[EIC 08] EICHBERG M., KLOPPENBURG S., KLOSE K., *et al.*, "Defining and continuous checking of structural program dependencies", *Proceedings of the 30th International Conference on Software Engineering (ICSE '08)*, ACM, pp. 391–400, 2008.

[ERL 09] ERL T., *SOA Design Patterns*, Prentice Hall, 2009.

[FAB 08] FABRESSE L., DONY C., HUCHARD M., "Foundations of a simple and unified component-oriented language", *Journal of Computer Languages, Systems & Structures*, vol. 34, no. 2–3, pp. 130–149, 2008.

[FAL 11]  FALESSI D., CANTONE G., KAZMAN R., *et al.*, "Decision-making techniques for software architecture design: a comparative survey", *ACM Computing Surveys (CSUR)*, vol. 43, no. 4, pp. 33:1–33:28, ACM, October 2011.

[FEI 12]  FEILER P.H., GLUCH D.P., *Model-Based Engineering with AADL: An Introduction to the SAE Architecture Analysis & Design Language*, Addison-Wesley Professional, 2012.

[GAM 95]  GAMMA E., HELM R., JOHNSON R., *et al.*, *Design Patterns: Elements of Reusable Object-Oriented Sofware*, Addison-Wesley Professional Computing Series, Addison Wesley Longman Inc., 1995.

[GAR 94]  GARLAN D., ALLEN R., OCKERBLOOM J., "Exploiting style in architectural design environments", *Proceedings of the ACM SIGSOFT Symposium on the Foundations of Software Engineering*, New Orleans, LA, pp. 175–188, 1994.

[GAR 00]  GARLAN D., MONROE R.T., WILE D., "Acme: architectural description of component-based systems", in LEAVENS G.T., SITARAMAN M. (eds.), *Foundations of Component-Based Systems*, Cambridge University Press, pp. 47–68, 2000.

[GIL 10]  GILLES O., HUGUES J., "Expressing and enforcing user-defined constraints of AADL models", *Proceedings of the 5th UML and AADL Workshop (UML and AADL 2010)*, 2010.

[HAR 07]  HARRISON N., AVGERIOU P., ZDUN U., "Using patterns to capture architectural decisions", *IEEE Software*, vol. 24, no. 4, pp. 38–45, July–August 2007.

[HOA 78]  HOARE C.A.R., "Communicating sequential processes", *Communications of the ACM*, vol. 21, no. 8, pp. 666–677, August 1978.

[JAN 05]  JANSEN A., BOSCH J., "Software architecture as a set of architectural design decisions", *Proceedings of the 5th IEEE/IFIP Working Conference on Software Architecture (WICSA '05)*, 2005.

[KLA 96]  KLARLUND N., KOISTINEN J., SCHWARTZBACH M.I., "Formal design constraints", *Proceedings of the 11th ACM SIGPLAN Conference on Object-Oriented Programming, Systems, Languages, and Applications*, ACM Press, San Jose, CA, pp. 370–383, 1996.

[KRU 09]  KRUCHTEN P., CAPILLA R., DUENAS J.C., "The decision view's role in software architecture practice", *IEEE Software*, vol. 26, no. 2, pp. 36–42, 2009.

[LUC 95]  LUCKHAM D.C., KENNEY J.L., AUGUSTIN L.M., *et al.*, "Specification and analysis of system architecture using Rapide", *IEEE Transactions on Software Engineering*, vol. 21, no. 4, pp. 336–355, 1995.

[MED 96]  MEDVIDOVIC N., OREIZY P., ROBBINS J.E., *et al.*, "Using object-oriented typing to support architectural design in the C2 style", *Proceedings of the 4th ACM SIGSOFT Symposium on the Foundations of Software Engineering (FSE '96)*, San Francisco, CA, pp. 24–32, October 1996.

[MED 00]  MEDVIDOVIC N., TAYLOR N.R., "A classification and comparison framework for software architecture description languages", *IEEE Transactions on Software Engineering*, vol. 26, no. 1, pp. 70–93, 2000.

[MED 02] MEDVIDOVIC N., ROSENBLUM D.S., REDMILES D.F., *et al.*, "Modeling software architectures in the Unified Modeling Language", *ACM Transactions on Software Engineering and Methodology*, vol. 11, no. 1, pp. 2–57, 2002.

[MIN 96] MINSKY N.H., "Law-governed regularities in object systems. Part I: an abstract model", *Theory and Practice of Object Systems*, vol. 2, no. 4, pp. 283–301, 1996.

[MIN 97] MINSKY N.H., PAL P.P., "Law-governed regularities in object systems. Part II: a concrete implementation", *Theory and Practice of Object Systems*, vol. 3, no. 2, pp. 87–101, 1997.

[MON 01] MONROE R.T., Capturing software architecture design expertise with Armani, Report, School of Computer Science, Carnegie Mellon University, Pittsburgh, PA, 2001.

[MOR 95] MORICONI M., QIAN X., RIEMENSCHNEIDER R.A., "Correct architecture refinement", *IEEE Transactions on Software Engineering*, vol. 21, no. 4, pp. 356–372, April 1995.

[MOR 97] MORICONI M., RIEMENSCHNEIDER R.A., Introduction to SADL 1.0: a language for specifying software architecture hierarchies, Report, Computer Science Laboratory, SRI International, 1997.

[OAS 07] OASIS, "Web services business process execution language version 2.0", available at http://docs.oasis-open.org/wsbpel/2.0/OS/wsbpel-v2.0-OS.pdf, 2007.

[OMG 08] OMG, "UML profile for CORBA and CORBA components (CCCMP), version 1.0 specification, document formal/08-04-07", Object Management Group, available at http://www.omg.org/spec/CCCMP/1.0/PDF, 2008.

[OMG 11] OMG, "Unified Modeling Language superstructure, version 2.4.1 specification, document formal/2011-08-06", Object Management Group, available at http://www.omg.org/spec/ UML/2.4.1/Superstructure/PDF, 2011.

[OMG 12] OMG, "Object Constraint Language specification, version 2.3.1, document formal/2012-01-01", Object Management Group, available at http://www.omg.org/spec/ OCL/2.3.1/PDF, 2012.

[REE 79] REENSKAUG T., Thing-model-view-editor: an example from a planning system, Report , Xerox Parc, CA , May 1979.

[SEC 08] SECO J.C., SILVA R., PIRIQUITO M., "ComponentJ: a cComponent-based programming language with dynamic reconfiguration", *Computer Science and Information Systems*, vol. 5, no. 2, pp. 65–86, 2008.

[SHA 96] SHAW M., GARLAN D., *Software Architecture: Perspectives on an Emerging Discipline*, Prentice Hall, 1996.

[SPA 12] SPACEK P., DONY C., TIBERMACINE C., *et al.*, "An inheritance system for structural & behavioral reuse in component-based software programming", *Proceedings of the 11th International Conference on Generative Programming and Component Engineering (GPCE '12)*, ACM Press, Dresden, Germany, September 2012.

[TAN 05] TANG A., BABAR M.A., GORTON I., *et al.*, "A survey of the use and documentation of architecture design rationale", *Proceedings of the 5th IEEE/IFIP Working Conference on Software Architecture (WICSA '05)*, Pittsburgh, PA, November 2005.

[TAN 09] TANG A., HAN J., VASA R., "Software architecture design reasoning: a case for improved methodology support", *IEEE Software*, vol. 26, no. 2, pp. 43–49, 2009.

[TER 09] TERRA R., DE OLIVEIRA VALENTE M.T., "A dependency constraint language to manage object-oriented software architectures", *Software Practice and Experience*, vol. 39, no. 12, pp. 1073–1094, 2009.

[TIB 06a] TIBERMACINE C., FLEURQUIN R., SADOU S., "On-demand quality-oriented assistance in component-based software evolution", *Proceedings of the 9th ACM SIGSOFT International Symposium on Component-Based Software Engineering (CBSE '06)*, Springer LNCS, Vasteras, Sweden, pp. 294–309, June 2006.

[TIB 06b] TIBERMACINE C., FLEURQUIN R., SADOU S., "Simplifying transformations of architectural constraints", *Proceedings of the ACM Symposium on Applied Computing (SAC '06), Track on Model Transformation*, ACM Press, Dijon, France, pp. 1240–1244, April 2006.

[TIB 10] TIBERMACINE C., FLEURQUIN R., SADOU S., "A family of languages for architecture constraint specification", *Journal of Systems and Software,* vol. 83, no. 1, pp. 815–831, 2010.

[TIB 11] TIBERMACINE C., SADOU S., DONY C., et al.,"Component-based specification of software architecture constraints", *Proceedings of the 14th International ACM Sigsoft Symposium on Component Based Software Engineering (CBSE '11)*, ACM, pp. 31–40, 2011.

[TYR 05] TYREE J., AKERMAN A., "Architecture decisions: demystifying architecture", *IEEE Software*, vol. 22, no. 2, pp. 19–27, March–April 2005.

Chapter 3

# Software Architectures and Multiple Variability

During the construction of software product lines (SPLs), variability management is a crucial activity. A large number of software variants must be produced, in most cases, by using extensible architectures. In this chapter, we present the various applications of a set of modular management variability tools (feature model script language for manipulation and automatic reasoning (FAMILIAR)) for different forms of architecture (component, service and plugin based), and at different stages of the software lifecycle. We discuss the lessons learnt from these studies and present guidelines for resolving recurring problems associated with multiple variability and software architecture.

## 3.1. Introduction

Many organizations today are faced with the challenge of constructing multiple, similar software products, which form SPLs.

It is no longer conceivable for these organizations to design software for only one client, one type of hardware, one operating system, one graphic interface, one country or in one language. Consequently, variability – or the

---

Chapter written by Mathieu ACHER, Philippe COLLET and Philippe LAHIRE.

ability of a software artifact to be extended, configured, personalized and adapted to the needs of clients and their specific contexts in a preplanned manner [SVA 05] – is in the process of becoming omnipresent in computer systems. Several hundreds, if not thousands, of configuration options can be seen in real projects, in which thousands of software variants can be produced, all by using extensible architecture.

As the majority of software applications are now large-scale, business-critical, operated 24/7, distributed and ubiquitous, their complexity is increasing at a rate that outpaces all major software engineering advances. Their complexity and diversity have become such that new paradigms and techniques are henceforth necessary. SPL engineering is one of the main approaches of the last decade seeking to address this problem.

An SPL can be defined as *"a set of software-intensive systems that share a common, managed set of features and that are developed from a common set of core assets in a prescribed way"* [CLE 01].

SPL engineering aims to generate tailor-made variants to meet the needs of particular customers or environments and promotes the systematic reuse of software core assets. Development generally begins with a domain analysis to identify the common points and points of variation of SPL elements. It is customary to express the variability of an SPL in terms of *features* (characteristics), which are abstractions of the field that are of interest for different participants in the systems captured by the SPL. A *feature model* (characteristics model) can be used to organize all the *features* of the SPL as well as a definition of their valid combinations, simply and compactly [SCH 07, CZA 07, DAV 13]. More details on the foundations of SPLs and feature models (FMs) will be given in section 3.2.

As software systems are now organized around relatively explicit architecture, which defines entities, their properties and relations, techniques and tools must be used to manage the variability of this architecture. When the product line principles are applied starting from the phases before development, variability can be managed by means of FMs, which can then be associated with different parts of the software architecture [PAR 10]. The points of variation of the architecture are then associated with certain features, allowing automatic composition of the architectural elements when features are selected to configure a specific variant of the SPL. An absolutely crucial resultant property is the guarantee that variability such as that expressed in the FM will be consistent in relation to the architecture [CZA 06, APE 09, LOP 10a]. If the variability is too permissive, e.g. when constraints between the *features* have been forgotten in the FM, non-valid architecture variants will then potentially be derived during compilation or runtime. If, on the contrary, the variability is too restrictive, the software architecture's capacity will be under-exploited and combinations of features, though hoped for by clients, will not be accessible.

The need to manage and reflect on architecture variability has been identified many times in the literature (section 3.3 will give more details). In this chapter, we discuss three case studies where variability techniques seemed to be necessary: for different architecture types (component, service oriented and plugin based), for different objectives (re-engineering and development of extensible architecture, combinations in scientific workflows of configurable services, combinations of parametrizable algorithms in a pipeline), with particular problems (for example the need to integrate services originating from different suppliers and the need to integrate the architect's knowledge), and in three different fields (video surveillance, medical imaging and the FraSCAti *open source* project). The shared aspect of these three case studies is the need to model, reflect on and manipulate a multiple variability in software architecture. By multiple, we mean:

– Multiple systems: when a multitude of subsystems (modular systems such as components or services) or artifacts (for example dependency files like those managed by the Maven tool, hierarchical architecture model) are present in a software architecture, different descriptions of the variability must be compared, organized and finally combined to form a consistent result [BUH 05, BOS 10, HAR 09, ROS 10, HOL 12].

– Multiple participants: increasingly frequently, the development of a software system brings several participants from the same company or several software component suppliers into play. For example, Reiser and Weber [REI 07] explain the need to manage variability via different structures of a company sharing the development of sub-systems in the automotive field. In the semiconductor field, Hartmann *et al.* [HAR 09] use several variability models to describe different suppliers' propositions, with the objective of configuring and implementing SPLs using the proposed software components.

– Multiple perspectives: different viewpoints can be defined by participants in the software project, in accordance with different criteria or concerns. Furthermore, variability can be perceived in different ways according to whether one is, for example, an end user (we would then refer to external variability) or a developer (we would then refer to internal variability) [MET 07, POH 05]. These viewpoints entail various uses [HUB 13a, ACH 12c, HUB 13b], i.e. the definitions of several layers of abstraction, the need to reflect the organizational structure with various participants, the support for a collaborative design or configuration in several stages [MAN 09, MEN 10, CZA 05b, FIL 12].

In summary, the major problem is being able to combine, separate and reflect on different architectural elements (for example services, components and plugins) exhibiting numerous points of variation and governed by complex rules. In addition, these artifacts may potentially be maintained by different suppliers or described in accordance with different perspectives.

In this chapter, we introduce several applications of a modular management variability toolkit (FAMILIAR) for different forms of architecture and at different stages of the software lifecycle. For each case study, we show:

– how the variability problem impacts on software architecture;

– what the techniques are, formalized and implemented in FAMILIAR, which can be used to deal with the problem;

– what the results (for example observed benefits) of applying these techniques have been.

In section 3.4, we first study the separation of needs and concerns in the framework of a video surveillance application, based on software components organized in a pipeline architecture. Pipeline components, each exhibiting their own variability, are combined to respond to different contexts and specific application scenarios. The variability management toolkit assists users of the video surveillance SPL by configuring the pipeline at different levels in a coherent and coordinated manner.

In a second study (see section 3.5), we are interested in the management of scientific workflows in service-oriented architecture (SOA). Different types of highly parametrizable services are provided by different suppliers and are considered as reusable SPLs. A workflow is then constructed as a multiple SPL in which different SPLs are combined. The toolkit enables incremental verification of the coherence of the workflow once this has been converted to architecture and configured.

A third study (see section 3.6) is concerned with the reverse engineering of architectural variability models applied to plugin-based systems. The toolkit then enables the software architect (SA) to semi-automatically extract, refine and develop a variability model of the real software architecture. The equipped process can be repeated for different versions of the architecture, and also allows its variability to be managed over time.

We conclude this chapter by taking some lessons from the three case studies and drawing some research prospects from them (see section 3.7).

This chapter will greatly interest software architecture and/or variability researchers as well as architects in charge of the design and development of highly configurable software systems. The case studies shown exhibit real, complex problems, impacting on three types of software architecture. We also hope that the techniques equipped (via FAMILIAR) will be reused by practitioners when they have to manage multiple variability in their architecture.

## 3.2. Variability: foundations and principles

In this section, we undertake a brief introduction of the notions of SPLs and variability. Then, we introduce FMs, one of the most widely used formalisms for describing variability.

### 3.2.1. *Variability and product lines*

Traditionally, as far as software engineering is concerned, software systems are developed individually, i.e. one at a time. The development process typically begins with an analysis of customer needs, then several stages of development (specification, design, implementation and tests) are realized and the result is a unique software product. On the contrary, SPL engineering focuses on techniques enabling the development of several similar software systems with a common code basis [BAS 98, CLE 01, POH 05].

This form of engineering especially relies on the idea of mass customization [PIN 99], known within many industries. For example, in the automotive industry, emphasis is placed on creating one production line, from which numerous variants of the same model are produced, both personalized and yet very similar. Mass customization benefits from the principle of similarity and a modular design for the large-scale production of personalized products. SPL engineering aims to develop variants of the same product in a systematic and coordinated way, by providing custom-made solutions for each client. Rather than individually developing each variant from zero, the shared parts are designed only once and the possibility of personalizing software products for different contexts opens up new prospects. For example, although resources are rare and the hardware is heterogeneous in embedded systems, effective variants can be adapted to a device or to specific scenarios [BEU 04]. Because of the co-development and systematic reuse, SPLs provide many advantages [BAS 98, CLE 01, POH 05], such as the speed at which they can be placed on the market, lower costs and better quality.

SPL engineering is generally organized in two complementary phases. Domain engineering is concerned with development "for reuse", whereas application engineering corresponds to development "by reuse". The targeted domain set and its potential needs are analyzed, especially to characterize the SPL and identify what differs between products. This allows the common points and differences between the expected variants, which are generally described in terms of *features*, to be specified. A feature is a first-class abstraction of the domain concerned. It typically involves a functionality element, which is important to the end user [APE 09]. Application engineering corresponds to product development. The end products are derived using artifacts developed in the domain engineering phase and by adapting the end product to specific demands.

Variability management is both a central and specific point in SPL engineering. It corresponds to the process of factorizing common points and the systematic highlighting of what varies, in terms of the documentation, needs, code, battery testing or models. Different approaches, formalisms and tools can be used for each stage of the process. For example, there are different approaches [JOH 09] and mechanisms for realizing domain analysis, modeling the variability of the model and realizing implementation. The objective of SPLs is primarily variability management in space (one entity can take various forms) [ERW 10], in contrast to variability over time that is concerned rather with the management of versions. Weiss and Lai hence define variability in SPLs as *"an assumption about how members of a family may differ from each other"* [WEI 99].

Thus, variability specifies the particularities of a system corresponding to the specific expectations of a client, whereas the parts found in each client's expectations correspond to the hypotheses that are true for all members of the product line. In [SVA 05], the authors define variability as *"the ability of a software system or artifact to be efficiently extended, changed, customized or configured for use in a particular context"*. It is recognized that modeling points of variation and their associated variants is necessary to express variability [JAC 97]. Thus, variability modeling languages (which can be graphic, textual or a blend of both) enables the production of dedicated models. These variability models describe points of variation and so facilitate the identification and impact of differences present within the same family. They are also used for the implementation of various approaches, the automatic generation of variants, error detection or to run automated reasoning.

### 3.2.2. *Feature models*

Feature modeling is a popular modeling technique that has attracted a great deal of interest since its introduction by Kang *et al.* [KAN 90] in the Feature-Oriented Domain Analysis (FODA) method. Even if we look at other approaches for isolating the variability description (for example the orthogonal variability model (OVM) [POH 05] or Covamof [SIN 06, SIN 08]), this approach is currently the *de facto* standard for describing variability. It also provides graphical representation through *feature diagrams*. FMs were henceforth very widely adopted with the presence of formal semantics, reasoning techniques and tools [SCH 07, CZA 07, APE 09, BEN 10]. Many extensions or dialects of FMs are proposed in the literature [KAN 98, GRI 98, RIE 03, BEU 04, CZA 05b, SCH 07, ASI 06, ASI 07]. We describe the essential principles and the foundations of FM semantics.

An FM defines both a hierarchy, which structures *features* in levels going from the more general to the most detailed, and variability elements, which are expressed through several mechanisms. Furthermore, every propositional constraint (for example *implies* or *excludes*) can be specified in order to express other complex dependencies between primitives. By dividing a feature into "subfeatures", these can be optional (*optional*), mandatory (*mandatory*) and constitute exclusive (*Xor*) or inclusive (*Or* groups) alternatives. For the purpose of our studies, we consider an FM to be composed of a *feature diagram* associated with a set of constraints described in propositional logic.

Figure 3.1a describes an FM example taken from [HUB 13a]. The *feature diagram* is displayed in accordance with a graphic notation similar to that in the FODA method [KAN 90]. This example relates to a vehicle product line and, in this respect, describes a subset of common and specific features of different variants of the Audi A3.

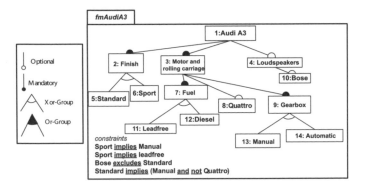

(a) *feature model*: FODA display

$\llbracket fmAudiA3 \rrbracket =$
$\{\{1, 2, 5, 3, 7, 11, 9, 13\},$
$\{1, 2, 5, 3, 7, 11, 9, 13, 4\},$
$\{1, 2, 5, 3, 7, 12, 9, 13\},$
$\{1, 2, 5, 3, 7, 12, 9, 13, 4\},$
$\{1, 2, 6, 3, 7, 11, 9, 13\},$
$\{1, 2, 6, 3, 7, 11, 9, 13, 4\},$
$\{1, 2, 6, 3, 7, 11, 9, 13, 4, 10\},$
$\{1, 2, 6, 3, 7, 11, 8, 9, 13\},$
$\{1, 2, 6, 3, 7, 11, 8, 9, 13, 4\},$
$\{1, 2, 6, 3, 7, 11, 8, 9, 13, 4, 10\}$
$\}$

(b) set of corresponding configurations

$\phi_{fmAudiA3} = 1 \; // \text{root}$
// Mandatory features
$\wedge \; (1 \Leftrightarrow 2) \wedge \; (1 \Leftrightarrow 3)$
$\wedge \; (7 \Leftrightarrow 3) \wedge \; (9 \Leftrightarrow 3)$
// Exclusive features (Xor - groups)
$\wedge \; (5 \Rightarrow (2 \wedge \neg 6)) \wedge (6 \Rightarrow (2 \wedge \neg 5))$
$\wedge \; (2 \Rightarrow (5 \vee 6)) \wedge (11 \Rightarrow (7 \wedge \neg 12))$
$\wedge \; (12 \Rightarrow (7 \wedge \neg 11)) \wedge (7 \Rightarrow (11 \vee 12))$
$\wedge \; (13 \Rightarrow (9 \wedge \neg 14)) \wedge (14 \Rightarrow (9 \wedge \neg 13))$
$\wedge \; (9 \Rightarrow (13 \vee 14))$
// Optional features
$\wedge \; (8 \Rightarrow 3) \wedge \; (10 \Rightarrow 4) \wedge \; (4 \Rightarrow 1)$
// Constraints
$\wedge \; (6 \Rightarrow 13) \wedge \; (6 \Rightarrow 11)$
$\wedge \; (10 \Rightarrow \neg 5) \wedge \; (5 \Rightarrow (13 \wedge \neg 8))$

(c) corresponding propositional formula

**Figure 3.1.** *Feature model, set of configurations and encoding in propositional logic*

An FM hierarchy is characterized by a tree $G = (\mathcal{F}, E, r)$, where $\mathcal{F}$ is a finite set of *features* and $E \subseteq \mathcal{F} \times \mathcal{F}$ is a finite set of edges (the edges display a hierarchy of *features* broken down from top to bottom, i.e of the parent–child relations between them); $r \in \mathcal{F}$ being the *feature* root. An FM defines a set of combinations of valid features as configurations. A valid configuration is obtained by selecting the features in such a manner that:

– if a feature is selected, its parents will also be;

– if a parent is selected, all mandatory "subfeatures", one "subfeature" only of each of its "Xor" groups and at least one feature of each "Or" group are selected;

– the propositional constraints are satisfied.

For example, in Figure 3.1a, {Audi A3 (1), Finish (2), Standard (5), Motor and rolling carriage (3), Fuel (7) and Without lead (11)} display a valid configuration. The features Standard (5) and Quattro (8) cannot be simultaneously selected and Diesel (12) cannot be selected without Fuel (7) because of the parent–child relation between them; it is the same for Sport (6), which cannot be selected without Without lead (11), due to the constraint added.

We define $g$, an FM configuration, as a set of selected features.[1] $[\![g]\!]$ corresponds to the set of valid $g$ FM configurations and it thus displays a set of sets of features. FMs are semantically linked to the propositional logic [CZA 07]. The set of configurations characterized by an FM can be described as a propositional formula $\phi$ defined on a set of Boolean variables, where each variable corresponds to a feature (see Figure 3.1c for the formula that corresponds to the FM in Figure 3.1a). Converting FMs in the logic allows the use of reasoning techniques for automatic analysis [BEN 10].

### 3.3. Framework of studies and connected work

One of the recurring objectives of SAs is to plan certain changes or variations by placing appropriate mechanisms in the architecture. Despite the

---

1 Attentive readers will note that the feature automatic (14) is not present in any of the configurations of Figure 3.1a, due to the constraints. Automatic (14) is called a "dead feature". We will address this notion in brief in section 3.4.2.2.

considerable research of software systems, in general, and software architecture, in particular [BAC 01], the problem of architectural variability management has certainly not received enough attention from the research community. In this section, we discuss the multiplicity of this variability, then review existing works related to architectural variability, its extraction and development, as well as its realization.

### 3.3.1. *From multiplicity to variability*

In an increasing number of use contexts, the need of support for composing concerns and their variability becomes crucial. There are then multiple elements to take into account to control the variability of an architecture.

#### 3.3.1.1. *Multiple systems*

When a multitude of subsystems (in component- or service-based architecture) or artifacts must be combined, several variability descriptions must be related, organized and lastly composed, to form a consistent result. This use context is broad, with the management of several SPLs with shared variabilities [BUH 05], which evolve to SPL composition [BOS 10], in which a complex domain is captured and organized [HOL 12] into multiple product lines [HAR 09, ROS 10] with relations between input product lines' variability models. Taking these relations into account necessitates reasoning on the configuration sets present, while maintaining an understandable organization of them, i.e. a feature hierarchy. The same thing occurs when we extract variability models, mainly FMs, from different software artifacts, e.g. system configuration files with the Linux Kernel [SHE 11], programs [HAS 13], software architectures [ACH 13b] or product descriptions [ACH 12a].

#### 3.3.1.2. *Multiple stakeholders*

Multiple product lines potentially require the assumption of responsibility for various different stakeholders on one or more SPLs. Techniques have been developed for FMs that enable organizational structures and tasks to be reflected. For example, Reiser and Weber [REI 07] address the problem of displaying and managing FMs in SPLs that are implemented by several companies in the automotive field. Several FMs are elaborated upon so that they can be managed independently by suppliers. FM composition is therefore concerned with the propagation of local changes throughout the hierarchy. Similarly, Hartmann and Trew [HAR 08] use an FM in the context of a multiple SPL with several dimensions and in need of the FM fusion process definition during their preconfiguration.

### 3.3.1.3. *Multiple perspectives*

The need to be able to reason on FM compositions, while also being able to manipulate a consistent FM hierarchy, is highlighted by the separation of concerns within variability models.

Taking into consideration their increasing complexity and uses, users can define different viewpoints depending on different criteria or concerns. The most used viewpoints are those that define a user-centered view (external variability) from technical features (internal variability) [POH 05]. These views have several uses, e.g. defining abstraction levels, reflecting organizational structures with specific stakeholders [MAN 09], enabling collaborative design [MEN 10] or multilevel configurations [CZA 05b]. The separation of these views also means that relations and compositions must be realized at a given moment in order to:

– reason on the whole SPL, with references, constraints, a minimal version of the composition model;

– to synthesize a full model in semi-automatic mode [ACH 12c, ACH 13b, ACH 13c, AND 12, ROS 11].

It is now observed in several fields of application that multiple variability dimensions will be used, with different objectives, in most activities relevant to SPL engineering.

### 3.3.2. *Extraction and evolution of architectural variability*

In general, the approaches that undertake a variability extraction take into account quite different entry artifacts, such as patrimonial systems documentation [JOH 06] or textual demands [ALV 08]. In this regard, She *et al.* [SHE 11] have suggested an approach based on reverse engineering combining two distinct sources of information: the textual feature description and the dependencies between features. Later, we will present an approach that also benefits from combining two other sources of information, namely the dependencies between *plugins* and the architecture fragments.

The FM analysis and reasoning techniques in this chapter reuse and extend previous work in SPL engineering [BEN 10]. Metzger *et al.* [MET 07] propose an approach to cross-checking product line variability and software variability models, thus assuming that such models (or views) are available. Janota and Botterweck propose a theoretical foundation for checking that an FM does not allow feature configurations that are not realizable by the architecture [JAN 08]. Lopez-Herrejon and Eyged [LOP 10b] address a related problem in the context of safe composition by checking the consistency of multiview variability models. In particular, they check whether an FM developed by a domain expert is a specialization or a refactoring of an FM representing the variability of multiple models.

The extraction of architectural variability is necessarily linked to the works on reverse engineering software architectures [DUC 09]. In the case with which we are concerned, we start with an explicit, potentially extensible, architecture description and recover implicit architectural knowledge from it, such as undocumented dependencies between components. It should also be noted here that this is not a question of recovering the full system architecture, but rather extracting an accurate variability model expressing the exact set of *valid* architectural configurations that can be obtained, e.g. from the composition of several system plugins.

In [DHU 10, PLE 12], Dhungana *et al.* report that evolution support becomes particularly important for engineering SPLs and other variability-intensive systems. They propose model-driven support at the feature level, using FM concepts [PLE 12]. They developed a set of operators to make FMs evolve, but no *reasoning and differencing techniques* are proposed for controlling the evolution of FMs. This is, particularly, important in our context for understanding the impact of the evolution of an FM. Moreover, Lotufo *et al.* have studied the evolution of the Linux kernel system [LOT 10]. They identify edit operations applied in practice and new automation challenges, including the detection of edits that break existing configurations.

## 3.4. Video surveillance component architecture

### 3.4.1. *Case study*

The objective of video surveillance is to analyze sequences of images to detect interesting situations or events. According to the application, the corresponding results can be saved for other processing or to raise alerts for human observers. There are different types of video surveillance tasks, according to the situation: detection of intrusion, object or event counting, surveillance of people, animals or cars, reconnaissance for specific scenarios, etc. The processing chains for video surveillance are complex software systems, exhibiting a strong degree of variability in accordance with different concerns [MOI 11]. On the software architecture side, the number of components, their variations due to various choices among the possible algorithms, the different ways of assembling them and the number of parameters that can be accepted make it so complex that configuring a processing chain is time consuming and error prone. Futhermore, the number of different applications that the video surveillance covers, the environments and contexts in which it can be run, the service quality required, increase this difficulty all the more. Finally, the context of an application can change in real time, necessitating a dynamic reconfiguration of the architecture. To make things even more complicated, variability factors are not separate: they are linked by a set of constraints.

---

### Why is it a multiple variability problem?

*Multiple systems*: the processing chain is composed of several components, each implementing a particular processing type: acquisition, segmentation, *clustering*, classification, etc. (see the top of Figure 3.2). For each processing chain, several variants of a component can be chosen. By way of an example, a model of the variability of segmentation, classification and lighting analysis components is described via three FMs aggregated into one (see the right of Figure 3.2, PFC).

*Multiple concerns*: the variability of software components is distinguished from the variability of the deployment context of the application (see the left of Figure 3.2, VSAR). Making the context model explicit allows a video surveillance expert to constrain the software variability: some contexts necessitate the selection of certain component features. These constraints can be seen as transformation rules. For example, person detection (see the Person feature in VSAR, on the left of Figure 3.2) indicates the activation of the Omega feature, a particular model used by the classification component.

---

### 3.4.2. *Accounting for multiple variability*

This large-sized variability poses architectural problems for the design (e.g. finding valid processing chains configurations, anticipating possible runtime contexts), at deployment (e.g. selecting the initial configuration) and during runtime (e.g. changing configurations in response to contextual changes).

3.4.2.1. *Modeling multiple variability*

The VSAR FM (on the left of Figure 3.2) describes the context variability. Several concerns are modeled in VSAR (objects of interest, scene characteristics, etc.).

The PFC FM describes the variability of different types of components. In practice, and following the principle of separation of concerns, a variability model is associated with each type. In the example in Figure 3.2 (right-hand side), there are: $SC$ (for segmentation), $C$ (for classification) and $T$ (for the specific task; as it happens, lighting analysis). Some constraints are expressed as well to reinforce the consistency of the three component families, for example the features *edge* and *density* cannot be selected together. The three FMs are then aggregated to form one single FM, i.e. PFC. Definition 3.1 describes the *aggregation* operator.

DEFINITION 3.1 (AGGREGATION).– *The aggregation operation, noted* $\times$, *takes a set of FM s* $fm_1, fm_2, \ldots, fm_n$ *and a set of Boolean constraints* $cst_1, cst_2, \ldots, cst_m$ *on the features as input, then produces a new FM* $fm_r$ *in which the constraints and the FMs are simply recopied and reattached to a synthetic root feature:* $fm_r = \times (\{fm_1, fm_2, \ldots, fm_n\}, \{cst_1, cst_2, \ldots, cst_m\})$.

From the example shown in Figure 3.2, we obtain:

$$\text{PFC} = \times (\{SC, C, T\}, \{\neg Edge \vee \neg Density\})$$

Placing in relation VSAR and PFC, via the transformation rules, also relies on this *aggregation* operator:

$$FM_{full} = \times (\{\text{VSAR}, \text{PFC}\}, \{LightingNoise \Rightarrow Edge \wedge LightingAnalysis, \ldots\})$$

Given the number of constraints and the great number of features, it is necessary to verify some properties and to assist the user during manipulation of these models.

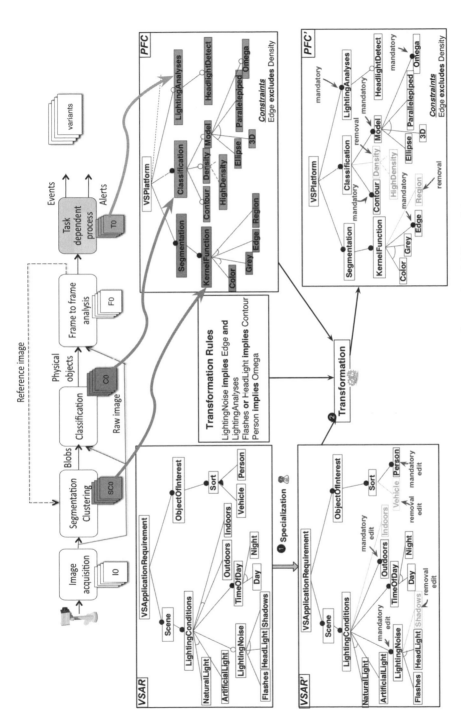

**Figure 3.2.** *Video surveillance processing chain and variability models. For color version of the figure, see www.iste.co.uk/oussalah/softwarearchitechtures2.zip*

### 3.4.2.2. *Reasoning*

Reasoning operations are run on the Boolean formula corresponding to the FM.

### 3.4.2.2.1. Checking consistency and anomalies detection

To verify the consistency of $FM_{full}$, in particular, it must be ensured that the corresponding $\phi_{full}$ Boolean formula is satisfiable, i.e. $[\![FM_{full}]\!] \neq \emptyset$.

DEFINITION 3.2 (DEAD FEATURES).– *A f feature is dead if it does not make up a part of any valid configuration of the FM. The set of dead features of an FM is denoted as* $deads(FM) = \{f \in \mathcal{F} \mid \forall c \in [\![FM]\!], f \notin c\}$.

DEFINITION 3.3 (CORE FEATURES).– *A f feature is "core" if it makes up a part of all valid configuration of the FM. The set of "core" features of an FM is denoted as* $cores(FM) = \{f \in \mathcal{F} \mid \forall c \in [\![FM]\!], f \in c\}$.

In the same way, *dead* and *core features* (see definitions 3.2 and 3.3) are reported to the user by operating $\phi_{full}$. By way of an example, the feature automatic (14) in Figure 3.1a is a dead feature. The detection of a dead feature can be assessed by the user as a modeling error (e.g. false transformation rule) or it can be intentional, since certain features are simply considered useless in a given context.

### 3.4.2.2.2. Checking realizability

The realizability property stipulates that, for each possible context of the application (as modeled in VSAR), there is at least one software configuration (as modeled in PFC). To check this property, it is necessary to:

1) aggregate PFC, VSAR and the transformation rules, which gives us $FM_{full}$;

2) check that each configuration authorized in VSAR is also valid in at least one $FM_{full}$ configuration only containing VSAR features. The intuition is that the property is true if the composition of VSAR and PFC has not reduced the VSAR configuration space.

$$\forall c \in [\![\text{VSAR}]\!], c \in [\![FM_{full}]\!]_{|\mathcal{F}_{\text{VSAR}}} \qquad\qquad [3.1]$$

where $\mathcal{F}_{\text{VSAR}}$ is the set of VSAR features and $A_{|B}$ denotes the projection of two sets: $A$ and $B$ suchas: $A_{|B} \overset{\triangle}{=} \{a' \mid a \in A \wedge a' = a \cap B\} = \{a \cap B \mid a \in A\}$.

To realize the projection, we use an operation called *slicing* (see definition 3.4). Given a subset of features, the *slicing* operator produces a new FM characterizing the projected set of configurations.

DEFINITION 3.4 (SLICING).– *We define slicing as an operation on an FM, denoted as* $\Pi_{\mathcal{F}_{slice}}(FM) = FM_{slice}$ *where* $\mathcal{F}_{slice} = \{ft_1, ft_2, ..., ft_n\} \subseteq \mathcal{F}$ *is a set of features (called the slicing criterion) and* $FM_{slice}$ *is the resulting FM (called the slice).* $FM_{slice}$ *characterizes the following projected set of configurations:* $[\![FM_{slice}]\!] = [\![FM]\!]_{|\mathcal{F}_{slice}}$. *Furthermore, we will take into consideration that* $FM_{slice}$ *must have a hierarchy as close as possible to the original hierarchy* $FM$*; in particular,* $FM_{slice}$ *features are connected to the nearest ancestor: a full formalization can be found in [ACH 13b].*

This FM is synthesized automatically from the "sliced" Boolean formula $\phi_{slice}$ and by applying satisfiability techniques described in [CZA 07, AND 12, ACH 13d]. $\phi_{slice}$ is obtained by eliminating the Boolean variables not included in the *slicing* criteria by existential quantification (see definition 3.5).

DEFINITION 3.5 (EXISTENTIAL QUANTIFICATION).– *Let* $v$ *a Boolean variable in* $\phi$. $\phi_{|v}$ *(respectively* $\phi_{|\bar{v}}$*) is* $\phi$ *where the* $v$ *variable is assigned to the value True (respectively False). Existential quantification is thus defined* $\exists v\, \phi =_{def} \phi_{|v} \vee \phi_{|\bar{v}}$.

It should be noted that $\phi_{slice}$ is also used to check the realizability property via satisfiability techniques.

### 3.4.2.3. *Specialization and updating of FMs*

VSAR (on the left in Figure 3.2) displays the set of possible contexts. To deploy a software application, VSAR must of course be *specialized*, for example by setting lighting conditions. These specialization operations make some *features* mandatory, removing *features*, or adding constraints. Thus, after this stage, a new FM, VSAR', is obtained.

Next, the modifications applied to VSAR on the software architecture, and thus PFC, must be transmitted. To realize this transformation of PFC into a simplified PFC' FM, the aggregation and *slicing* operators are applied: $FM_{full'}$ $=\times$ $(\{\text{VSAR'}, \text{PFC'}\}, \{LightingNoise$ $\Rightarrow$ $Edge\wedge$ $LightingAnalysis, \ldots\})$ PFC' being defined by the following relation: $\Pi_{\mathcal{F}_{\text{PFC}}}(FM_{full'}) = $ PFC'.

### 3.4.3. Results

We have tested the modeling process on six real deployment scenarios (detection of intrusion in a building and in a parking lot, headcount, etc.) with the help of a video surveillance expert.

The VSAR FM used for testing has 77 features and its number of valid configurations is greater than $10^8$. The PFC FM used for testing has 51 features and its number of valid configurations is greater than $10^6$. A total of 22 transformation rules have been taken into consideration. We have checked that the realizability property described above was really valid.

The idea behind the testing is to evaluate in what proportion software architecture configurations, which will be taken into consideration, during runtime are simplified via the work of a video surveillance expert on the specification part. We have considered a scenario where the video surveillance expert only operates on features present in the VSAR specification model. In other words, only the VSAR FM specialization is applied, whereas the direct PFC FM specialization is not considered. Next, the inter- and intramodel constraints are automatically taken into account and no additional manual operation is applied.

For each scenario, we used automatic techniques described in the previous section to transform the PFC FM into a PFC' FM given a sequence of edits, which apply on the VSAR model. In Table 3.1, for each scenario, we report:

– #edits: the number of edit operations applied to specialize VSAR;

– #configurations: the number of valid configurations in PFC';

– #removes: the number of features not present in PFC' but originally present in the PFC FM;

– #core: the number of "core" features present in PFC';

– #VPs: the number of remaining features to be chosen during runtime in PFC'. Note that $\#VPs = 51 - (\#cores + \#removes)$.

| Scenario | #Edits | #Configurations | #Cores | #Removes | #VPs |
|:--------:|:------:|:---------------:|:------:|:--------:|:----:|
| 1 | 13 | 48,384 | 19 | 4 | 28 |
| 2 | 18 | 106,560 | 18 | 2 | 31 |
| 3 | 12 | 24,192 | 18 | 4 | 29 |
| 4 | 18 | 118,656 | 18 | 1 | 32 |
| 5 | 16 | 32,256 | 24 | 4 | 23 |
| 6 | 15 | 22,608 | 21 | 2 | 28 |
| PFC | - | $\geq 10^6$ | 13 | - | 38 |

**Table 3.1.** *Measurements on the process application*

The results show that for all scenarios, after specialization and transformation, the number of valid configurations in PFC' is less important than the number of valid configurations originally defined in PFC, by at least one order of magnitude. In particular, at least five, and at most 11, features have been able to be set during design. #VPs vary from 23 (scenario 5) to 31 (scenario 2), which means that at least seven and at most 15 choices are no longer taken into consideration during runtime.

In addition, the effective separation of FMs enables the video surveillance expert to work on an adapted abstraction level, focusing on its expertise and its know-how by manipulating concepts specific to its domain.

The separation of FMs also enables the variability of different components to be manipulated and managed. This makes these specifications more easily *reusable* in the framework of a video surveillance application deployment, i.e. in the six scenarios, the different FMs have simply been reused.

Finally, the approach ensures a consistency of FMs all throughout the modeling process.

## 3.5. SOA for scientific *workflows*

### 3.5.1. *Case study*

Scientific *workflows* are increasingly being used for integrating current tools and algorithms with the aim of constructing large and complex applications such as *pipelines* for scientific data analysis [GIL 07, MCP 09].

We will illustrate the use of scientific *workflows* in the medical imaging field where distributed infrastructures such as computing grids have become necessary for running very costly scientific processing in time and space. To facilitate the running of scientific *workflows* in this field, SOA is used increasingly and has the objectives:

– of producing distributed, reusable imaging services, uncoupled from technical grid platforms;

– of providing standardized interfaces to call application codes as well as information exchange protocols;

– of composing these atomic services to describe complex processing channel (*workflows*).

By using SOA, imaging experts essentially compose different image processing types, each provided by a service.

Numerous services are available on the grid for each stage of the *workflow*, and vary according to different concerns: support for different image formats (Digital Imaging and Communications in Medicine (DICOM), Nifti, Analyze, etc.), acquisition modalities (Magnetic Resonance (MR), Computed Tomography (CT), Positron Emission Tomography (PET), etc.), network protocols, algorithmic methods for processing an image, anatomical structures (brain, kidney, etc.) for which the services are assumed to be the most efficient. In general, scientific services exhibiting a large number of data ports with specificities on input and output data, as well as various functional and non-functional characteristics. The general problem for *workflow* designers is choosing a set of services, among the many available on the grid, all while taking into account their variabilities, and this too, according to different interrelated concerns. Given the complexity of the problem, manual variability management is not realistic, since it requires considerable time and effort all while being subject to errors [ACH 12b].

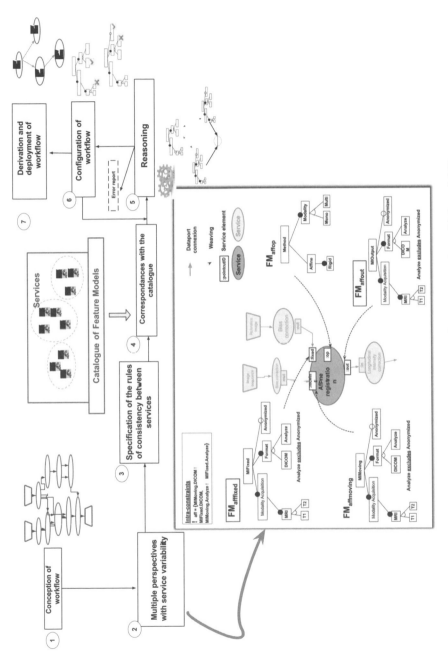

**Figure 3.3.** *Modeling, management and reasoning on the multiple variability of a workflow based on SOA. For a color version of the figure, see www.iste.co.uk/oussalah/softwarearchitectures2.zip*

---

### Why is it a multiple variability problem?

*Multiple systems*: a scientific *workflow* is composed of several services, each service exhibiting variability. Thus, it is necessary to combine the variability information attached to each service. These relations can be defined by the user via constraints between the FMs of each service.

*Multiple concerns*: several concerns, each exhibiting variability, describe a medical imaging service. For example, an affine *registration* service is capable of processing various types of input images, producing different types of output images, with a variability on the method (see the bottom of Figure 3.3).

*Multiple participants*:  several service providers (scientists, institutes/ research teams, specialized businesses, etc.) propose algorithms or medical imaging processing and are all equal candidates for realizing a part of the *workflow*, depending on the condition that they have the right variability.

---

### 3.5.2. *Accounting for multiple variability*

The aim of our approach is to derive a consistent *workflow*, composed of services organized in a catalog, from a description of the *workflow* completed by a variability demand specification.

Figure 3.3 gives an overview of the modeling process that takes multiple variability into account. First (see ①), the architect develops a workflow description that defines the different calculation stages (e.g. data analysis), which must be run, as well as the relations between these stages (e.g. running order).

The workflow description is next reinforced with a display of variability demands with the objective of facilitating the discovery, creation and running of services realizing the calculation stages.

Then, the workflow architect identifies and models different concerns (e.g. medical image format, algorithmic method) for each stage of the scientific workflow (see ②).

Several FMs are formed during different parts of a stage (e.g. data port, functional interface) to specify the variability demands specific to a given application.

When several features of one viewpoint interact with one or more features of one or more viewpoints, constraints within or between services are specified (see ③). Furthermore, constraints of compatibility between services (e.g. between data ports) can be deduced from the workflow structure and activated by the architect.

To ensure that the variability demands can be matched with combinations of features offered by the catalog, the FMs formed in the workflow are compared with the FMs of the catalog (see ④).

The configuration sets are compared (see definition 3.6) with a very efficient algorithm in particular, described in [THU 09], operating on FM formulas. This technique is used especially when we want to check whether all the configurations demanded by the architect and specified at workflow level are implemented by at least one configuration of a catalog service. Advanced techniques, described in [ACH 12d], can also be used for a more subtle understanding of the differences.

DEFINITION 3.6 (COMPARISON BETWEEN TWO FMS).– $fm_1$ and $fm_2$ $fm_1$ is a specialization of $fm_2$ if $[\![fm_1]\!] \subset [\![fm_2]\!]$ ; $fm_1$ is a generalization of $fm_2$ if $[\![fm_1]\!] \subset [\![fm_2]\!]$ ; $fm_1$ is a refactoring of $fm_2$ if $[\![fm_1]\!] = [\![fm_2]\!]$ ; $fm_1$ is an arbitrary edit of $fm_2$ in the other cases.

Finally, it is sometimes necessary to calculate configurations demanded by the architect and realizable in the catalog at the same time. This corresponds to calculating the intersection of configuration sets of two FMs. The merging operator is used in this framework (see definition 3.7).

DEFINITION 3.7 (MERGING OF TWO FMS).– $fm_1$ and $fm_2$ The merging of two FMs, in intersection mode², produces a new FM, $fm_m$, such as: $[\![fm_m]\!] = [\![fm_1]\!] \cap [\![fm_2]\!]$.

---

2 There are other merging modes: union, diff, etc. [ACH 13c].

In stage ⑤, we reason automatically on FMs and constraints, as specified by the workflow architect, in stages ① and ②. This assists the architect in detecting errors, automatically selecting features, ruling out service providers incapable of supporting the specified variability, etc.

By way of an example, the bottom of Figure 3.3 shows four viewpoints of the *affine registration* service documented by four FMs: $FM_{afffixed}$, $FM_{affop}$, $FM_{affmoving}$ and $FM_{affout}$. To reason on these four viewpoints, the aggregation operation (see definition 3.1) is first undertaken:

$$FM_{AffineRegistration} \;=\; \times(\{FM_{afffixed}, FM_{affop}, FM_{affmoving}, FM_{affout}\}, \phi_{aff})$$

where $phi_{aff}$ is the set of constraints between the viewpoints of the service.

Next, $FM_{AffineRegistration}$ is operated to ensure the satisfiability of the viewpoint set, calculate the *core* and *dead features* (see definitions 3.3 and 3.2). The architect can verify all this information and, if necessary, edit the variability specifications.

To complete the workflow configuration (see ⑥), the architect must make choices on the remaining points of variation. At each stage of the process, reasoning operations (consistency, propagation, etc.) are run to assist the architect.

Finally, the architect chooses services in the catalog (in the case of there being several candidates for a given combination of features), which are next combined to deploy the final workflow (see ⑦).

### 3.5.3. *Results*

We have tested the approach on three real scientific workflows with different sizes (from 9 to 24 services) and topologies, varying the number of dependencies (see Table 3.2, #services and #dependencies). The number of

FMs (#FMs), the number of total features (#features), the number of *core features* (#core), the number of points of variation (#VPs = # core features - #) and the number of configurations (#configurations) are also noted for each workflow in Table 3.2 (see initial specification).

| | | Workflow ① | Workflow ② | Workflow ③ |
|---|---|---|---|---|
| Workflow | #Services | 9 | 14 | 24 |
| | #Dependencies | 16 | 20 | 41 |
| Initial specification | #FMs | 12 | 8 | 25 |
| | #Features | 131 | 97 | 286 |
| | #Core | 52 | 43 | 110 |
| | #VPs | 79 | 54 | 176 |
| | #Configurations | $10^{12}$ | $10^9$ | $10^{25}$ |
| After reasoning | #Features | 104 | 79 | 213 |
| | #Core | 72 | 48 | 146 |
| | #VPs | 32 | 31 | 67 |
| | #Configurations | $10^4$ | $10^5$ | $10^9$ |

**Table 3.2.** *Test results on three workflows*

We report this same information on the variability of each workflow after running automatic reasoning techniques. The decrease in the number of points of variation for the architect to take into account is an average of 58%. The configuration space is decreased by several orders of magnitude. These tests show that reasoning mechanisms significantly reduce the major variability and great complexity of the workflow.

Thus, the support we propose enables a decrease in effort and time. This support is not only desirable; in practice, it is indispensable, considering the orders of complexity as shown in Table 3.2.

The satisfiability of an FM is known to be a difficult and NP-full complex problem [SCH 07]. As argued by several authors, in these cases, the decision-making process must be simplified and automatized [MEN 09a, MEN 10, HUB 10, JAN 10]. In our case, many dozens of FMs must be considered, with complex rules between models. Our observations, in this case study, reinforce the need of tackling multiple variability, whereas the techniques proposed make it possible to accurately assist the user.

## 3.6. Reverse engineering *plugin*-based architecture

### 3.6.1. *Case study*

The FraSCAti platform [FRA 09] is an open-source implementation of the OASIS standard *service component architecture* (SCA) [ARC 06]. SCA is independent of any technology and its objective is to construct distributed applications based on composite services and components. A variety of programming languages and *frameworks* (Java, C, C++, WS-BPEL, Spring Framework, etc.), interface definition languages (WSDL, Java, etc.) and network communication protocols (*Web Service, Java Messaging Service*, etc.) are available for implementing, describing and *interconnecting* these services and components.

The development of FraSCAti began in 2007 and numerous functionalities have been added on an ongoing basis. After six major *releases*, FraSCAti now provides different SCA specifications (*Assembly Model, Java Common Annotations & APIs, Java Component Implementation, Spring Component Implementation, WS-BPEL Client & Implementation, Web Services Binding, JMS Binding, Transaction Policy*), a set of extensions as standard, including different types of component implementation (SCA composite, Java, EJB, WS-BPEL, C, Spring, Fractal, OSGi, Scala, BeanShell, FScript, Groovy, JavaScript, JRuby, Jy-thon, XQuery, Velocity scripting languages), different types of *bindings* (SOAP, JMS, Java RMI, HTTP, REST, JITS-RPC, JNA, UPnP, OSGi, JGroups), and different types of description interfaces (WSDL, Java, UPnP, C headers), as well as APIs for introspection and reconfiguration at runtime [SEI 09].

It should be noted that FraSCAti itself is designed wholly as an SCA application, i.e. as an assembly of SCA components. With all these abilities, the FraSCAti project has become highly configurable on various parts of its architecture [ACH 11, ACH 13a]. Thus, different variants of FraSCAti responding to particular needs and target system constraints can be derived. By way of an example, a FraSCAti variant can be deployed that would compile Java code on the fly, with advanced introspection possibilities and a wide choice of implementation languages. A more minimalist version would necessarily not include these system features. All FraSCAti features are implemented as SCA components that are next plugged into the FraSCAti architecture. The dependencies of these plugins are captured via Apache Maven, a project management tool based on XML descriptors.

---

### Why is it a multiple variability problem?

*Multiple artifacts*:  in the case of FraSCAti, two project artifacts are considered: (1) a hierarchical architectural model of FraSCAti, expressed in SCA; (2) the available plugins described in Maven files as well as their variability (i.e. the dependencies between plugins).

*Multiple viewpoints*:  the architect of the FraSCAti project has an implicit and *a priori* knowledge of the architecture and thus potentially a different viewpoint from that automatically calculated by an extraction procedure. Furthermore, the FMs extracted from different versions of FraSCAti constitute as many viewpoints on the variability of FraSCAti (see Figure 3.5).

---

With regard to the complexity of FraSCAti (version 1.5 contains approximately 250,000 lines of code and more than 60 plugins) and its architecture, we think that it is representative of large, complex, plugin-based systems. The variability of FraSCAti has become so complex that management based on the principles and techniques of SPLs seemed necessary. The objectives are to be able to:

– facilitate configuration: a central FM will allow an architect to choose the features that they want to include in the FraSCAti variant, without having to consult and check different technical artifacts (e.g. Maven file), all with a suitable abstraction level on the architecture. The derivation of a FraSCAti variant can next be automated on the condition that it has a valid configuration and the traceability links of features with FraSCAti plugins[3];

– manage its evolution: this variability management must be systematized over time to facilitate maintenance of the project. The architect can also verify that the evolution of its architecture is correct, e.g. that the dependencies

---

3 Generating variants from a feature model configuration is not addressed in this section.

between previously established features are still correct in the current version of FraSCAti.

### 3.6.2. *Accounting for multiple variability*

The main challenge we are tackling is the extraction of the FM of the FraSCAti architecture. This architectural FM is indeed vital to facilitate its systematic configuration and manage its evolution. If the set of configurations modeled is too large, then some variants of FraSCAti will be authorized and will not compile or be run correctly. If the set of configurations is too narrow, the richness of the FraSCAti platform will not be fully exploited.

A purely manual extraction is not desirable, since it is subject to errors and is time consuming. On a large scale, it is thus necessary to rely on automatic extraction methods and to combine them with the architects knowledge.

#### 3.6.2.1. *Automatic extraction by combining artifacts*

The SCA model documents the architecture variability only very approximately, whereas the *plugins* are very far from the architectural viewpoint (it is simply a flat list). The two sources of information are complementary. The idea is then to combine them with the aim of synthesizing a new, full FM displaying both the features and hierarchy of the architecture (as documented in the SCA model), as well as the variability and technical constraints (as documented in the Maven files).

Figure 3.4 summarizes the stages necessary for realizing automatic extraction. In the first stage, an architectural FM, denoted as $fm_{Arch_{150}}$, is extracted following the analysis of the SCA model. We call it 150% architecture since it is a rough approximation of the variability really supported by the architecture – the constraints between architectural elements are not made explicit in the SCA model, certain combinations (configurations) are authorized in this model. In fact, another FM, denoted as $fm_{Plug}$, is extracted and displays the FraSCAti plugins as well as their dependencies. $fm_{Plug}$ models the plugins as features, exhibiting a hierarchy at one level only and numerous transverse constraints are present. Traceability links between $fm_{Plug}$ and $fm_{Arch_{150}}$ are automatically deducted and formalized in the form of logic constraints between features.

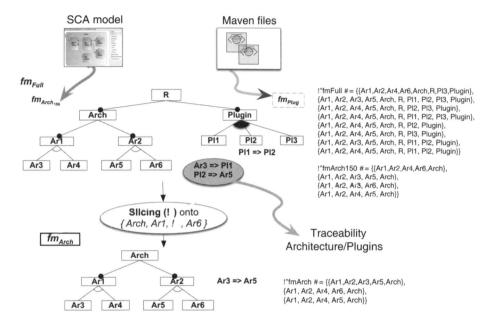

**Figure 3.4.** *Automatic extraction by aggregation and slicing. For a color version of the figure, see www.iste.co.uk/oussalah/softwarearchitectures2.zip*

The two FMs $fm_{Plug}$ and $fm_{Arch_{150}}$ as well as the traceability links are aggregated next, producing a new FM $fm_{Full}$ (see Figure 3.4). To project the technical constraints on the architectural part of $fm_{Full}$, we calculate a new FM with the help of slicing operator (see definition 3.4).

In the example in Figure 3.4, the resulting slice is denoted as $fm_{Arch}$. Thus, we obtain: $\Pi_{\mathcal{F}_{fm_{Arch_{150}}}}(fm_{Full}) = fm_{Arch}$ where $\mathcal{F}_{fm_{Arch_{150}}} = \{Arch, Ar1, \ldots, Ar6\}$.

In particular, we can observe that a configuration of the architectural FM $fm_{Arch_{150}}$ is no longer in $fm_{Arch}$: $[\![fm_{Arch_{150}}]\!] \setminus [\![fm_{Arch}]\!] = \{Ar1, Ar2, Ar3, Ar6, Arch\}$. Indeed, the slice $fm_{Arch}$ contains an additional constraint $Ar3 \Rightarrow Ar5$, which was not originally present in $fm_{Arch_{150}}$. This very simple example shows the advantage of combining two sources of information. On a larger scale, the number of constraints deducted in $fm_{Arch}$ and the decrease in its configuration space are significant (see section 3.6.3).

3.6.2.2. *Validation of the extraction and evolutions by the architect*

For each version of FraSCAti (see Figure 3.5), the architectural FM synthesized by the extraction procedure must be validated by the SA. In particular, the SA must ensure that the variability information and set of configurations characterized by $fm_{Arch}$ do not contradict his/her intention and knowledge of the architecture.

Here, we support the idea that $fm_{Arch}$, the FM extracted, must be compared with the architect's internal vision on the one hand, made explicit by an FM, $fm_{SA}$, and with the previous version of the architectural FM on the other hand, for example $fm_{Arch_2}$ (version 1.4) is compared with $fm_{Arch_1}$ (version 1.3).

At the root of the re-engineering of FraSCAti as an SPL, the SA manually developed an intentional model of the architecture variability (see $fm_{SA}$, at the top of Figure 3.5) for version 1.3. We have applied the extraction procedure on this very version and obtained $fm_{Arch_1}$. In the same way that $fm_{Arch_2}$ is an evolution of $fm_{Arch_1}$, $fm_{Arch_1}$ can be seen as an evolution of $fm_{SA}$. Thus, the same problem arises as much when reasoning on the evolution of FraSCAti as when validating the model originally defined by the SA.

The absence of ground truth, i.e. of an FM for which we are absolutely certain that each combination of features authorized is provided by the architecture, makes defining the variability specification unpredictable in both $fm_{Arch_1}$ and $fm_{SA}$. Comparison techniques can be applied and this information is then reported to the architect so that he/she can determine whether he/she has made an error or whether the extraction procedure was defective.

However, the variability information can be displayed differently in the two FMs – the level of detail and vocabulary used can vary strongly from one model to another. First, operations to reconcile two FMs are applied. Next, the architect can refine the FMs in accordance with the differences' information obtained.

### 3.6.3. *Results*

We have applied the extraction procedure and the evolution management techniques on three successive major versions of FraSCAti. Philippe Merle, architect of the project since 2007, designed the starting FM and validated the models extracted.

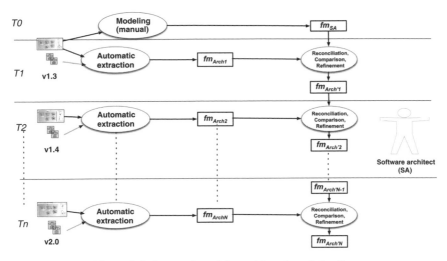

**Figure 3.5.** *Integration of the architect knowledge for different FraSCAti evolutions*

The FraSCAti case study offers an interesting look at the reverse engineering of variability in software architecture.

First, although the gap between intentional variability (as expressed by the architect) and the FM extracted seems acceptable, it has proven necessary to assist the architect with automatic support:

– Basic string comparison techniques were sufficient for establishing correspondences between the FMs.

– The most time-consuming task was surmounting the problem of the differing granularity of details in each FM. Advanced techniques, such as secure deletion of features by slicing, were necessary for doing this, the syntax editing techniques of the FM not being sufficient.

– Automatic differencing techniques are crucial to integrate the knowledge of the architect and validate the evolution of the architecture. A manual inspection is not possible and the techniques proposed in the literature prove to be useful, but insufficient.

Second, the extraction procedure produces very promising results. Most of the variability information originally specified by the architect was recovered. A manual check of several variability decisions imposed by the software architect shows that the extraction is not at fault and working in accordance with his/her intentions. The FM extracted, and analysis of differences, have even encouraged the architect to correct his initial model. These results have been observed on many versions of FraSCAti by repeating the extraction procedure [ACH 13a].

Third, the knowledge of the architect is required to restrict the set of configurations of the FM extracted, in particular when software artifacts (e.g. Maven files) do not document the architecture variability correctly, and to verify and validate the automatic procedure. Thus, we will take into consideration that fully automating the extraction is neither realistic nor desirable for subsequent versions of the FraSCAti architecture.

The results that we report in this FraSCAti case study show that the FMs obtained are more precise than those developed manually. Because of the difference information, the architect can also refine the FMs extracted. We are interested in highlighting the key role of automatic extraction methods capable of combining several sources of variability and tooled support to help the architect to integrate his/her knowledge and check the evolution of the architecture.

## 3.7. Evaluation

### 3.7.1. *The necessity of tooling*

To manage SPLs on a large scale obliges users to run complex tasks: the FMs to be composed are generally located in different files; it is necessary to reason on FMs (e.g. to check validity or search for dead functionalities, i.e. those which will never be included in a configuration), after having run several composition operations. More generally, it is important that SPL developers be provided with tools that allow them to capture and reuse a sequence of operations participating in the management of an SPL.

We have thus designed and implemented FAMILIAR, a *domain-specific language* dedicated to the management of feature models [ACH 13b]. It is an executable language that takes on manipulation and reasoning on multiple FMs. It provides high-level operators for:

– the deconstruction and composition of FMs (several merger operators and operators for extraction and aggregation);

– aligning FMs (insertion, renaming and removal of functionalities);

– reasoning on FMs and their configurations (validity of an FM, comparison of FMs, number of valid configurations in an FM, etc.).

FAMILIAR also has instructions for describing iterations, conditions and writing and running parametrizable scripts. FAMILIAR accepts multiple notations for specifying FMs (GUIDSL/FeatureIDE [BAT 05, THU 14], SPLOT [MEN 09b], a subset of TVL [BOU 10], etc.).

SAT solvers (SAT4J) and a library for *Binary Decision Diagrams* (BDDs) or JavaBDD are used internally in FAMILIAR in order to implement the runtime of some operations (e.g. merger of FMs or configuration operations). The proposed tool also allows users to import FMs or configurations from their own environments. The output generated by FAMILIAR can be used by other tools, e.g. in order to relate FMs to other artifacts (e.g. end of code, models) [CZA 05a, HEI 10].

In terms of support for tools, we provide a textual editor for the Eclipse environment and an interpreter that runs the various scripts. The interpreter can also be used in interactive mode so as to facilitate prototyping. Furthermore, the language has also been integrated with the graphic editor from FeatureIDE [THU 14] and, thus, all the graphic edits are synchronized with the environmental variables and the set of interactive commands is synchronized with the graphic editors.

### 3.7.2. *Summary of case studies*

The three case studies share a common problem: how to model, manage and reason on the multiple variability of a software architecture. Table 3.3 lists types of multiple variability encountered (multiple participants, systems, concerns, viewpoints) on one side. Case study ① is particularly complex, since three types of multiple variability must be managed. The two other case studies, ② and ③, exhibit two types.

This multiple variability has posed common (e.g. the need to check the consistency of the FMs for the three case studies) yet also specific (e.g. checking the realizability property for the case study ②) case study difficulties.

| Case study | Multiple variability | Techniques |
|---|---|---|
| ① (see section 3.4) | *Multiple participants*: several medical imaging service providers can be chosen to realize the workflow<br>*Multiple concerns*: several concerns, each exhibiting variability, describe a medical imaging service<br>*Multiple systems*: several services, each exhibiting variability, must be chosen and combined to construct the workflow | Consistency of the variability in the workflow Propagating choices and updating feature models Interactive support for a configuration in several stages |
| ② (see section 3.5) | *Multiple concerns*: the variability of software components is distinguished from the variability of application contexts<br>*Multiple systems*: several components, each exhibiting variability, must be configured to implement the processing channel | Consistency of the variability in the pipeline, checking properties such as realizability Incremental specialization and updating feature models |
| ③ (see section 3.6) | *Multiple viewpoints*: two variability models, one being the architect and the other obtained by automatic extraction, are compared.<br>*Multiple systems*: two artifacts (Maven files of the dependencies and model architectural) are combined to synthesize an architectural model with variability | Alignment and reasoning on different viewpoints Step-by-step refinement of variability models by the architect after operating automatically calculated differences |

**Table 3.3.** *Multiple variability in the case studies and techniques applied*

The techniques proposed and applied in the three case studies are, however, generic in the sense that they rely on a set of composition, deconstruction, reasoning and editing operators. Combined together, these operators enable different variability scenarios to be implemented by bringing the following multiple FMs into play:

– Updating of FMs: several FMs, each focusing on a viewpoint or subsystem of the architecture, are interrelated by complex constraints. Updating the variability information in each FM is then especially necessary to correct or simplify possible anomalies. The aggregate and slice operators in FAMILIAR are used: the former operator serves to compose the different interrelated FMs, and the latter serves to deconstruct the FMs again. Intermediate composition is thus exploited by the slicing operator to correct the FM. Note that the merger operator can also be used to calculate a composition.

– Production of viewpoints on FMs: given an FM or a set of FMs, a participant wants to focus on a particular concern related to their expertise, role in the organization or the configuration tasks assigned to them. The slicing operator is used: the slice criterion is a subset of features. FAMILIAR provides facilities for specifying the slice criterion, with a dedicated notation.

– Reconciliation of FMs: when two or more FMs cannot be directly combined or merged, they must be reconciled. Editing operations for renaming the features are useful, but insufficient (see the case studies in sections 3.5 and 3.6). It is also necessary to remove some features, as they are not included in one of the FMs to be reconciled. The slicing operator is used again in this context.

– Reasoning on several FMs: reasoning techniques are necessary to determine the satisfiability of an FM, detect the dead features or calculate the realizability property. The aggregation operator serves to produce an intermediate FM on which FAMILIAR reasoning operations (isValid, dead, etc.) can next be applied. For the realizability property, the aggregation, slicing and differencing operators are combined.

## 3.8. Conclusion

By their very nature, software architectures rely on an explicit organization, capable of taking into account a certain number of changes. With the variability of software systems achieving an unprecedented size and complexity, controlling different aspects of variability in software architectures is a top requirement.

In this chapter, we have described several applications of a modular variability management toolkit for different forms of architectures (component-, service- and plugin based) and at different stages of the software lifecycle. This tool takes the form of a dedicated language, called FAMILIAR, as well as a development environment. Three case studies relative to software architectures have been presented and analyzed.

In the context of a video surveillance product line, the separation of needs and concerns has been applied to controlling variability in a pipeline software component architecture. Video surveillance users are thus assisted in multilevel configuration of the pipeline. In an SOA for scientific computation, strongly parametrizable services are considered to be product lines and the resulting scientific workflows multiple product lines. The consistent combination of product lines is ensured through the process of constructing the workflow architecture. Finally, an experiment in reverse engineering architectural variability models is discussed. It concerns a plugin-based architecture for which the SA was able to not only semi-automatically extract and refine a variability model of the real software architecture, but even control its evolution.

Through these studies, we observe that different operators provided by the FAMILIAR language allow different variability modeling scenarios to be managed in relation with the software architectures, e.g. the updating of FMs in accordance with modifications to the architecture, production of views on these FMs, reasoning on several FMs, as well as reconciliation of the FM with the architect's vision and real architectures.

Among the many prospects opened up by this work, we find it particularly relevant to the future to address the issues of on the one hand, deriving consistent architectures from higher level variability models [CZA 06, FIL 12, FIL 13, PAR 10], and on the other hand managing attributes and non-functional properties to the variability of a software architecture [KOL 13, SIE 12], and finally, handling the dynamic adaptation of architectures [FOU 12, MOR 09].

## 3.9. Bibliography

[ACH 11]  ACHER M., CLEVE A., COLLET P., *et al.*, "Reverse engineering architectural feature models", *ECSA '11*, *LNCS*, Springer, Berlin, Heidelberg, vol. 6903, pp. 220–235, 2011.

[ACH 12a]  ACHER M., CLEVE A., PERROUIN G., *et al.*, "On extracting feature models from product descriptions", *VaMoS '12*, ACM, Leipzig, Germany, pp. 45–54, 2012.

[ACH 12b]  ACHER M., COLLET P., GAIGNARD A., *et al.*, "Composing multiple variability artifacts to assemble coherent workflows", *Software Quality Journal*, vol. 20, nos. 3–4, pp. 689–734, 2012.

[ACH 12c]  ACHER M., COLLET P., LAHIRE P., *et al.*, "Separation of concerns in feature modeling: support and applications", *Aspect-Oriented Software Development (AOSD '12)*, ACM, New York, NY, pp. 1–12, March 2012.

[ACH 12d]  ACHER M., HEYMANS P., QUINTAN C., *et al.*, "Feature model differences", *Proceedings of the 24th International Conference on Advanced Information Systems Engineering (CAiSE '12)*, Springer, New York, NY, pp. 629–645, 2012.

[ACH 13a]  ACHER M., CLEVE A., COLLET P., *et al.*, "Extraction and evolution of architectural variability models in plugin-based systems", *Software and Systems Modeling*, 14 July 2013.

[ACH 13b]  ACHER M., COLLET P., LAHIRE P., *et al.*, "FAMILIAR: a domain-specific language for large scale management of feature models", *Science of Computer Programming*, vol. 78, no. 6, pp. 657–681, 2013.

[ACH 13c]  ACHER M., COMBEMALLE B., COLLET P., *et al.*, "Composing your compositions of variability models", *ACM/IEEE 16th International Conference on Model Driven Engineering Languages and Systems (MODELS '13)*, Springer, New York, NY, 2013.

[ACH 13d]  ACHER M., HEYMANS P., CLEVE A., *et al.*, "Support for reverse engineering and maintaining feature models", *7th International Workshop on Variability Modelling of Software-Intensive Systems (VaMoS '13)*, ACM, Pisa, Italy, January 2013.

[ALV 08]  ALVES V., SCHWANNINGER C., BARBOSA L., *et al.*, "An exploratory study of information retrieval rechniques in domain analysis", *SPLC '08*, IEEE, New York, NY, pp. 67–76, 2008.

[AND 12]  ANDERSEN N., CZARNECKI K., SHE S., *et al.*, "Efficient synthesis of feature models", *Proceedings of SPLC'12*, ACM Press, New York, NY, pp. 97–106, 2012.

[APE 09]  APEL S., KÄSTNER C., "An overview of feature-oriented software development", *Journal of Object Technology*, vol. 8, no. 5, pp. 49–84, July–August 2009.

[ARC 06]  ARCHITECTURE O.S.C., OASIS Service Component Architecture, available at "www.oasis-opencsa.org/sca", 2006.

[ASI 06]  ASIKAINEN T., MANNISTO T., SOININEN T., "A unified conceptual foundation for feature modelling", *Proceedings of the 10th International on Software Product Line Conference (SPLC '06)*, IEEE Computer Society, Washington, DC, pp. 31–40, 2006.

[ASI 07]  ASIKAINEN T., MÄNNISTÖ T., SOININEN T., "Kumbang: a domain ontology for modelling variability in software product families", *Advanced Engineering Informatics*, vol. 21, no. 1, pp. 23–40, 2007.

[BAC 01]  BACHMANN F., BASS L., "Managing variability in software architectures", *SIGSOFT Software Engineering Notes*, vol. 26, pp. 126–132, May 2001.

[BAS 98]  BASS L., CLEMENTS P., KAZMAN R., *Software Architecture in Practice*, Addison-Wesley, Boston, MA, 1998.

[BAT 05]  BATORY D.S., "Feature models, grammars, and propositional formulas", *SPLC '05*, LNCS, Springer-verlag, Rennes, France, vol. 3714, pp. 7–20, 2005.

[BEN 10] BENAVIDES D., SEGURA S., RUIZ-CORTES A., "Automated analysis of feature models 20 years later: a literature review", *Information Systems*, vol. 35, no. 6, pp. 615–636, 2010.

[BEU 04] BEUCHE D., PAPAJEWSKI H., SCHRADER-PREIKSCHAT W., "Variability management with feature models", *Science of Computer Programming*, vol. 53, no. 3, pp. 333–352, December 2004.

[BOS 10] BOSCH J., "Toward compositional software product lines", *IEEE Software*, vol. 27, pp. 29–34, 2010.

[BOU 10] BOUCHER Q., CLASSEN A., FABER P., *et al.*, "Introducing TVL, a text-based feature modelling language", *International Workshop on Variability Modelling of Software-Intensive Systems (VaMoS '10)*, ACM, Linz, Austria, pp. 159–162, 2010.

[BUH 05] BUHNE S., LAUENROTH K., POHL K., "Modelling requirements variability across product lines", *Proceedings of the 13th IEEE International Conference on Requirements Engineering (RE '05)*, IEEE Computer Society, Washington, DC, pp. 41–52, 2005.

[CLE 01] CLEMENTS P., NORTHROP L.M., *Software Product Lines: Practices and Patterns*, Addison-Wesley, 2001.

[CZA 05a] CZARNECKI K., ANTKIEWICZ M., "Mapping features to models: a template approach based on superimposed variants", *GPCE '05*, LNCS, Springer-Verlag, Tallinn, Estonia, vol. 3676, pp. 422–437, 2005.

[CZA 05b] CZARNECKI K., HELSEN S., EISENECKER U., "Staged configuration through specialization and multilevel configuration of feature models", *Software Process: Improvement and Practice*, vol. 10, no. 2, pp. 143–169, 2005.

[CZA 06] CZARNECKI K., PIETROSZEK K., "Verifying feature-based model templates against well-formedness OCL constraints", *GPCE '06*, ACM, Portland, OR, pp. 211–220, 2006.

[CZA 07] CZARNECKI K., WASOWSKI A., "Feature diagrams and logics: there and back again", *SPLC '07*, IEEE, Kyoto, Japan, pp. 23–34, 2007.

[DAV 13] DAVRIL J.-M., DELFOSSE E., HARIRI N., *et al.*, "Feature model extraction from large collections of informal product descriptions", *European Software Engineering Conference and the ACM SIGSOFT Symposium on the Foundations of Software Engineering (ESEC/FSE '13)*, pp. 290–300, 2013.

[DHU 10] DHUNGANA D., GRÜNBACHER P., RABISER R., *et al.*, "Structuring the modeling space and supporting evolution in software product line engineering", *Journal of Systems and Software*, vol. 83, no. 7, pp. 1108–1122, 2010.

[DUC 09] DUCASSE S., POLLET D., "Software architecture reconstruction: a process-oriented taxonomy", *IEEE Transactions on Software Engineering*, vol. 35, no. 4, pp. 573–591, 2009.

[ERW 10] ERWIG M., "A language for software variation research", *Proceedings of the 9th International Conference on Generative Programming and Component Engineering, GPCE '10*, ACM, New York, NY, pp. 3–12, 2010.

[FIL 12] FILHO J., BARAIS O., BAUDRY B., *et al.*, "Leveraging variability modeling for multi-dimensional model-driven software product lines", *3rd International Workshop on Product Line Approaches in Software Engineering (PLEASE)*, ACM, Zurich, Switzerland, pp. 5–8, June 2012.

[FIL 13] FILHO J.B.F., BARAIS O., ACHER M., *et al.*, "Generating counter examples of model-based software product lines: an exploratory study", *17th International Conference on Software Product Lines (SPLC '13)*, ACM, Tokyo, Japan, pp. 72–81, 2013.

[FOU 12] FOUQUET F., NAIN G., MORIN B., *et al.*, "An eclipse modelling framework alternative to meet the models@runtime requirements", *Proceedings of the 15th International Conference on Model Driven Engineering Languages and Systems (MODELS '12)*, Springer-Verlag, pp. 87–101, 2012.

[FRA 09] FRASCATI, available at "frascati.ow2.org", 2009.

[GIL 07] GIL Y., DEELMAN E., ELLISMAN M.H., *et al.*, "Examining the challenges of scientific workflows", *IEEE Computer*, vol. 40, no. 12, pp. 24–32, 2007.

[GRI 98] GRISS M.L., FAVARO J., D'ALESSANDRO M., "Integrating feature modeling with the RSEB", *ICSR '98*, IEEE Computer Society, Washington, DC, p. 76, 1998.

[HAR 08] HARTMANN H., TREW T., "Using feature diagrams with context variability to model multiple product lines for software supply chains", *SPLC '08*, IEEE, Limerick, Ireland, pp. 12–21, 2008.

[HAR 09] HARTMANN H., TREW T., MATSINGER A., "Supplier independent feature modelling", *SPLC '09*, IEEE, San Franscisco, CA, pp. 191–200, 2009.

[HAS 13] HASLINGER E.N., LOPEZ-HERREJON R.E., EGYED A., "On extracting feature models from sets of valid feature combinations", *Proceedings of FASE '13*, Springer, Rome, Itlay, pp. 53–67, 2013.

[HEI 10] HEIDENREICH F., SANCHEZ P., SANTOS J., *et al.*, "Relating feature models to other models of a software product line: a comparative study of featureMapper and VML", *Transactions on Aspect-Oriented Software Development VII*, Special Issue on A Common Case Study for Aspect-Oriented Modeling, Springer, vol. 6210, pp. 69–114, 2010.

[HOL 12] HOLL G., GRÜNBACHER P., RABISER R., "A systematic review and an expert survey on capabilities supporting multi product lines", *Information and Software Technology*, Elsevier B.V., vol. 54, no. 8, pp. 828-852, August 2012.

[HUB 10] HUBAUX A., HEYMANS P., SCHOBBENS P.-Y., *et al.*, "Towards multi-view feature-based configuration", *REFSQ '10*, LNCS, Springer-Verlag, New York, NY, vol. 6182, pp. 106–112, 2010.

[HUB 13a] HUBAUX A., ACHER M., TUN T.T., *et al.*, "Separating concerns in feature models: retrospective and multi-view support", (eds.), REINHARTZ-BERGER I., STURM A., CLARK T., *et al.*, *Domain Engineering: Product Lines, Conceptual Models, and Languages*, Springer, New York, NY, pp. 3–28, 2013.

[HUB 13b] HUBAUX A., HEYMANS P., SCHOBBENS P.Y., *et al.*, "Supporting multiple perspectives in feature-based configuration", *Software and Systems Modeling*, vol. 12, no. 3, pp. 641–663, 2013.

[JAC 97] JACOBSON I., GRISS M., JONSSON P., *Software Reuse: Architecture, Process and Organization for Business Success*, ACM Press/Addison-Wesley, New York, NY, 1997.

[JAN 08] JANOTA M., BOTTERWECK G., "Formal approach to integrating feature and architecture models", *Fundamental Approaches to Software Engineering*, vol. 4961, pp. 31–45, 2008.

[JAN 10] JANOTA M., SAT solving in interactive configuration, PhD Thesis, Department of Computer Science at University College Dublin, September 2010.

[JOH 06] JOHN I., "Capturing product line information from legacy user documentation", *Software Product Lines*, Springer, Berlin, Germany, pp. 127–159, 2006.

[JOH 09] JOHN I., EISENBARTH M., "A decade of scoping: a survey", *SPLC '09*, ICPS, ACM, San Franscisco, CA, vol. 446, pp. 31–40, 2009.

[KAN 90] KANG K., COHEN S., HESS J., *et al.*, Feature-oriented domain analysis (FODA), Report no. CMU/SEI-90-TR-21, SEI, Pittsburgh, PA, November 1990.

[KAN 98] KANG K., KIM S., LEE J., *et al.*, "FORM: a feature-oriented reuse method with domain-specific reference architectures", *Annals of Software Engineering*, vol. 5, no. 1, pp. 143–168, 1998.

[KOL 13] KOLESNIKOV S.S., APEL S., SIEGMUND N., *et al.*, "Predicting quality attributes of software product lines using software and network measures and sampling", *VaMoS*, ACM, Pisa, Italy, p. 6, 2013.

[LOP 10a] LOPEZ-HERREJON R.E., EGYED A., "On the need of safe software product line architectures", *ECSA '10*, LNCS, vol. 6285, Springer, Copenhagen, Denmark, pp. 493–496, 2010.

[LOP 10b] LOPEZ-HERREJON R.E., EGYED A., "Detecting inconsistencies in multi-view models with variability", *6th European Conference on Modelling Foundations and Applications, (ECMFA '2010)*, pp. 217–232, Paris, France, 2010.

[LOT 10] LOTUFO R., SHE S., BERGER T., *et al.*, "Evolution of the linux kernel variability model", *SPLC '10*, LNCS, vol. 6287, ACM, Jeju, South Korea, pp. 136–150, 2010.

[MAN 09] MANNION M., SAVOLAINEN J., ASIKAINEN T., "Viewpoint-oriented variability modeling", *Proceedings of the 33rd International Computer Software and Applications Conference (COMPSAC '09)*, IEEE, Seattle, Washington, DC, pp. 67–72, 2009.

[MCP 09] MCPHILLIPS T., BOWERS S., ZINN D., *et al.*, "Scientific workflow design for mere mortals", *Future Generation Computer Systems*, vol. 25, pp. 541–551, May 2009.

[MEN 09a] MENDONÇA M., Efficient reasoning techniques for large scale feature models, Master's Thesis, University of Waterloo, Ontario, Canada, 2009.

[MEN 09b] MENDONCA M., BRANCO M., COWAN D., "S.P.L.O.T.: software product lines online tools", *OOPSLA '09 (companion)*, ACM, Orlando, FL, 2009.

[MEN 10] MENDONCA M., COWAN D., "Decision-making coordination and efficient reasoning techniques for feature-based configuration", *Science of Computer Programming*, vol. 75, no. 5, pp. 311–332, 2010.

[MET 07]  METZGER A., POHL K., HEYMANS P., *et al.*, "Disambiguating the documentation of variability in software product lines: a separation of concerns, formalization and automated analysis", *RE '07*, IEEE, New Delhi, India, pp. 243–253, 2007.

[MOI 11]  MOISAN S., RIGAULT J.-P., ACHER M., *et al.*, "Run time adaptation of video-surveillance systems: a software modeling approach", *8th International Conference on Computer Vision Systems (ICVS '2011)*, LNCS, Springer Verlag, Sophia Antipolis, France, September 2011.

[MOR 09]  MORIN B., BARAIS O., NAIN G., *et al.*, "Taming dynamically adaptive systems using models and aspects", *ICSE '09*, IEEE, Vancouver, Canada, pp. 122–132, 2009.

[PAR 10]  PARRA C.A., CLEVE A., BLANC X., *et al.*, "Feature-based composition of software architectures", *ECSA '10*, LNCS, vol. 6285, Springer, Copenhagen, Denmark, pp. 230–245, 2010.

[PIN 99]  PINE B.J., *Mass Customization: The New Frontier in Business Competition*, Harvard Business School Press, Watertown, MA, 1999.

[PLE 12]  PLEUSS A., BOTTERWECK G., DHUNGANA D., *et al.*, "Model-driven support for product line evolution on feature level", *Journal of Systems and Software*, vol. 85, no. 10, pp. 2261–2274, October 2012.

[POH 05]  POHL K., BÖCKLE G., DER LINDEN F.J.V., *Software Product Line Engineering: Foundations, Principles and Techniques*, Springer-Verlag, Berlin, 2005.

[REI 07]  REISER M.-O., WEBER M., "Multi-level feature trees: a pragmatic approach to managing highly complex product families", *Requirement Engineering*, vol. 12, no. 2, pp. 57–75, 2007.

[RIE 03]  RIEBISCH M., "Towards a more precise definition of feature models", *Modelling Variability for Object-Oriented Product Lines*, BookOnDemand, Norderstedt, pp. 64–76, 2003.

[ROS 10]  ROSENMÜLLER M., SIEGMUND N., "Automating the configuration of multi software product lines", *Variability Modelling of Software intensive Systems VaMoS*, ACM, Linz, Austria, 2010.

[ROS 11]  ROSENMÜLLER M., SIEGMUND N., THÜM T., *et al.*, "Multi-dimensional variability modeling", *VaMoS '11*, ACM, Namur, Belgiumpp. 11–20, 2011.

[SCH 07]  SCHOBBENS P.-Y., HEYMANS P., TRIGAUX J.-C., *et al.*, "Generic semantics of feature diagrams", *Computer Networks*, vol. 51, no. 2, pp. 456–479, 2007.

[SEI 09]  SEINTURIER L., MERLE P., FOURNIER D., *et al.*, "Reconfigurable SCA applications with the FraSCAti Platform", *SCC '09*, IEEE, Bangalore, India, pp. 268–275, 2009.

[SHE 11]  SHE S., LOTUFO R., BERGER T., *et al.*, "Reverse engineering feature models", *ICSE '11*, ACM, San Francisco, CA, pp. 461–470, 2011.

[SIE 12]  SIEGMUND N., KOLESNIKOV S.S., KÄSTNER C., *et al.*, "Predicting performance via automated feature-interaction detection", *34th International Conference on Software Engineering (ICSE '12)*, IEEE, Zurich, Switzerland, pp. 167–177, 2012.

[SIN 06]  SINNEMA M., DEELSTRA S., HOEKSTRA P., "The COVAMOF derivation process", *ICSR*, Springer-Verlag, Turin, Italy, pp. 101–114, 2006.

[SIN 08] SINNEMA M., DEELSTRA S., "Industrial validation of COVAMOF", *Journal of Systems and Software*, vol. 81, no. 4, pp. 584–600, 2008.

[SVA 05] SVAHNBERG M., VAN GURP J., BOSCH J., "A taxonomy of variability realization techniques: research articles", *Software, Practice and Experience*, vol. 35, no. 8, pp. 705–754, 2005.

[THU 09] THUM T., BATORY D., KÄSTNER C., "Reasoning about edits to feature models", *ICSE '09*, ACM, Vancouver, Canada, pp. 254–264, 2009.

[THU 14] THUM T., KÄSTNER C., BENDUHN F., *et al.*, "FeatureIDE: an extensible framework for feature-oriented software development", *Science of Computer Programming*, vol. 79, no. 1, pp. 70–85, 2014.

[WEI 99] WEISS D.M., LAI C.T.R., *Software Product-Line Engineering: A Family-Based Software Development Process*, Addison-Wesley Longman, Boston, MA, 1999.

Chapter 4

# Architecture and Quality of Software Systems

Defining the architecture of a software system is a critical step in making design decisions. This is where decisions will be particularly made on non-functional requirements (NFRs), including those of quality. When it comes to building a new system, it is advantageous to utilize the knowledge gained in the development of other similar systems, i.e. belonging to the same functional domain. Our purpose is to study how it is possible to build on a given functional domain knowledge to secure the desired goal, namely the architecture quality. We propose a quality-driven architecture design approach and apply it as a first step for the development of the reference architecture of a functional domain and then to that of a specific system. We develop a real case study from the health sector.

## 4.1. Introduction

Defining the architecture is a major step in developing a software system. It is the first step in making design decisions. This is where both the decomposition of components and the way in which they will communicate are decided. Poor decomposition will affect product quality, which will be very difficult or expensive to correct later. Therefore, it is important at this stage to use tools for assessing the system's future quality and to make choices knowingly. If it is not possible to estimate *a priori* an architecture globally, it is, however, possible to compare it with alternative solutions.

Chapter written by Nicole LÉVY, Francisca LOSAVIO and Yann POLLET.

The objective is to move toward the best possible architecture, the one that best meets functional requirements (FRs) and NFRs expressed in the requirements analysis. Various propositions exist to guide the development of an architectural solution. Most methods advocate a top–down approach by decomposition. However, such an approach is difficult to carry out end-to-end. The architect rarely starts his construction from scratch; he/she reuses an approach, existing developments, systems from the same domain, or components in a more or less explicit manner.

In a given sector (e.g. banking and the health sector), systems ensure similar missions, and in order to do so, they provide very similar, if not identical, functionalities from one context to another. Here, we name such a set the "functional domain". This notion is more restrictive than the classical "domain" notion, where system functionalities to be defined can be very different. For example, for the "health" sector, "shared medical record" is a functional domain.

When it comes to developing a new system, it is interesting to take advantage of knowledge gained in the development of similar systems, those belonging to the same functional domain. This applies particularly to required functions, quality requirements common to all systems and enterprises or the context of use design choices. Current methods for developing architectures are not able to do this and essentially offer development methods from scratch [HOF 07, RAS 11]. However, experience shows that close functions are reflected by architectural choices that are reusable in other contexts. But there are quite significant differences in solutions to implement due to, on the one hand, functions to ensure and, on the other hand, NFRs specific to each specific context.

Our purpose is to study how knowledge capitalization related to a given functional domain can achieve the desired objective, namely good quality architecture. For this, in section 4.2, we will introduce the concept of quality of architectures. Then in section 4.3, we will present the proposed approach of quality-driven architecture development. We will first apply this approach in section 4.4 for reference architecture development for a functional domain, and then in section 4.5 for a specific system. We develop a real case study from the health sector to illustrate our overall approach. Section 4.6 describes related work.

## 4.2. Quality approach

### 4.2.1. *ISO 25010 quality*

Software quality focuses on the study of quality factors for software products and on the capacity to use these products in a particular context of usage [CAL 97]. Quality is typically defined in terms of conformance to specification and fitness for purpose ([CRO 84, DEM 00] among many others). However, this definition has its limitations: in case of a poor or deficient specification, the product will be conformed to its specification, but it will not hold the required quality; in case of the fitness for purpose, a product can accomplish its functionality better than another one. As an example, we will cite here two definitions taken from the well-known standards: IEEE [IEE 83] and ISO/IEC 25030 [ISO 06].

According to the IEEE standard [IEE 98], software quality is the set of properties and characteristics of a software product that relates to its ability to satisfy given requirements, as conformed to specifications. According to ISO/IEC 25030, software quality is the ability of the software product to satisfy explicit and implicit requirements when used under specified conditions.

ISO/IEC 9126-1 and the updated ISO/IEC 25010 [ISO 11], which are part of the SQuaRE standard series [ISO 06], by the "Joint Technical Committee ISO/IEC JTC 1, information technology, Subcommittee SC 7, Software and Systems Engineering", define quality properties that can be used to describe software products. Properties of quality are represented by a quality model composed of a hierarchy of characteristics based on eight main characteristics (Figure 4.1): functional suitability, performance efficiency, compatibility, usability, reliability, security, maintainability and portability. These characteristics, called abstract, are then further refined to achieve measurable characteristics called quality attributes. For example, functional suitability implies the existence of a set of functions that satisfy a particular requirement. It is refined into subcharacteristics such as completeness, correctness and appropriateness. These subcharacteristics may themselves be refined according to the targeted application domain. The hierarchy of characteristics of the ISO/IEC 25010 standard makes up the quality model of an application or software system in a given domain. It should be noted that a software product could also be a by-product of development, for example, a use-case model or an architecture model.

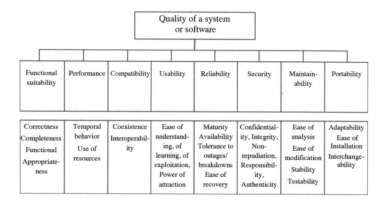

**Figure 4.1.** *Software quality model according to ISO/IEC 25010 [ISO 11]*

With regard to the quality of the software architecture, software quality characteristics (which are often referred to as quality attributes in the literature, whereas in ISO/IEC 25010 the term "attribute" is restricted to measurable characteristics) can be considered as benchmarks that describe the system-intended behavior within the environment for which it is built. These are standards by which results can be measured or assessed. The quality characteristics, specified as a quality model, can provide the means for measuring the fitness and suitability of the architecture, and hence affect the whole system quality. Software architecture has a profound effect on most system qualities in one way or another. However, there are no rules to determine precisely what are the quality requirements directly involved with the architecture, and the software architect, through his knowledge of the domain, must play an important role in the definition of the quality model associated with the architecture.

In general, the quality of a software system depends on the quality of its components and their interactions. This can be measured internally during the construction of the system or externally when the system is tested before delivery and, finally, can be measured by the end user when the system is in use. Software properties may be inherent properties of the system, which exist permanently in the software product but whose value may change if the system evolves. They may also be assigned properties that can change without changing the software (see Table 4.1). In this case, it is generally the case of properties required by the customer. System requirements are stated by the software engineer developing the software system and concern mainly the required configuration.

| Software Properties | Inherent properties | Domain-specific functional properties |
|---|---|---|
| | | Quality properties (functional suitability, reliability, performance efficiency, usability, security, compatibility, maintainability, portability, etc.) |
| | Assigned properties | Managerial properties (price, delivery date, product supplier, etc. ) |

**Table 4.1.** *Software properties classification [ISO 06]*

According to the SQuARE classification, software quality requirements represent NFRs stated by the client as software properties, at the same level of FRs; both types of requirements are considered as properties inherent to software requirements. The quality of a software product in a particular context of use is determined by its inherent properties. Domain-specific functional properties are generally concerned with transforming input data into output data. Additional functions or implicit functionalities may be needed to implement quality requirements and constraints required to accomplish a functionality. Quality requirements are also associated with FRs. A *quality characteristic* is the term used by the ISO/IEC 25010 quality model standard [ISO 11] (see Figure 4.1); it indicates a software quality requirement that can be refined until the quality attributes or measurable elements are attained. General metrics for internal, external and in use quality requirements are also provided by this standard; they were defined in ISO/IEC 9126-2, 3 and 4 and they have not been changed in the standard's recent update. In this chapter, we only consider internal quality defined by [ISO 11] to measure the software product artifacts developed during the system development process; software architecture is one of these products and the measures at this level are very abstract. For example, a Boolean value will indicate the presence of a mechanism taking into account a quality characteristic [LOS 03].

### 4.2.2. *Quality reference*

Ensuring the quality of a system requires studying the quality attributes at each stage of the development process. During the requirements analysis, the non-functional properties of the future system are described: the quality model of the system is defined, including quality requirements associated with functionalities. When designing the architecture, it is important to verify that each required quality criterion will be taken into account during the system development: the quality model of the architecture is then defined. We will study these two quality models by studying how the second one refines the first one and describes how the future system should be evaluated to check the satisfaction of the required properties.

In the requirements analysis, the expected non-functional properties described must be analyzed to associate with them a quality characteristic from the standard used (e.g. ISO 25010). In the requirements analysis, expected non-functional properties are restrictions on the future system and its development process as well as external constraints (legal, economic, technological, etc.) that the system must satisfy [KOT 98].

The ISO 25010 standard [ISO 06] considers the inherent product properties: functional properties related to the domain and quality properties, as well as assigned properties that are external properties that will have no direct impact on the product. Our aim is to study what the requirements are, which, when taken into account, will have an impact on the software architecture development. We will only consider those as they are the ones that must be taken into account by the architecture in order to guarantee their satisfaction by the future system. They are the requirements that are related to the product: the future system. They are often constraints on its behavior, e.g. concerning its performance or capacity. These properties can be easily quantified, and a measure as well as a value can be specified in the requirements analysis. They will have a direct impact on the way to realize the system. Other non-functional properties such as usability, maintainability and reusability are less easily quantified. Requirements analysis can be very vague on this subject or can specify what is meant by these terms and at what level of abstraction they are used; on the other hand, if the ISO/IEC 25010 is used, these terms are defined in the standard. In this case, the analysis will indicate how they will be evaluated. Whether it is in the requirements analysis or after, it will anyway have to be specified. From these properties, the quality model of the system must be derived. We will now study this model.

### 4.2.3. *Quality model of a system*

The quality model of a system describes its requirements in terms of quality. We consider the ISO/IEC 25010 model and propose to use a table where, for each characteristic and subcharacteristic of the standard, it is specified how it should be considered in the system: the requirements mentioning it; a priority assigned (e.g. a 5-point scale, the highest being 1); how to evaluate it (measure); a fixed value defined as a goal for the measure (see Table 4.2).

| Quality characteristics/ Subcharacteristics | Priority | Requir-ement | Measured Quality Attribute | Valued Objective |
|---|---|---|---|---|
| *Performance efficiency / Time behavior* | 1 | [i], [j] | Response time | 1 s, 1 s |
| *Usability/Operability* | 2 | [k] | Time taken by the user to write his request | 3 min |

**Table 4.2.** *Quality model shown in a table*

For example, let us consider the following requirements:

[i] the system will respond to the query "search availability for a specific flight" in less than 1 s;

[j] the system will respond to the query "search for available seats in a certain flight" in less than 1 s;

[k] the user will be able to perform its search request of availability for a specific flight in less than 3 min.

A quality model derived from these requirements is described in Table 4.2. However, we note that sometimes the measurement cannot be or is only vaguely indicated in the requirement statement. For example, it will be indicated that the system should be able to resist external attacks without further specification, or that the system will respond to a particular standard. In this case, the architecture should indicate how these needs are understood and taken into account. This information will be specified in the architecture quality model.

### 4.2.4. *Functional quality model*

The functional quality model (FQM) is used to link FRs and quality properties that may be required in order to fully perform each function. Table 4.3 shows an FQM example for the m-bank sector. For legibility reasons, the measured attributes and the expected order of magnitude are not shown.

| Functional requirements | | Quality characteristics/subcharacteristics |
|---|---|---|
| Authentication | Token card + PIN | Usability (accessibility, operability, protection against user errors), reliability (availability), security (authenticity), efficiency (time behavior – response time) |
| | Barcode | |
| | Short court | |
| Financial information services | Data consultation and operations not involving payment | Usability (accessibility), reliability, security (integrity), efficiency (time behavior – response time) |
| Accounting | Transfer between bank accounts | Reliability (availability), security (integrity, authenticity, confidentiality), efficiency (time – response time), functional suitability (correction) |
| | Credit card transactions | Reliability (availability), security (integrity, authenticity, confidentiality), efficiency (time behavior – response time), functional suitability (correction) |
| | Payment of services | Reliability (availability), security (integrity, authenticity, confidentiality), efficiency (time – response time), functional suitability (correction) |

**Table 4.3.** *Functional quality model of m-bank [LOS 13]*

## 4.2.5. *Quality model of the architecture*

The software architecture is a specification of the structure of the future system in terms of components and communicating connectors [SG 96]. It is important to clearly show how the architecture takes into account the requirements from the quality model of the system. It is a matter of affecting responsibilities: "who does what?". Table 4.4 describes the architectural quality model (AQM) as follows: the non-functional requirements (NFR) related to the architecture are associated with the corresponding ISO/IEC 25010 quality requirements and the chosen architectural solution. It can be a component or a group of components. For example, for performance, this is often indicated for a use scenario. Upon its execution, several components will be affected. The table should also indicate more precisely the measure applied and the value derived from the value mentioned in the system model. In the previous case of the performance, each component must know what its required performance should be. This table is used to identify the exact origin of quality properties in relation to NFRs of the architecture, from the requirements analysis to components that manage them, introducing traceability links that facilitate the verification. It is required to ensure that all requirements are taken into account by the architecture even before assessing whether they will be properly satisfied. The table also tells the designer how the different qualities will be measured, which will help to define how to achieve them. Sometimes, the presence of a component ensures that some quality will be taken into account. For example, this is the case of the security property to be provided by information encryption/decryption modules or a pattern, an architectural solution or a style [BUS 96]. In this case, the measurement is Boolean: the presence of a device supporting the property. Table 4.4 shows an example of AQM for the domain of the m-bank or mobile bank, to access all banking transactions from a mobile phone. For readability reasons, the measured attributes and the expected order of magnitude are not shown.

| Requirements related to architecture | | Architectural solution or style | Quality characteristics/ subcharacteristics (AQM) |
|---|---|---|---|
| The server database must be centralized | | *Repository* | Security (integrity), maintainability (modifiability – scalability), reliability (availability) |
| The communication layer for data access must be extensible and secure | | *Event channel – proxy* | Maintainability (modifiability, scalability), security (authenticity, confidentiality, integrity), efficiency (time behavior) |
| The communication layer must be implemented using Web Services | | SOA | Compatibility (interoperability), security (authenticity), functional suitability (relevance, accuracy), reliability (availability), maintainability (modifiability – scalability), portability (adaptability) |
| Transmission | SMS | Event Channel | Channel security (integrity, confidentiality), the reliability of channels (if available) |
| | Web Mobile | | |
| | Application Client | | |
| | Mobile | | |
| | Secured SMS | | |

**Table 4.4.** *Architectural quality model of the m-bank domain, shown as a set of scenarios [LOS 13]*

The use of standards is recommended in various books, identifying best practices of software engineering. Indeed, they facilitate communication between stakeholders and understanding. However, their use is not a common practice because standards often lack the user guidelines. This is particularly the case for standards on software quality, amplified by the fact that there is no agreement on terminology. In practice, each domain uses its own definitions of requirements and quality parameters. An ontology allowing the comparison of different quality standards has been proposed in [LOS 09] and [JEA 12].

## 4.3. Approach for architecture development of a domain

In this section, we present a generic approach for developing systems architectures by taking into account both the FQM and AQM models defined above.

### 4.3.1. *General principles*

From a general point of view, the process of building a domain architecture takes as input a set of requirements, which comprises:

– some domain-specific FRs, expressing the functions to be provided by future systems;

– some NFRs (including "quality requirements"), whose concern is how these functions should be provided under the aspects of quality of the provided service, in addition to particular requested aptitudes of future systems;

– some design requirements from the enterprise requiring the system or the system context of use, i.e. a set of constraints that should be imposed, for any reason whatsoever, on future systems in terms of design, mode of implementation, interfaces with existing systems, etc. This set may also contain constraints applying to the future architecture such as types of components, types of connectors between them (synchronous, asynchronous), etc.

The design of a new system aims at defining a system architecture satisfying such requirements. In particular, this includes:

– the definition of an architectural configuration. Such a configuration may be expressed as a graph [LOS 12] whose vertices are the components of the system, and whose edges are the connectors supporting interactions between components;

– the definitions of the components. This includes the definition of the interfaces provided by each component, as well as the different FRs and NFRs that must be satisfied by each component individually.

The links kept between the defined architectural elements and the system requirements justifying them ensure the traceability of design choices. This traceability is crucial in the design of any system[1].

The approach proposed here focuses on building the architecture of a new system in two steps; the first step is domain specific and, therefore, common to all systems of the domain; the second step is specific to the particular context of each system to be built. These two phases are:

– construction of the domain architecture proposed as a common basis for further realization of some system of the domain;

– adaptation of this domain architecture to a system to be built on the basis of its specific requirements.

### 4.3.1.1. *Domain architecture*

Domain architecture is the architecture of an "ideal" system that would satisfy requirements that are common to the class of all considered systems. This architecture is abstract because it is not produced for a single concrete system. For example, in a shared medical record (which may be present in many contexts, ranging from an individual medical practitioner software to a complete Hospital Information System of some large institution), there exists a common kernel of services or FRs expected from any system, and known as absolutely required. For example: consult a patient's file, add a medical event to it, etc. There is also a basic set of NFRs common to all systems such as security, minimum performance, etc.

Sometimes, a generic requirement which applies to a quality attribute will be present in all systems of the considered domain, but the expected value of this attribute will *a priori* differ from one system to another. In the context of software product lines such as described in Chapter 5, this would be a variation point denoting the fact that various alternatives are known at the domain level. One of them has to be selected at the non-functional level [BAR 10, POH 05]. Thus, the approach based on a quality model enables us to know exactly the functionality realizing the quality requirement. At the

---

1 It should be noted here that a component may be a basic software component, i.e. directly produced by a software development team, or a software subsystem, which must in turn be broken down into finer granularity components. The second case involves the definitions of internal architectures for the various identified subsystems. The decomposition into sub-systems continues until basic software components are obtained. The approach of building the system architecture therefore appears as essentially recursive.

functional domain level, an attribute will be characterized by an expected order of magnitude or by an expected property. This particular value should be specified at the system level. For example, in the case of a medical records management system, a measured attribute will be the volume supported by the system in terms of number of managed records; this requirement will have to be instantiated for each system of the domain, but with different values from one system to another. In this case, the requirement is selected at the domain level with a parameter value being set for each particular system. Its value not being determined at the domain level, the corresponding requirement should be taken into account later, i.e. at the "system" level.

The domain reference architecture is defined beforehand. It constitutes the basis for the construction of some particular concrete system architecture. This architecture is to be exceptionally questioned for enrichment purposes.

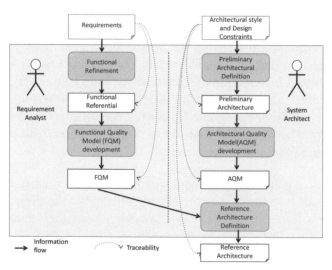

**Figure 4.2.** *Development of architecture*

The development of both domain architecture and that of some particular system architecture follow exactly the same approach, the principle of which is described by Figure 4.2. First, the approach considers two sets of activities, according to two parallel branches. In this sense, it is closer to the Y cycle approach [ROC 01]. But, if in both cases, the first part concerns the functional aspects, the other is not related to the same level of abstraction as it relates to the technical aspects of the Y cycle and here, the architecture.

The activities of the left branch of the diagram correspond to the tasks undertaken by an analyst (requirement analyst), i.e. tasks that require knowledge related to the domain, while those of the right branch of the diagram require the skills of a system architect.

### 4.3.2. *Functional quality model*

The functional refinement activity analyzes user requirements in functional terms, and formalizes them under the form of a set of functions. In the case of the functional domain, they will be classified properly into (1) functions necessary for all systems in the domain or (2) functions that are possible only, i.e. applicable only to particular systems. Only the first ones will be retained.

Based on the user requirements, the preliminary architectural definition guides the choice of a relevant architectural style and thus proposes a first system architecture draft that will be the basis for future adaptations.

### 4.3.3. *Architectural quality model*

Starting from this first version of the architecture, the activity called "AQM Development" takes into account the NFRs not linked to specific functions and so applying to the overall system. Their impact on the architecture is analyzed by translating them into adaptations of the previous architecture, with, in particular, applicable quality characteristics assertions assigned to components.

### 4.3.4. *Reference architecture*

The joint results issued from these two branches enable the development of the final architecture. So, according to the phase where this activity is located, the result is either the functional domain reference architecture, or the specifically studied system architecture. Let us recall that the reference domain architecture is the basis for the development of specific architectures of new systems, based on context-specific architectural adaptations. The presentation of these activities as two entirely separate branches is of course an ideal view, as in practice there may be interactions between the two branches. It is important to maintain traceability links between quality assertions and the different models.

Once the domain architecture has been developed, the approach followed for the development of the architecture of a particular system follows an approach quite similar to the one just described. The starting point then consists of both the specific user requirements related to this new system and the reference architecture of the considered functional domain. Each activity appears as an enrichment activity of a model in the specific context of the new system and of its requirements. It aims at delivering a new quality model applicable to the target system.

### 4.3.4.1. *Principle of the architectural integration approach*

In order to build an architecture specifically tailored to some particular system requirements, including both FRs and NFRs, the proposed approach, in its principle, consists of the following steps:

– First, build an initial architecture meeting the FRs, relaxing the constraints induced by the quality requirements. This is the "ideal" architecture, which addresses the problem without taking into account the NFRs, i.e. regardless of security, performance requirements, etc. Such an architecture is thus only justified by FRs and architectural style(s) that may be associated with the functional domain. The choice of an architectural style implies that the architecture will meet all the quality requirements related to the chosen style.

– Progressively integrate the different quality requirements. This is performed by (1) looking, at each step, for the different possible ways of taking into account a considered requirement in the architecture related to the current step, (2) selecting one of them, and consequently adapting the architecture, and (3) ensuring that the architecture thus amended still satisfies all quality requirements considered at the previous steps.

The architectural modifications introduced at each stage can be:

– additions of new components: typically, an added component meets a functional requirement or a quality requirement that will guarantee the considered quality characteristic at system level;

– additions of FRs or NFRs on a component already present in the architecture;

– addition of new requirements on the execution infrastructure;

– changes in the architecture topology (connections between components). This case requires checking again the validity of the previous selected architecture adaptations, and possibly doing backtracks in the process in order to challenge them;

– combinations of the above possibilities.

Note that, at the functional domain level, changes can either have a direct or delayed impact on the architecture. Contrary to a product line approach, all the choices are not *a priori* known, and, in any case, it is always possible to define *a posteriori* a new one. Our approach then may be seen as a heuristic approach justified by experience. This does not, of course, guarantee that a solution is obtained with certainty, nor the best solution (best in the sense of lower complexity). The approach is essentially iterative and may require backtracking during iterations, as is the case in most architectural design methods [ARA 02, BAS 02a, BOS 99, KRU 99].

Finally, it is also clear that the order in which the various quality requirements are considered has an influence on both the process and possibly the outcome. That is why it is important to take quality requirements in an order that generally leads to the lowest modifications in the architecture. To do so, the architect should determine an order that corresponds to a decreasing order of difficulty in potential adaptations, or to a decreasing potential impact on the architecture. The classification of requirements is of course based primarily on the architect's expertise, involving references to similar cases issued from his/her experience.

### 4.3.5. *Transition from domain level to system level*

We have developed a two-step approach: the first step applies to the functional domain level and the second step applies to the system level.

The consideration of the functional domain level results from the need of facilitating reuse, both from the point of view of common functionalities (that one may consider as characteristics of a domain), as well as from the point of view of the structure of the various system architectures. This level is very similar to that considered in product line approaches, but here the set of all possible solutions has not been *a priori* exhaustively explored, which makes the functional domain more open or adaptable to unexpected evolutions. The functional domain level may be seen as a factorization of common aspects of a certain family of systems, but keeping the possibility of creating further new developments.

The system level is the level considered in most classical approaches. The process of defining a system architecture starts, on the one hand, from the user's requirements concerning the system and, on the other hand, from the reference architecture resulting from the previous process at the functional domain level. FRs and NFRs are here completely specified. If required, concrete values of quality attributes can be provided. Technical constraints on the implementation are taken into account.

## 4.4. Development of the reference architecture in a functional domain

### 4.4.1. *Example of functional domain*

Our approach will be illustrated by an example of health information systems whose purpose is to manage shared patients' records as a support to medical practitioners' activities [LLO 03]. For this purpose, a set of functions is provided to different users: medical practitioners, system administrators and, for some particular systems, the patients themselves. In fact, we consider a set of various possible but similar systems having a common core of functionalities, and differing mainly by the expected NFRs (with, if necessary, a set of additional FRs). In our functional domain, we consider two particular examples of systems:

– Dopamine, a system in charge of managing patients' records in an administrative region (with a very large number of records to be managed, user access via the Internet, strong requirement for availability, etc.).

– Samarkand, a software package dedicated to private medical practitioners (with a smaller number of patients' records to be managed, user workstations and servers located in the same building, sharing of patients' records only among known associated practitioners, etc.).

### 4.4.2. *Functional refinement*

As a first step, we collect all functions identified for systems of the considered domain. By highlighting the common elements, i.e. taking the intersection of the various sets of functions associated with each system, we get a set of common functions, which is the common functional core of the functional domain. This common core is a domain-specific functional invariant.

In our example, the functional core will include the possibility on the part of a medical practitioner to get connected to the system to retrieve patients' reference matching given criteria, to view a medical record (if he/she has the rights to do so) and to add new items to this record (new symptoms, diagnosis, prescription, etc.). A medical practitioner, having the particular status of medical administrator, will be able to register a practitioner as a user of the system, or to remove one from the list of registered users. Moreover, for a reason of extensibility, it must be possible (for any system of the functional domain) to enrich the present medical reference data (symptoms, diagnoses and prescriptions issued from possible evolutions of medical standards). This requires the system to provide an additional function allowing reference repository enrichment to be done by the medical administrator. Finally, the functional core should also include the ability to perform data archiving under the control of a technical operator.

| Function class | Function | User | Comment |
|---|---|---|---|
| User authentication | Practitioner Login | Medical practitioner | *Implicit function* |
| Access to a patient's record and add items to it | Search for a patient's record | Medical practitioner | |
| | Consult a patient's record | | |
| | Add item to a patient's record | | |
| Administrate | Enrich medical repository | Medical administrator | *Implicit function* |
| | Add or remove a user | | |
| Save data | Save data | Technical operator | *Implicit function* |

**Table 4.5.** *Functions at domain level*

Table 4.5 summarizes the main common functionalities, grouped by functional classes. The functions annotated as "implicit" are introduced to meet a requirement perceived in a first analysis (at user level) as non-functional. For example, this is the case of the "Practitioner Login" function, which contributes to meet an initial security requirement, as mentioned in the example of Table 4.4.

### 4.4.3. *Development of the FQM*

The FQM summarizes all the quality requirements associated with the various functions identified in the functional domain. For each function, the model specifies the expected non-functional requirement(s) that possibly constrain(s) it (such as requirements of performance, security, etc.). Some domain-level requirements may be completely defined with a perfect accuracy. They apply to any system in the domain (in particular, this is the case of requirements closely related to the considered professional practices). They constitute the domain-level specific requirements. Other domain-level requirements are defined in a generic way, and so, require being instantiated assigning them specific values for the considered system. This is the case when some requirement must be present in every system of the domain, but with some variation on either the level of the requirement or on its precise technicalities. These are the generic requirements. The FQM for our example is summarized in Table 4.6.

| Function | Quality characteristic/sub-characteristic | Measured quality attribute [parameter] | Parameter range |
|---|---|---|---|
| Practitioner Login | *Security/Authenticity* | Medical practitioner Login [Authentication method] | – |
| Search for a patient's record | *Performance efficiency/Time behavior* | Maximum time to locate the patient's record from a set of given criteria [Maximum time value] | Maximum time value $\leq 5$ s |
|  | *Performance efficiency/Resources utilization* | Storage capacity in terms of patient's records [Minimum number of managed folders] | Min Number $\geq$ 10,000 |
| Consult a patient's record | *Performance efficiency/Time behavior* | Access to a patient's record from its identifier [Maximum time value] | Maximum time value $\leq 5$ s |
|  | *Security/ Confidentiality* | Practitioner access restriction to records or items based on rights [Rights management policy] | – |
| Add a new item to the repository | *Maintainability/ Modifiability* | Possibility to modify the repository (with medical standards evolution) | – |

**Table 4.6.** *Functional quality model of domain level*

### 4.4.4. *Definition of the preliminary architecture*

This activity aims at defining a first draft of the system architecture, which does not yet take into account the applicable quality requirements. It is called the "preliminary architecture". It results from the selection of an architectural style and identification of basic components, tracing identified components from FRs. This activity can be started in parallel with the functional refinement activity; so far as the selected architectural style does not depend directly on the description of the expected functionalities.

In our example, the choice is a three-tier architecture, as shown in Figure 4.3. The only constraint, for the moment, is to geographically separate a data server from client workstations. The software components are the following:

– In the client tier, the "Practitioner MMI" (Man–Machine Interface) and the "Administrator MMI" components, which implement, respectively, the practitioner's and medical administrator's man–machine interfaces.

– In the application tier, the "Service Access" component handles different types of queries issued from man–machine interfaces, and the "Medical Data" component in charge of the applicative objects considered in a patient's record.

– In the persistence tier, the Administrative Database (administrative data related to medical practitioners and patients), the Medical Database (data related to patients' medical history) and the Repository Database (repository of standard symptoms, diagnoses and prescriptions).

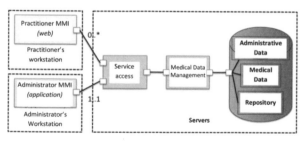

**Figure 4.3.** *Preliminary architecture*

The AQM of the functional domain of our example is described in Table 4.7. For a particular system to be built, each element of Table 4.7

determines a quality requirement issued from the domain, either directly, or via an instantiation through values to be assigned to parameters.

### 4.4.5. *Development of architectural quality model*

| Quality characteristic/ subcharacteristic | Measured quality attribute [parameter] | Parameter range |
|---|---|---|
| *Security/Confidentiality* | Confidentiality of stored data | – |
| *Reliability/Availability* | Guarantee of accessibility [Rate] | [0..1] |
| *Reliability/Recoverability* | Guarantee of an RTO [Time][2] | [0..10] |
| | Guarantee of an RPO [Time][3] | [0..10] |
| *Usability/User interface aesthetic* | Compliance with an ergonomic chart | – |

**Table 4.7.** *Architectural quality model of the domain level*

### 4.4.6. *Integration of the reference architecture of the domain*

| Source (FQM/ AQM) | Function (if FQM) | Quality characteristic/ subcharacteristic | Measured quality attribute [parameter] | Parameter range |
|---|---|---|---|---|
| FQM | Practitioner Login | *Security/Authenticity* | Practitioner authentication | – |
| FQM | Consult a patient's record | *Security/ Confidentiality* | Access restricted to certain records or items based on a chosen rights management policy | – |
| AQM | – | *Security/ Confidentiality* | Confidentiality of stored data | – |
| AQM | – | *Reliability/ Availability* | Guarantee of availability [RateValue] | [0..1] |
| AQM | – | *Reliability/ Recoverability* | Guarantee of an RTO [TimeValue] | [0..10] |
| AQM | – | *Reliability/* | Guarantee of an RPO | [0..10] |

2 RTO: Recovery time objective.

3 RPO: Recovery point objective.

| | | *Recoverability* | [time] | |
|---|---|---|---|---|
| FQM | Searching a patient record | *Performance efficiency/Time behavior* | Maximum time to find a patient records identifier from a set of criteria [Value] | value ≤ 5 s |
| FQM | Consult a patient's record | *Performance efficiency/Time behavior* | Maximum time access to patient records from its ID [Value] | Value ≤ 5 s |
| FQM | Searching a patient record | *Performance efficiency/Resource utilization* | Storage of record [Minimum number of managed records] | Min number ≥ 10,000) |
| AQM | – | *Usability/User interface aesthetic* | Compliance with an ergonomic chart | – |
| FQM | Adding a new item to the repository | *Maintainability/ Modifiability* | Possibility to modify the repository (in the case of changing health standards) | – |

**Table 4.8.** *Overall quality model of the domain level*

This activity aims to define the system architecture satisfying all the domain-level requirements. This architecture will be obtained by successive adjustments of the previous preliminary architecture. The approach consists of:

– taking as an initial basis the "preliminary architecture" already built;

– integrating in to the architecture successively different quality requirements;

– searching at each step for various possible fits meeting the concerned requirement;

– choosing one and consequently modifying the architecture;

– ensuring that the architecture still meets the quality requirements considered in the previous steps;

– possibly backtracking and challenging a design choice made at an earlier step.

The overall quality model is obtained by merging the requirements resulting from both FQM and AQM models. Table 4.8 thus shows such a specification, where requirements are sorted by order of priority, the order being based on the architect's experience. Architectural adaptation is performed successively by taking into account the requirements. At each step, the various ways of taking into account the considered requirement are identified, as well as the consequent impact on the architecture. This impact may be immediate, i.e. it immediately applies to any system in the domain, or deferred, i.e. the choice is marked in order to be kept for a further step; this choice has to be specific for each particular future system. Our approach is illustrated below. Table 4.8 illustrates only the first elements of the resulting table; we then summarize the results.

The "Medical Practitioners Login" requirement remains generic, different practical ways of authentication being possible. Each system will have to specify its own authentication method. As the choices to be made are independent of the Login mode, specific authentication mechanisms are encapsulated in an added "Login" component. This approach is summarized in Tables 4.9 and 4.10. It is possible to check the impact on the architecture not modifying the previous properties.

| Requirement number | 1 |
|---|---|
| Quality characteristic/subcharacteristic | *Security/authenticity* |
| Quality requirement | Practitioner access subject to authentication |
| Taking requirement into account & design decision | *Functional level*: possible choices<br>– Login and password stored in the administrative database<br>– Authentication by an health professional card and password<br>– Other authentication modes (biometric, etc.)<br>– *Decision*: adding a "Login" component, deferral of the choice of the Login mode at the "system" level |
| Impact on the architecture | *Immediate:*<br>– *Adding a "Login" component*, with allocation of the functional requirement "Login" [Authentication method]<br>– *Adding a requirement to the administrative database*: management of "professional ID" and "password" encrypted<br>*Deferred*:<br>– *Adding a functional requirement* to the "Login" component: implementation of an authentication method<br>– *Adding a requirement on infrastructure*: possible integration of a card reader with its associated driver |

**Table 4.9.** *Architectural impact of the login requirement*

| Requirement number | 2 |
|---|---|
| Quality characteristic/ sub-characteristic | *Security/confidentiality* |
| Quality requirement | Restrict access to patient's records according to rights |
| Taking requirement into account & design decision | *Functional level*: possible choices<br>– access policy based on rights given by the doctor who created the patient's record (context of a doctor office in Samarkand)<br>– access policy based on practitioners' role on patients' record (context of a health network in Dopamine)<br>*Architectural level*: possible choices to determinate rights (using chosen policy):<br>– for each request on a patient's record<br>– only once at access time, then memorized in a managed context (involves managing contexts and associated time-out) |
| Impact on the architecture | *Immediate:*<br>– adding a "Rights Management" component with a functional requirement "Manage rights [policy]"<br>– adding functional requirement on the administrative database component: manage a set of entities "Right of a practitioner on a record"<br>*Deferred:*<br>– adding functional requirement on the "Rights Management" component: policy implementation specified at system level |

**Table 4.10.** *Architectural impact of the access restriction requirement*

The reference architecture of the functional domain, shown in Figure 4.4, is obtained after taking into account all the requirements. The main requirements applied to components (immediate choices) are indicated.

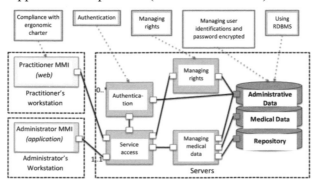

**Figure 4.4.** *Reference architecture of the functional domain*

## 4.5. Architectures at system level

Based on the above analysis of the functional domain, we will now study the architecture definitions of two systems issued from the same domain. It involves Dopamine, a regional health information system, and Samarkand, a medical information system dedicated to independent practitioners. The activities that will be described are, of course, specific to each of the two systems being considered, and therefore conducted in an absolutely independent manner. To clearly represent this, here we choose to show at the same time and comparatively these two analyses, activity-by-activity.

### 4.5.1. *Functional refinement*

For each system, the table of domain level common functions is completed with the specific functions of the considered system. Table 4.11 shows the overall results obtained for each of the two systems, the last column indicating whether the identified function is required in one or another system, or in both (domain). Terms present in the gray boxes indicate the new system-specific functions.

| Class of functionality | Function | User | Applies to |
|---|---|---|---|
| Authentication | Practitioner Login | Medical practitioner | Domain |
| | Patient Login | Patient | Dopamine |
| Access to a patient's record and add items to it | Searching a record | Medical practitioner | Domain |
| | Consulting a record | | Domain |
| | Adding an item to a record | | Domain |
| | Read own (simplified) record | Patient | Dopamine |
| | Grant another practitioner's rights to a record | Medical practitioner | Samarkand |
| Administer | Enrich the medical repository | Medical administrator | Domain |
| | Add or remove a user | | Domain |
| | Audit accesses to system | | Dopamine |
| Save data | Save data | Operator | Domain |

**Table 4.11.** *Functions at system level for Dopamine and Samarkand systems*

In Dopamine, the patient is provided with a way to access a simplified version of his/her own record. Note that the sharing of patients' records between practitioners is governed by two different policies depending on the considered systems: explicitly granted by the practitioner creator of the record in Samarkand, but managed automatically by the system based on practitioner role in Dopamine.

### 4.5.2. Functional quality model

Table 4.12 presents the FQMs of the two systems. It complements that of the domain, by adding the domain-specific functions of each system as well as the quality attributes attached to each function. The last column indicates the value definitions required for each of the two systems, attribute by attribute. Note that, in addition, a design requirement is added in Dopamine: the system will have the capability of being distributed over the Internet, on a Web server and on different client workstations spread geographically.

| Function | Quality characteristic/sub-characteristic | Measured quality attribute [parameter] | Required value |
|---|---|---|---|
| Practitioner Login | *Security/authenticity* | Practitioner Login [Authentication method] | D: Login & password S: Card |
| Login patient | *Security/authenticity* | Patient Login [Authentication method] | D: Login password |
| Searching for a patient record | *Performance efficiency/time behavior* | Maximum time to find an ID record using criteria [Maximum time] | D: 5 s S: 3 s |
| | *Use of resources* | Storage capacity of record [Minimum number of managed records] | D: 1,000,000 S: 10,000 |
| Consulting a record (Practitioner) | *Performance efficiency/time behavior* | Access time to a record from its ID [Maximum time] | D: 4 s S: 3 s |
| | *Security/confidentiality* | Restricted practitioner access to certain records or items of record based on rights [Access management policy] | D: policy based on grants S: policy based on roles |
| Consulting one's own record | *Performance efficiency/time behavior* | Time for accessing a record [Maximum time] | D: 5 s |

**Table 4.12.** *Functional quality model of the Dopamine and Samarkand systems*

### 4.5.3. Basic architecture

In a very similar manner to the process of defining the functional domain reference architecture, the architecture of a particular system is built by successive adjustments of the functional domain reference architecture, based on the quality requirements specified for each system.

| Characteristic/ sub-characteristic | Measured quality attribute (parameter) | Required value |
|---|---|---|
| *Security/confidentiality/ integrity* | Confidentiality et integrity related to communications | Applies to: D |
| *Reliability/availability* | Guarantee of availability [Rate] | D: 0.999 S: 0.99 |
| *Reliability/recoverability* | Guarantee of an RTO [Time] | D: 10 mn S: 30 mn |
| | Guarantee of an RPO [Time] | D: 1 mn S: 30 mn |
| *Usability/user interface aesthetic* | Compliance to an ergonomic chart | D: practitioner and patient ergonomic charts S: practitioner ergonomic chart |

**Table 4.13.** *Architectural quality model of the Dopamine and Samarkand systems*

### 4.5.4. Architectural quality model

Table 4.13 summarizes the AQM of the two systems in a single framework, incorporating the AQM of the domain, adding specific architectural quality requirements of the considered systems. The values of the parameters enabling us to instantiate the generic requirements are specified. An architectural quality requirement added in Dopamine concerns the security of communications (the system being deployed on the Internet), unlike Samarkand (based on a private network, on only one geographical location). Other requirements of Table 4.13 are domain-level generic requirements, which are to be instantiated in the specific context of each system. Note that some requirements are omitted, those already taken into account at the domain level, i.e. having no deferred choice.

In a very similar manner to the construction of the reference domain architecture, each of the system architectures is built on the basis of a subsequent number of architecture adaptation decisions, each one resulting in component additions and/or additions of new requirements on components already identified and/or on the execution infrastructure. As an example, in Table 4.14, we show a summary of the results obtained for the first processed requirements (the first fiverequirements of a total of 11), stating which one applies to one or the other system.

### 4.5.5. *Architecture of the Dopamine and Samarkand systems*

For a given system, the FQM and AQM are merged into a global quality model, which incorporates all the requirements issued from the two models. As for the domain level, this work relies on the architect's expertise and fixes an order for taking each requirement into account in the adapting processes. In order to simplify discussion, and to continue drawing a parallel between the two architectures to be built, we assume here this order is the same for both systems.

The resulting architectures of the Samarkand and Dopamine systems are presented in Figures 4.5 and 4.6.

These two examples of systems issued from the same functional domain highlight the fact that two very close sets of functional requirements (here, in our case, one is a superset of another), but with different quality requirements, lead to very different architectures. Thus, the two architectures differ by additional components required in the second architecture (here, to ensure the required availability). They also differ by the topology of the connections between components and by different variants of the same basic components (which provide the same function, but are based on different quality requirements and different constraints).

| Requirement | Analysis/decision | Impact |
|---|---|---|
| *Security/Authenticity* Medical Practitioners Authentication [Authentication method] (Function: Practitioner Login) | *Analysis & decision*: "Login" component implements the selected authentication method for the considered system | Dopamine: addition – functional requirement: on the "Authentication" component (authentication by Login and password) Samarkand: addition – functional requirement: on the "Login" component (Authentication by card) – infrastructure requirement: addition of a card reader |
| *Security/authenticity* Patient Login [Authentication method] (Function: patient Login) | *Analysis & decision*: Dopamine: "Login" component implements the authentication method for patients Samarkand: nil | Dopamine: addition – functional requirement: on the "Authentication" component (Authentication by Login and password) Samarkand: – |
| *Security/confidentiality* Access restricted to certain records or data according to rights [Right management policy] (Function: read patient's record) | *Analysis and decision*: The "management of access rights" component implements the rights management policy required for the system | Dopamine: addition – functional requirement: "management of access rights" component Samarkand: addition – functional requirement: "management of access rights" component |
| *Security/confidentiality & integrity* confidentiality & integrity of communications | Analysis and decision: Dopamine: secure protocols and PKI management Samarkand: nil (private network) | Dopamine: addition – infrastructure requirement: secure protocols and PKI management Samarkand: nil |
| *Reliability/availability* Required availability [Availability ratio] | Analysis and decision: choice of a suitable server for the required availability property Dopamine: suitable server Samarkand: nil (standard server) | Dopamine: addition – infrastructure requirement: suitable server Samarkand: nil |

**Table 4.14.** *Sample design decisions and their impact on architectures for the Dopamine and Samarkand systems*

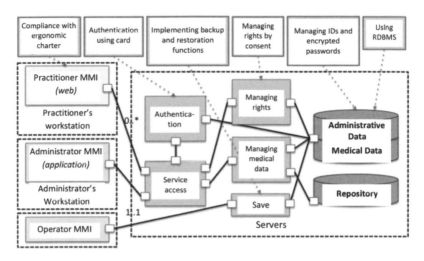

**Figure 4.5.** *Architecture of the Samarkand system*

## 4.6. Related work

In architectural design, it is crucial to maintain a link between requirements and architectural solution. Castro *et al.* [CAS 12] mentioned the problems of informal and/or incomplete requirements and the complexity of maintaining traceability links. Despite these challenges, it is unusual to have a systematic approach that is concerned with analyzing and understanding the requirements and producing a suitable set of architectural solutions that satisfactorily meet the requirements, illustrated by a complete example. The techniques and methods used for software development should include a way of systematically dealing with the relationship between requirements models and architectural models.

Functional requirements are taken into account at the system specification level and the NFRs by the architecture. The architectural design chooses and implements a solution that best meets the quality requirements. As a consequence, all architectural design methods have to deal with quality requirements and include an evaluation process of the resulting quality. Many architectural evaluation methods are presented in [RAS 11], all based on the architecture tradeoff analysis method (ATAM) [BAS 02a] that we will comment upon, and a version adapted from the product family approach, i.e. family architecture analysis method (FAAM) [DOL 02].

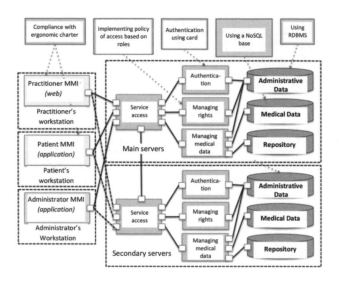

**Figure 4.6.** *Architecture of the Dopamine system*

ATAM [BAS 02a] is a well-known architectural evaluation method proposed by the SEI[4]. The ATAM process consists of gathering stakeholders together (brainstorming) to analyze business drivers (requirements) and to extract quality attributes from these drivers (quality characteristics in the ISO/IEC 25010 terminology) that will be used to define scenarios. These will be related to architectural solutions, constraints and metrics through a utility tree. The scenarios are prioritized for each quality attribute and used in conjunction with the architectural solutions to create an analysis of trade-offs, sensitivity points and risks [BAR 98]. ATAM uses the Attribute-Based Architectural Analysis (ABAS) structure, which is a framework to specify architectural solutions and related quality attributes; it was defined before the "utility tree" notion. ATAM does not use a quality model; however the "utility tree" is conceptually similar. A standard quality model can be used in ABAS to specify the quality requirements for the architectural solution [LOS 03]. The ATAM analysis is qualitative, being based on the experience of the software architect and work team.

Scenario-based approaches enable the definition of the quality model of a software system [TAN 12]. These represent a way to relate the FRs and NFRs with their requirements in terms of quality. Conventional methods of

---

4 Software Engineering Institute, Carnegie Mellon University.

architectural design, such as ADD [BAS 02, WOJ 06], consider the defined quality requirements using scenarios based on the structure of the architecture. For example, security, reliability or performance will be described in terms of outcomes related to a particular implementation identified and described on the basis of interactions between the components of the architecture. These scenarios drive the architecture design [KOT 98]. However, these design methods do not consider the fact that some functions also require qualities that are similar to implicit or resolved functions, or functions supported by specific mechanisms, architectural solutions or patterns. It is important to consider and remember these mechanisms or components implementing or supporting a quality requirement. Examples of such components are proxies or event channels that are used for guaranteeing security (integrity, authenticity, and confidentiality) of a communication. The product line approaches with their model of characteristics (feature models) containing the variability points are used to store the choices that can be made for a particular component.

Among the well-known classical architecture design methods, two main trends can be distinguished:

– functionality-based methods such as Bosch [BOS 99] and RUP [KRU 99]; these start capturing the system's functionality relevant to the architecture, and then this initial architecture is transformed responding to the system quality requirements, by adding/removing components;

– quality-based methods, such as the goal-oriented approaches of van Lamsweerde [VAN 03] and Chung *et al.* [CHU 03]. These methods identify FRs and NFRs together with their quality properties, for a specific functionality. NFRs are, in general, architectural requirements that apply to the whole system. Other quality-based methods are those of Weiss [ARA 02] and Bass [BAS 02b] which are incremental and iterative and are based on scenarios related to the structure of the architecture; at each iteration, functions are introduced as an instantiation of components and connectors.

Microsoft [MIC 09] recommends an iterative and incremental approach for a general software architecture design process. It is characterized by:

– the use of clear architectural objectives and key scenarios;

– identification of the type of applications, techniques and styles (similar to our domain description);

– identification of key issues based on quality attributes and crosscutting concerns;

– the definition of a first candidate solution from which it is then possible to iterate in order to evaluate the current solution vis-a-vis the main scenarios.

The key scenarios are those that are considered as the most important for the success of the application. They can be defined as any scenario that meets one or more of the following criteria: it represents an issue – a significant unknown area or an area of potential risks; it refers to an architecturally significant use case; it represents the intersection of quality attributes with functionality; it represents a trade-off between quality attributes. This architectural process is meant to be an iterative and incremental approach. The first candidate architecture will be a high-level design that can be tested against key scenarios, requirements, known constraints, quality attributes and the architectural frame. As the candidate architecture is refined, more details will be learned about the design and key scenarios, application overview, and approach to issues can be expanded.

An approach highly popular in industry is the product line approach. The big difference from our approach is that functional domain is open to new functions or systems, while in a product line all functions are *a priori* provided and described. The decisions are known from the start and the focus is placed on where the variability should be taken into account. Our approach is more focused on the systematic consideration of quality properties that are necessary and critical to building a basic architecture. This artifact is a reusable asset, and can be seen as a reference architecture or a product line architecture. It expresses an important part of the domain knowledge. Let us note that refinement of quality characteristics from ISO 25010 allows us to take into account a kind of non-functional variability. Thus, for each subcharacteristic, several solutions are presented that can be implemented in different products. Another kind of non-functional variability is the alternatives originated, for example, by different values of parameters of a quality attribute that can be solved by different implementations. This non-functional aspect is not treated very well in the software product line approaches, where it is usually left aside or not explicitly taken into account [BAR 10, BEN 05, SIE 08, TAN 12].

In [HOF 07], five architectural design methods used in the industry for the construction of product family architectures are discussed and compared: Attribute-Driven Design (ADD) [BAS 02b], Siemens four-views (SV4) [HOF 99], RUP 4 +1 views [KRU 99], Business Architecture Process and Organization (BAPO/CAFCR) considering Customer, Application, Functional, Conceptual and Realization (CAFCR) issues [AME 03] and Architectural Separation of Concerns (ARES or ASC) [RAN 00] from Nokia. A general architectural model for an architecture-centric design is derived from this comparison. It includes assessment and analysis activities that can be used either for a family of products, or for a single system, as in our approach. The method has non-sequential design activities:

– Architectural analysis serves to define the problem to be solved by the architecture.

– Architectural synthesis proposes architectural solutions to a set of architectural significant requirements, moving from the problem space to the solution space.

– Architectural evaluation ensures that the architectural design decisions made are the right ones; the candidate solutions are measured against the architectural requirements.

The following artifacts are produced during the activities:

– architectural concerns: this is expressed in general as quality requirements on the system and how they should be implemented, they may include the use of existing standards;

– the context: this is a general business goal or characteristic of the organization; however, a business goal for the architecture is a concern;

– architectural significant requirements (ASR): these may arise from other architectural concern or from the system context;

– candidate architectural solutions: this presents an alternative solution or partial solutions; they include information about the design rationale (decisions made, traceability of decisions with requirements, etc.).

Some less explicit inputs are:

– design knowledge: this comes from the architect, organizational memory or the architecture community;

– analysis knowledge: analysis patterns and analytic models, workflow methods and techniques;

– realization knowledge: technology, components, project management.

In general, this knowledge is used to evaluate the design of the system to ensure it can be constructed or to estimate the quality of the result. This method summarizes the existing expertise of architects. However, let us note that, on the one hand, it describes, as for the methods from which it is derived, the process for architectural design of new systems, and not, as in our approach, by reuse of domain knowledge and of existing systems; on the other hand, there is no mention of quality requirements by using quality standards, our approach being based on ISO/IEC 25010.

## 4.7. Conclusion

The development of a system is a complex task and multiple approaches have been described with systematic steps in order to ensure a better understanding of the result with respect to user's requirements. In this chapter, we are interested in the architecture development of a future system, a step where NFRs and quality are taken into account.

In practice, it is rare to develop a system from scratch. However, conventional methods generally do not describe how to capitalize on a project team's knowledge. Methods describe either new work or evolutions of a system, either in the context of product lines, with all possible variants of a product, or by reusing existing components. Our approach is different in that it proposes to capitalize on the knowledge in what we have called a functional domain. Variability points may be introduced if they are known, but this is not the important part. Knowledge of a functional domain is that shared by all systems in a certain domain; it is a core of knowledge that allows us to define a reference architecture. The different systems will be developed from this capitalized knowledge and shared architecture.

We have proposed a method of developing systems architecture by placing them in the context of systems family having related functions. Our method applies to define both the reference architecture of a functional domain and that of a particular derived system. Our approach is described as a Y cycle. During the parallel work, the analyst studies the functional properties and the architect works on the technical aspects. Their work is summarized at the end of the approach in an architecture in which functions are assigned to components, as are the non-functional properties.

Thus, to define a system, the first step is to define its functional domain, and then to derive from it its specific architecture.

We applied and detailed the two steps of our method in a case study resulting from the professional healthcare sector, the development of both the Dopamine and the Samarkand systems that aim at sharing patient records. Both systems exist and were originally developed in an *ad hoc* manner, without a precise approach. However, the capitalization of knowledge shows that on this occasion, the two systems share many things and could have been developed as shown here. Our approach applies to many cases where the systems differ but their architecture and major functions are similar.

To go further in development assistance, it is necessary to formalize the approach. For this, it is necessary to manage the traceability links between the different levels of abstraction, the more or less formal languages and not the necessarily shared systems. Current methods do not allow such flexibility to manage traceability links between requirements and architectural components. Formalizing our approach will allow support tools to be defined in order to guide architects and analysts and enable evaluation of non-functional properties at the architectural level to be performed. Concerning the definition of the reference architecture from functionally similar existing systems, some work has already begun [LOS 12] which may build on the present work.

## 4.8. Bibliography

[AME 03] AMERICA P., OBBINK H., ROMMES E., "Multi-view variation modeling for scenario analysis", *Fifth Workshop on Product Family Engineering (PFE-5)*, Sienne, Italy, Springer Verlag, pp. 44–55, 2003.

[ARA 02] ARAUJO J., WEISS M., "Using the NFR framework to represent patterns", *PLoP-02*, Monticello, IL, 2002.

[BAR 98] BARBACCI M., FEILER P., KLEIN M., *et al.*, *Steps in an Architecture Tradeoff Analysis Method: Quality Attribute Models and Analysis (CMU/SEI-97-TR-029)*, SEI, Carnegie Mellon University, 1998.

[BAS 02a] BASS L., KLEIN M., BACHMANN F., "Quality attribute design primitives and the attribute driven design method", *Software Product Family Engineering International Workshop (PFE)*, Bilbao, Spain, 2001, LNCS 2290, pp. 169–186, 2002.

[BAS 02b] BASS L., KLEIN M., BACHMANN F., *Attribute Driven Design Method (ADD)*, SEI, Carnegie Mellon University, 2002.

[BAR 10] BARTHOLDT J., OBERHAUSER R., MEDAK M., *et al.*, "Integrating quality modeling in software product lines", *International Journal on Advances in Software*, vol. 3, no. 1&A, pp. 161–174, 2010.

[BEN 05] BENAVIDES D., TRINIDAD P., RUIZ-CORTÉS A., "Automated reasoning on feature models", *LNCS Advanced Information Systems Conference: 17th International Conference (CAISE '05)*, Porto, Portugal, June 2005.

[BOS 99] BOSCH J., *Design and Use of Software Architecture*, Addison-Wesley, Harlow, 2000.

[BUS 96] BUSCHMANN F., MEUNIER R., RHONERT H., *et al.*, *Pattern-Oriented Software Architecture: A System of Patterns*, John Wiley & Sons, New York, 1996.

[CAL 97] MCCALL J., RICHARDS P., WALTERS D., *Factors in Software Quality*, Aide Defense Center, Rome, Italy, 1997.

[CAS 12] CASTRO J., LUCENA M., SILVA C., *et al.*, "Changing attitudes towards the generation of architectural models", *Journal of Systems and Software*, vol. 85, no. 3, pp. 463–479, March 2012.

[CHU 03] CHUNG L., COOPER K., YI A., "Developing adaptable software architectures using design patterns: an NFR approach", *Computer Standards & Interfaces*, no. 25, pp. 253–260, 2003.

[CRO 84] CROSBY P.B., *Quality without Tears*, McGraw-Hill, New York, 1984.

[DEM 00] DEMING W.E., *Out of the Crisis*, MIT Press, Cambridge, pp. 168–169, 2000.

[DOL 02] DOLAN T., Architecture assessment of information-system families, PhD Thesis, University of Technology, Eindhoven, Netherlands, 2002.

[HOF 07] HOFMEISTER C., KRUTCHEN P., NORD R.L., *et al.*, "A general model of software architecture design derived from five industrial approaches", *Journal of Systems and Software*, vol. 80, pp. 106–126, 2007.

[HOF 99] HOFMEISTER C., NORD R., SONI D., *Applied Software Architecture*, Addison-Wesley, Boston, 1999.

[IEE 83] IEEE STD 729, 1983.

[IEE 98] IEEE-std-1061-1998, Standard for a Software Quality Methodology, Technical Report, IEEE Computer Society, 1998.

[ISO 06] ISO, *FDIS 25030: Systems and Software Engineering – Systems and Software Quality Requirements and Evaluation (SQuaRE) – Quality Requirements*, ISO/IECJTC1/SC7/N3632, 2006.

[ISO 11] ISO, *ISO/IEC 25010: Systems and Software Engineering – Systems and Software Quality Requirements and Evaluation (SQuaRE) – System and Software Quality Models*, ISO/IECJTC1/SC7/WG6, 2011.

[JEA 12] JEAN S., LOSAVIO F., MATTEO A., *et al.*, "Standards de qualité et préférences utilisateurs pour la modélisation des propriétés non fonctionnelles dans OWL-S", *Techniques et Science Informatique (TSI)*, vol. 21, no. 1, pp. 39–70, 2012.

[KOT 98] KOTONYA G., SOMMERVILLE I., *Requirements Engineering, Processes and Techniques*, John Wiley & Sons, Chichester, 1998.

[KRU 99] KRUTCHEN P., *The Rational Unified Process an Introduction*, Addison-Wesley-Longman, Reading, 1999.

[LLO 03] LLOYD D., KALRA D., EHR requirements, Centre for Health Informatics and Multi-professional Education, University College, London, 2003. Available at http://discovery.ucl.ac.uk/1583/1/A5.pdf.

[LOS 03] LOSAVIO F., CHIRINOS L., LÉVY N., *et al.*, "Quality characteristics for software architecture", *Journal of Object Technology*, vol. 2, no. 2, pp. 133–150, March/April, 2003.

[LOS 09] LOSAVIO F., MATTEO A., LÉVY N., "Web services domain knowledge with an ontology on software quality standards", *ITA'09*, Glyndwr University, Wrexham, UK, September 2009.

[LOS 12] LOSAVIO F., ORDAZ O., LÉVY N., *et al.*, "Refactoring process for product line architecture design", *Journée Lignes de Produits (JDLP'12)*, Lille, France, November 2012. Available at http://jldp.org/2012/images/jldp2012-actes.pdf.

[LOS 13] LOSAVIO F., MATTEO A., "Reference architecture design using domain quality view", *Journal of Software Engineering and Methodology*, vol. 3, no. 1, pp. 47–61, March 2013.

[MIC 09] MICROSOFT, *Microsoft Application Architecture Guide – Software Architecture and Design*, 2nd ed., Chapter 4, 2009. Available at http://msdn.microsoft.com/en-us/library/ee658084.aspx.

[POH 05] POHL K., BÖCKLE G., VAN DER LINDEN F., *Software Product Line Engineering – Foundations, Principles, and Techniques*, Springer IXXVI, pp. 1–467, 2005.

[ROC 01] ROCQUES P., VALLÉE F., *UML en action*, 2nd ed., Eyrolles, Paris, 2001.

[RAN 00] RAN A., "ARES conceptual framework for software architecture", in JAZAYERI M., RAN A., VAN DER LINDEN F. (eds), *Software Architecture for Product Families Principles and Practice*, Addison-Wesley, Boston, 2000.

[RAS 11] RASHID A., ROYER J.C., RUMMLER A. (eds), *Aspect-Oriented Model-Driven Software Product Lines: The AMPLE Way*, Chapter 5, Cambridge University Press, Cambridge, 2011.

[SIE 08] SIEGMUND N., KUHLEMANN M., ROSENMULLER M., *et al.*, "Integrated product line model for semi-automated product derivation using non-functional properties", *VaMoS*, Essen, Germany, pp. 16–18, January 2008.

[SHA 96] SHAW M., GARLAN D., *Software Architecture: Perspectives of an Emerging Discipline*, Prentice-Hall, Upper Saddle River, NJ, 1996.

[TAN 12] TAN L., LIN Y., YE H., "Quality-Oriented software product line architecture design", *Journal of Software Engineering and Applications*, vol. 5, pp. 472–476, 2012.

[VAN 03] VAN LAMSWEERDE A., "From system goals to software architecture", in BERNARDO M., INVERARDI P. (eds.), *Formal Methods for Software Architectures*, LNCS, Springer-Verlag, Bertinoro, Italy, September 2003.

[WOJ 06] WOJCIK R., *et al.*, *Attribute-Driven Design (ADD)*, Version 2.0, Carnegie Mellon Software Engineering Institute, 2006. Available at www.sei.cmu.edu/reports/06tr023.pdf.

Chapter 5

# Software Architectures and Multiagent Systems

Multiagent systems (MAS) are software systems consisting of autonomous and independent entities in interaction. Realizing an application in the form of a MAS is an architectural response that takes into account certain major requirements, such as complexity, distribution, scalability, dynamicity or even adaptation. This chapter presents the basic concepts of MAS, and then positions them as a software architecture style that essentially concerns the "component and connector" category of views. Its principal unique features concern the abstraction level, modes of coupling between entities, autonomy and decentralization. However, MAS is more than just an architecture style; more precisely, it covers a family of architectural styles depending on the varied nature of the entities and their relations. An architectural gap between the design and implementation of MAS results from this variation. The last part of this chapter shows how to fill this gap by defining two architectural views (macro and microlevel) and by relying on a software component model for realization.

Chapter written by Jean-Paul ARCANGELI, Victor NOËL and Frédéric MIGEON.

## 5.1. Introduction

MAS are software systems, whose function is realized by a set of autonomous and independent entities in interaction. The first works in the field date from the end of the 1980s. MAS takes root in "artificial intelligence", particularly in "distributed artificial intelligence", but also in works on concurrent and distributed programming paradigms and languages. In the mid-1990s, the community began to be interested in the question of MAS development, and in addressing "software engineering" problems. However, MAS development has rarely been addressed from the point of view of software architectures.

Producing an application by using MAS technology as the basis for the solution is an architectural design choice that meets certain requirements such as complexity, distribution, dynamicity, scalability or adaptation. The objective of this chapter is to present MAS as a software architecture style, to position this style in relation to other known styles (objects, software components, services, actors), to identify its unique features as well as the particular development problems that this style poses, and, finally, to show the principles of a solution to these problems.

This chapter is organized as follows. Section 5.2 presents the MAS paradigm and the main concepts of the field, as well as a state of the art on agent-based software engineering (readers familiar with MAS can skip this section). MAS is next analyzed and positioned as an architectural style in section 5.3, where its advantages and drawbacks as a support for architectural design are summarized. Section 5.4 deals with the existence and the nature of an architectural gap between the design and the implementation of MAS, leading to development difficulties and a loss of quality in software products. In response to this problem, the outline of a solution is presented in section 5.5. Finally, a conclusion is given in section 5.6.

## 5.2. MAS and agent-oriented software engineering

The concept of agents is present in different computer science fields and the term "agent" is overloaded with meaning. There is no single, universally accepted definition, including in the "multiagent systems" community. Nevertheless, it is commonly accepted that the term "agent" refers to entities characterized by a certain level of autonomy and an ability to act or react to situations, events, messages, etc. According to Weiss [WEI 99], an agent is an autonomous, reactive and proactive entity capable of communicating. According to Ferber [FER 99], an agent is an entity (physical or virtual) capable of partially perceiving its environment. It is also able to act in it and communicate with other agents, possibly reproducing itself. It aims at satisfying a set of objectives depending on its resources and its own abilities, as well as the partial representation it has of its environment.

There are also multiple definitions of what constitutes a MAS [FER 99, WEI 99, WOO 09]. For example, for Weiss, it is a system composed of multiple agents in interaction.

The objective of this section is to present and discuss these concepts in more detail, to show some fields of application and then to give an overview of agent-oriented development methods and techniques.

### 5.2.1. *Agent*

From a software point of view, the agent is a building block for the design and programming of concurrent and/or distributed applications, in which control is strongly decentralized. Hence, object-oriented design can be substituted by agent-oriented design, for example, to meet the modeling needs of real systems or for the distributed solving of problems. From the point of view of programming, let us note that the ancestor of agents is the Hewitt actor model [HEW 77], refined by Agha in the context of distributed systems [AGH 86]. The "distributed systems" community has, moreover, tackled the concept of agents to develop that of mobile agents [FUG 98].

Each agent has a specific activity defined by its individual behavior and realized in the context of a "lifecycle", which orders its perception, decision and action operations. Agents are autonomous regarding control and "selection of action" concerns [BRI 14]: taking a situation or a message into account (or not) is decided by the agent at runtime, as well as the choice of actions that will be realized. Hence, agents can be proactive (not just reactive), i.e. they can act of their own initiative.

It is the work in traditional artificial intelligence that can give agents the methods needed for decision-making. Cognitive or deliberative (or even intelligent) agents are equipped with knowledge and logical reasoning methods. Most often, they pursue an explicit aim and their capacity for reasoning allows them to choose the actions in order to achieve this aim. For example, belief, desire, intentions (BDI) agents [RAO 95] rely on revisable knowledge about the state of the world surrounding them and on the aims (desires) for producing intentions, the latter being behind the choice of actions that the agents realize. Concerning the design of the agents, complexity sometimes resides within the intelligence of the agents (for example, advanced decision or learning mechanisms), and the application can only be composed of a small number of "intelligent" agents (even only one). Let us note, however, that some mechanisms, such as reflection or the ability of actors to change their behavior, provide agents with means of autonomous evolution, while they are not considered as having intelligence.

Moreover, it is important to note that intelligence is not a mandatory property of the agents in a MAS: for example "reflex" agents act and react without any intelligence.

### 5.2.2. System and interactions

Fundamentally, the agents operate and interact within a system in which control and data are decentralized.

From an abstract point of view, agents are equipped with sensors and effectors (also called actuators) that enable them to interact and act. The agent (partially) perceives the system that surrounds it via its sensors and acts on it via its effectors. Sensors and effectors support the exchange of information between the agent and the rest of the system in *push* or *pull* mode according to who is initiating the exchange. Hence, an agent can be seen as an abstract machine, whose internal architecture defines how information is processed, produced, enters and leaves the agent. There are multiple types of agents (the MAS community sometimes employs the term "agent architecture") according to the way in which the information is perceived and processed and actions are preformed in the surrounding system.

These interaction mechanisms also contribute to update the agent's knowledge with which it can take decisions. This knowledge is thus "contextualized": the agent acts depending on the representation it has of its environment and the state that it perceives. It can also receive feedbacks from its actions, which contributes to improving the quality of its future decisions.

Nonetheless, its interaction capacities are frequently limited to a simple mode of point-to-point, unidirectional and asynchronous communication by message (as in the case of actors). These interactions by message can, however, be used in the context of complex exchanges governed by communication protocols. For this, there are agent communication languages (ACL), which define message and protocol types for organizing the conversations between agents. The most well-known of these languages, FIPA-ACL [FIP 02], was defined and standardized by the Foundation for Intelligent Physical Agents (FIPA)[1].

We have seen that, conceptually, an agent is autonomous in terms of activity and that it can trigger its actions itself. In a system, the agents are thus naturally executed in asynchronous mode. In practice, the reality of the operational autonomy depends on the implementation and the policy of the runtime system resource allocation (for example multithreading). It should be noted that the distribution of control and the lack of synchronization can quite naturally lead to non-deterministic systems, but this is neither mandatory nor necessarily desirable.

### 5.2.3. *MAS*

One of the main reasons of existence of MAS is to distribute intelligence (here, we are at the center of distributed artificial intelligence), knowledge and control. In a MAS, no agent controls the system on its own and none possesses all the information: it is the collective that prevails over the individual and that realizes the task for which the system was designed. Beyond this "collective intelligence", MAS displays the following two major characteristics:

– the existence of an organization that regulates system functioning and within which the agents are "social" entities;

– the presence in the system of a particular element, the environment, consisting of entities that are not agents.

These two characteristics are set differently in the multiple approaches, which have been defined by the MAS community. An approach defines a consistent set of concepts that enable a problem to be addressed and support

---

1 www.fipa.org.

design of the solution in the form of a MAS. An approach may rely on a theory and its use can be supervised using a method (models, processes, etc.) as we will see in section 5.2.5.

### 5.2.3.1. *Organization*

The way in which agents are organized within the system is of the utmost importance when it comes to design and functioning. Organization defines a framework for interaction, collaboration and the sharing of tasks between agents, possibly by using "social laws", which are not under agents' control. It can take different forms according to the approaches, but every organization is based on the concept of roles (whether explicit or not), which abstractly describe the behavior (function) of agents in the collective. For example, the agent-group-role (AGR) model is an organizational model based on roles for dynamic and open MAS [FER 04]. An agent can generally play several roles and one role can be played by several agents, and these associations can be dynamically realized at runtime [ODE 03].

For a given application, some approaches define an organization that does not change during the system runtime, whereas others rely on the agents' capacity for reorganization or self-organization: being equipped with a "social" behavior enables them to change roles at runtime. Thus, organization is the way to compose the different system elements, and the functionality of the system results from the organization of agents. Then by changing this organization, the system can adapt its functionality [DEM 95]. Hence, some approaches seek to exploit self-organization as a way to make suitable organizations emerge, with the outcome that the system realizes the expected functionality [DIM 11].

For a presentation and analysis of the various current approaches for designing, defining, modifying and adapting the organization of a MAS, whether with the agents themselves or with an external observer, readers can refer to [PIC 09].

### 5.2.3.2. *Environment*

In a MAS, the environment is a shared space that supports the exchange of information: it is the medium for the interaction and coordination between agents, through which the latter can act and interact. It possesses its own dynamics and processes, independently of the dynamics of agents. We can distinguish the logical environment, which is entirely part of the MAS, and the system environment, which is external to the MAS (defined by the system deployment context and users). For Weyns *et al.*, the environment is a first-class abstraction that provides the agents with the means of their existence and simultaneously serves as a mediator for the interaction between agents and the access to resources [WEY 07]. A typical example is "situated" MAS where agents have a position in the environment: they are bound to a locally accessible part of the environment that they perceive and act on.

The environment can support complex interactions, e.g. indirect bioinspired "stigmergic" communication [GRA 59]: in this mode of communication, the environment contains markers (for example inspired by the pheromones of ant colonies) that can be perceived or deposited by the agents.

Generally, we find passive or active entities in the environment, which do not have autonomy. In particular, some approaches consider and design the organization as a software entity that makes up part of the environment and is responsible for the regulation of interactions between agents.

### 5.2.4. *Examples of MAS*

There are numerous MAS applications with the aim of solving problems in a distributed way (optimization, decision support systems, etc.), simulating complex phenomena (social or natural) or managing resources and complex systems. These applications involve multiple fields: robotics, transportation, securing facilities, crisis management, video games, factory systems and processes, embedded systems, ambient intelligence, etc.

Among these examples, we can cite manufacturing control [SHE 06] where the problem is about assigning products to manufacture to machines, which are controlled by operators, all while adhering to certain constraints, such as an order in the stages of manufacturing. Because this order is not foreseeable, the machines are only able to deal with one product at a time and the operators piloting the machines are not permanently available for all of them, so the function of the MAS is to optimize, potentially in real time, these product-machine and machine-operator allocations in a way that minimizes the production time and adheres to strict deadlines. A classic modeling of the problem consists of representing the machines, products and operators as agents and giving them a behavior that enables them to organize themselves to meet manufacturing requirements. The arrival of new manufacturing requirements and the unforeseen unavailability of operators or machines is represented through the addition and removal of agents in the system, and consequently, by the adaptation and the dynamic reorganization of the system in order to satisfy the requirements.

Another favored field of application for MAS is "individual-centered" simulation [PHA 07] in which, to model a collective phenomenon, there is a focus on behaviors and interactions at the level of individuals. Each individual is an agent immersed in an environment. The aim is to observe and explain the collective phenomena that are produced at the system level as well as identifying the individual behaviors behind the collective phenomenon and their impact on the latter.

Most MAS applications were developed in an academic context. Amid the real MAS use cases in an industry context, we can cite that of the firm Massive Software[2] that uses the paradigm of MAS in the field of virtual reality to offer its clients the means of directing action scenes in films: crowds of people are defined with agents (one agent for one person), each of which follows a predefined behavior. An editor allows the movements of the agents in the environment to be defined, to interactively develop the decisions that an agent can make, without any programming knowledge. Hence, it is possible to direct animations or simulations in which thousands of agents interact to give a realistic scene[3].

## 5.2.5. *Agent-oriented software engineering*

Agent-oriented software engineering (AOSE) is a generic term characterizing all agent-oriented system development, but not necessarily MAS. To talk about methodological aspects requires us to talk about the software process, notation and metamodel used, as well as the tools available, a considerable part of which concerns development platforms. Here, we only address those that relate to MAS.

---

2 www.massivesoftware.com.
3 www.youtube.com/watch?v=ZwkjW4bmpYE.

As in classic software engineering, a method comes to support an approach adopted for the development. Hence, for a given MAS approach (such as that presented in sections 5.2.1–5.2.3), we can find several methods that follow the principles of it more or less faithfully. In theory, given the requirements expressed by the stakeholders, the development team must determine which approach is most suitable and which method to use for instantiating it. In practice, the preferences that a development team may have for a method hinder development as much as they help it.

The very first methods appeared in the mid-1990s but serious research in this field has only been undertaken from the 2000s onwards. The most common methods, emerging from software engineering, are inspired by object-oriented development methods (see Figure 5.1). Others (not presented here) emerged from knowledge engineering, or were defined specifically to support developments promoted by some approaches.

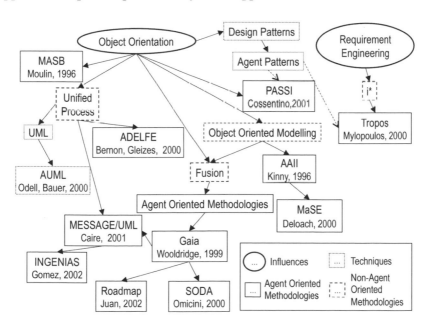

**Figure 5.1.** *The influence of object-oriented development methods [GLE 08]*

### 5.2.5.1. *Process*

In this section, we provide an overview of some of the most notable development processes (that readers will find references to in [NOE 12]), which does not constitute an exhaustive list. For more detail on development methods, readers can refer to [BER 04].

We define a process as a succession of phases divided into coordinated activities (an activity itself can be divided into stages) that can produce and/or consume software artifacts under the responsibility of people assuming a role. Most MAS development methods being inspired by object-oriented engineering, it is natural that the lifecycles and processes used in the design of such systems are of the types classically used in modular design: in a wave, iterative, V-shaped, in a spiral, etc.

Furthermore, for the vast majority, these methods integrate the following major development phases: extraction and requirements analysis, architectural design and implementation, even if they are not always clearly identified as such. For example, ADELFE and INGENIAS rely on the unified process (UP) and integrate new stages and definitions of work specific to the multiagent field into this process, whereas PASSI and ASPECS rely on their own iterative process. Some methods only cover one part of the process, such as Gaia or SODA, which concentrate exclusively on the requirements analysis and design, or Prometheus and MaSE, which do not address requirements analysis. In general, the methods do not offer processes up to the deployment, relying on the principle that multiagent modeling is mostly a question of analysis (especially for Tropos, emerging from requirement engineering) and design, with the exception of PASSI or INGENIAS (which cover the whole development cycle).

Besides the phases covered by the processes, it is also interesting to identify what the processes offer by way of deliverables, quality management and organization. Methods relying on the UP, such as ADELFE or INGENIAS, inherit from its quality and risk management. Some methods focus particularly on the definition of processes and the software artifacts, especially by using dedicated formalisms such as the software process engineering metamodel (SPEM)[4]. Finally, we must note a strong desire within the MAS community to clearly document the set of defined processes in a standardized form, as it is the case with the work of the FIPA on the

---

4 www.omg.org/spec/SPEM/.

design processes documentation and fragmentation (DPDF) themed group, which has defined the SC00097B standard[5].

### 5.2.5.2. *Notations and metamodels*

As with processes, the broad spectrum of notations used in development methods illustrates the vast diversity of approaches. We find a unified vision of these approaches there, emerging mainly from the object world, which has given rise to the use of generic modeling language (generic purpose modeling language (GPML)) such as UML2 or SysML. They are often used in the traditional phases of processes but also, most often in the form of UML profiles, in more specific activities. However, for development activities very specific to an approach, the use of domain-specific modeling languages (DSML), in which the domain agent concepts are reified, is becoming more common. We then find numerous modeling languages (e.g. AUML, INGENIAS, AMAS-ML for ADELFE) in this offshoot of model-driven engineering [FAV 04].

From the study of the metamodels of these design models, it is possible to analyze what the key concepts of a notation are, and thus of an AOSE method and the approach that it promotes. We then measure the diversity of metamodels and the weak coverage that each offers of the set of existing concepts. In Table 5.1, taken from [NOE 12] where it is studied in more detail, we present a comparative analysis of the abstractions provided by the design models used in the methods presented previously. This table considers three aspects of the design of a MAS: the internal architecture of the agent, environment and interaction. For each of these aspects, the models offer various abstractions that are identified with the presence of a tick mark in the table. The scattering of tick marks illustrates in itself the diversity of approaches and abstractions used.

### 5.2.5.3. *Tools*

The very nature of the MAS paradigm and the richness of its approaches makes MAS implantation difficult directly from standard programming languages. Development is then facilitated with the use of tools and platforms (which, among other things, help with reuse). As with the use of notations, the choice of development platforms and tools goes through an identification

---

5 www.fipa.org/specs/fipa00097/SC00097B.pdf.

of the characteristic key concepts of the approaches promoted. In the production of the MAS community, we find many platforms specific to an approach. Some attempts at unification exist, but come up against the richness of the MAS paradigm: taking the common denominator reduces the result of a too abstract description of the paradigm, and conversely, the aggregation of multiple concepts poses problems for consistency and compatibility.

| Available abstractions | Design models | | | | | | | | | | | | | | | | |
|---|---|---|---|---|---|---|---|---|---|---|---|---|---|---|---|---|---|
| | SeSAmUML | PASSI | ASPECS | AgentUML | AML | ADELFE | A&A | Macodo | AGR | MASQ | VOWELS | MOISE+ | Opera | MESSAGE | GAIA | CRIO | Tropos |
| **Internal** | | | | | | | | | | | | | | | | | |
| Goals | | | | | | | | | | | | | | | ✓ | | |
| UML | ✓ | ✓ | ✓ | | | ✓ | | | | | | | | | | | |
| BDI | | | | ✓ | ✓ | | | | | | | | | | | | |
| Rules | ✓ | | | | | ✓ | | | | | | | | | | | |
| Skills | | | ✓ | | | ✓ | | | | | | | | | | | |
| Recursivity | | | ✓ | | | ✓ | | | | | | | | | | | |
| **Environment** | | | | | | | | | | | | | | | | | |
| Org. struct. | | | ✓ | | | | ✓ | ✓ | | | | ✓ | ✓ | | | | ✓ |
| Org. dyn. | | | ✓ | | | | | ✓ | | | | | ✓ | | | | |
| Situated | ✓ | | | | | ✓ | | | | | | | | | | | |
| Entities | ✓ | | | | ✓ | ✓ | | | ✓ | ✓ | | | | | | | |
| **Interaction** | | | | | | | | | | | | | | | | | |
| Messages | | | ✓ | ✓ | ✓ | ✓ | ✓ | | | | | ✓ | | ✓ | ✓ | | ✓ |
| Sens./act. | ✓ | | | | | | ✓ | ✓ | | | | | | | | | |
| Role | | | ✓ | | | | | | ✓ | ✓ | | ✓ | ✓ | ✓ | ✓ | ✓ | ✓ |

**Table 5.1.** *Characterization of design models with respect to available abstractions*

### 5.2.5.4. *Assessment*

As we have shown in this section, the MAS paradigm reveals a great richness, which is illustrated by the diversity of existing approaches and platforms supporting them. Nevertheless, the development of MAS has its own unique features, usages and difficulties that are still to be detailed in architectural terms (and in terms of the associated requirements). Culturally, the MAS community has only recently begun to contemplate software architecture questions. We can, however, cite the works of Weyns on the design and documentation of situated MAS and their environment [WEY 10]. In the next section, we will see that the choice of a particular approach, the consequences for the architecture to be designed, and the effort to bridge the distance between the domain of the problem and that of the solution are all constraints imposed on the developer of a MAS.

## 5.3. MAS as an architectural style

In the previous section, we presented the concepts of agent and MAS, interaction, organization and environment. We explained the dynamics of these systems in terms of sociality as well as the dynamics of the agents in terms of the cycle "perception – decision – action". The objective of this section is to give an understanding of these elements from a "software architecture" point of view and to show how the "MAS style" resembles and differs from other architectural styles such as object-oriented, component-oriented, service- and actor-based styles. Here, we compare their structural properties, their way of addressing problems and their solutions, as well as the requirements met by these architectural choices.

After positioning the MAS style in architectural terms, we analyze it from the point of view of the abstractions that characterize it, then from the point of view of composition and structural aspects. Next, we propose a summary of its advantages and disadvantages, relative to the requirements on the product, its documentation and its development.

Here, we also show that depending on the chosen MAS approach, this paradigm and style can be refined differently. We deduce from this that, rather than just one style, there is a family of MAS architectural styles.

### 5.3.1. *Positioning the "MAS" style*

First, it must be noted that the solutions expressed using the MAS paradigm enter quasi-exclusively into the "component and connector" category of architectural views [CLE 03]: at the system level and the agent level, the organizational structure and system dynamics at runtime are what is described. However, although little-explored, the benefits of the MAS style to the "module" and "allocation" views are not negligible. We return to this point in section 5.3.4.2.

Following the nomenclature for describing styles used in [CLE 03], we observe that elements of the MAS style are various (depending on the approaches and problem to be dealt with), but generally the following main categories can be found:

– agents;

– environment entities;

– interaction connectors (perception and action).

There are at least as many types of interaction connectors as there are interaction mechanisms such as those described in section 5.2.5. We distinguish those for direct interaction (from agent to agent, e.g. asynchronous message sending) and indirect interaction (from agent to environment, e.g. stigmergy, perception or movements in a situated environment). We will return to these elements and their use to document the architecture of a MAS section 5.3.4.3.

### 5.3.2. *Characteristics in terms of abstraction*

Here, we analyze the MAS style from the point of view of the abstractions and the elements that characterize it, and then the consequences it has on implementation supports and the possibilities of reuse.

#### 5.3.2.1. *A high level of abstraction*

Traditional paradigms are strongly influenced by the machine and the support used for implementation: from the first imperative languages up to the software components and services, the abstractions offered have always been constructed in compliance with the lower layers already available. Conversely, due to their roots in artificial intelligence, and like the "logic" programming style, MAS is differentiated by a decorrelated vision of the machine (as illustrated in section 5.2.5) and a high level of abstraction in the model; the system and its elements present characteristics that we can characterize as anthropomorphic (autonomy, interaction, sociality). Methodologically speaking, the design of such systems is thus particularly concerned with social characteristics, whether this is regarding communication, organization, roles, etc. This results in a clear and explicit separation, first in the system between the agents and the environment and second in the agents between their sociality (perception and action) and their autonomy (decision).

Every design activity aims to translate concepts manipulated in the problem domain into concepts belonging to the domain of the approach chosen to construct the solution. In the case of the MAS style, the distance between these two domains is short and design most often comes down to structuring the solution in a form close to that of the problem itself. This proximity is more pronounced than in the case of objects, in particular because of the integration of the activity within the agents (which contributes to their autonomy and anthropomorphism), and to the use of diverse and various interaction mechanisms within an environment adapted to the agents. Thus, by minimizing the conceptual gap between the two domains, design is facilitated: modeled elements and the agents represent the problem entities and their behavior (in particular social) represents how the system function is realized. The designer must, however, choose the right abstractions to model his/her solution, and this depends on his/her problem (for example by using interaction mechanisms adapted to the structure of the problem).

For example, in the manufacturing control domain it is common with MAS to model the machines, operators and products as agents and the product path as the environment (see section 5.2.4). Allocations being very dynamic and changing, a management of the agent's social relations by the agents themselves and the use of interactions via message are preferred. Hence, the elements of the problem (machines, operators and products) make up an integral part of the solution. Conversely, in a more traditional approach, the solution is expressed using concepts far from the problem, but close to a generic solving algorithm. The latter is not specific to the problem: for example, to do constraint-based optimization, from the expression of constraints on discrete variables (values belonging to a finite set), a generic algorithm finds an allocation of values for these variables. This requires a reformulation of the problem. When instantiated for manufacturing control, variables represent product-machine and machine-operator allocations as well as order relations between these allocations. And the constraints express which temporal relations are possible and impossible – or preferred – between the values of these variables.

This high level of abstraction and the proximity between the concepts of the domains of the problem and the solution create in exchange a gap between the designed solution and its implementation. We return to this point in section 5.4.

## 5.3.2.2. *Modular abstraction level*

The design of a MAS, thus, relies on high-level abstractions: agents, environment and interaction mechanisms. These can, nonetheless, take very various forms. Hence, some abstractions must be subjected to a refinement, conforming simultaneously to the approach chosen and the requirements to be met.

Typically, to meet requirements regarding decentralization, the focus will be on the agents' capacities for autonomy and perception; to meet requirements regarding interoperability, the focus will be on the interaction and communication mechanisms; to meet requirements regarding adaptation, the focus will be on the organization dynamic, etc. For example, in the context of manufacturing control where the first requirement is on-the-fly allocation of tasks to machines and operators, the focus will be on the organization dynamic and especially on reorganization (the organization here is realizing the allocation choices made by agents at a given moment, it evolves with each event such as the appearance of a new task or the unavailability of a machine or an operator).

This property differentiates the MAS style from other traditional styles, as it makes it, in a way, an "open" style with which the designer has the freedom (but also the restriction) to choose which abstractions he/she wishes to use and refine, and which abstractions he/she considers non-architectural in the design of his/her MAS. In some applications, we cannot, for example, disregard the scheduling of agents (typically, in multiagent simulation): while defining the system, the designer assumes certain hypotheses regarding scheduling (without necessarily making them explicit); he/she must thus "descend" to the scheduling level to correctly design his/her software. In many applications, however, the problem of scheduling does not arise. The reliability of message passing is another example of a concern that can be taken into account, or not, according to the nature of the application: depending on the case, the designer assumes or does not assume the hypothesis that the messages sent are reliably received.

Depending on the problem, the MAS designer thus chooses whether or not to take certain concerns into account, and for this, he/she chooses which abstractions to refine for his/her needs.

### 5.3.2.3. *Consequences on the implementation support*

In general, the choice of an architectural style and associated implementation support (for example a programming language, a middleware or a framework) meets major requirements and guarantees some essential properties of the software product produced. In return, it constrains the solution and its realization. For example, the choice of an object-oriented architecture constrains the expression of every interaction in the form of a method call.

In the context of the MAS style, the problem is posed the opposite way: because the style's abstractions are of high level and undergo a refinement during the design, the constraint resides in the fact that the abstractions employed (typically, various interaction mechanisms) must be made available by an implementation support adapted to the approach and the field of application. For example, for an interaction via message sending, we can directly use the abstractions offered by the implementation support (which is generally the case with the supports proposed by the MAS community), but for a stigmergy-based interaction, a specific component providing this abstraction must be available (which is generally not the case). It is as an attempt to meet these needs that the production of agent-oriented platforms has taken such a place in the MAS community (see section 5.2.5.3).

This impacts on the design of a MAS and the choices made during this phase restrict the implementation support that can be used. In general, the diversity of available types of agents, environment types and interaction mechanisms enables (and imposes on) the architect to define and separate:

– MAS aspects, concerning the design of the system with respect to the MAS paradigm chosen to respond to the problem;

– "operational" aspects, concerning the abstractions used by the MAS design, i.e. how the agents and the mechanisms, which they rely on to act and interact, function.

An additional effort is thus needed, which will be more or less considerable according to the implementation support used, and it is not possible to have an adequate implementation support systematically available. Here, we return to the idea of the gap between design and implementation previously raised, which is dealt with in section 5.4.

5.3.2.4. *Reuse and design patterns*

The efforts of the MAS community to provide reusable elements are mostly confined to the production of implementation supports.

Some patterns have, however, been proposed by the community [OLU 07]. Traditionally, collections of design and architectural patterns are developed in response to recurring design problems: design patterns enable us to enrich the "native" abstractions of a paradigm to express new higher level abstractions, whereas architectural patterns rely on available abstractions for modeling reusable organizational solutions. Abstractions offered in the context of the MAS style being, by their nature, already of high level and refinable, the majority of patterns offered by the MAS community are architectural. The typical patterns that can be found are, for example, indirect communication patterns through various environment topologies, organization patterns with generic roles and behaviors to be instantiated with respect to the problems, patterns applicable to classes of problems, etc.

These patterns do not meet, or hardly meet, the requirements relative to the organization of the development, the flexibility and the extensibility of the software produced, unlike design patterns in the object world.

### 5.3.3. *Characteristics in terms of (de)composition*

In this section, we discuss some characteristics of the MAS style in terms of decomposition into autonomous entities, of composition and of coupling.

5.3.3.1. *Decentralization and autonomy*

An essential characteristic of the MAS style is combining the decentralization of control and the autonomy of agents. Within a MAS, agents play roles and these roles structure the MAS. Hence, the agent is a component with a social character, but also autonomous. This results in the following properties:

– the agent can manage itself and its relations with other agents;

– the agent has the capacity to determine its actions itself (i.e. to do or not do what other agents expect of him/her).

The first point makes agents closer to objects that contain and internally manage the references for objects whose services they require, and makes them farther from software components (or services) for which, on the contrary, composition is externalized. Thus, coupling is of the same level as in the case of objects, but autonomy also introduces some advantages (discussed below). This management of social relations can, nonetheless, be externalized in the environment and constrained by it, as in situated MAS or with organizations in the environment. However, this remains a design choice, not imposed by the MAS style (but possibly by a specific approach) as is the case in components or service styles.

The second point is based on the decoupling between information retrieval (for example receiving a message) and the processing of this information (processing of the message). It makes the agents closer to actors (from Hewitt actor model) but with a greater variety of interaction means, and makes them clearly farther from more traditional paradigms and styles, where the service providers have no choice regarding response to a request. In the end, with the MAS style, we are quite far from the structuring of applications into subprograms that underpin most traditional approaches. This veritable "inversion of control" is not only structural, as it is for the object-oriented design pattern of the same name, but genuinely semantic.

### 5.3.3.2. *Composition and coupling*

In composition, the interaction means specify the nature of the exchanges between agents but do not serve to specify the services rendered by the agent, contrary to traditional (more or less rich) interfaces and connectors, which are more explicit in that way. Indeed, while in traditional approaches interactions between the system elements represent requests regarding functionalities, in MAS the agents exchange information (whether directly or indirectly) which enables them to decide whether or not to undertake actions and render their service. This point underlines a paradigm shift and the composition of agents (to form a system) results in a "semantic coupling" guided by the knowledge and the social organization of the work [BRI 14]. From an architectural point of view, this is particularly apparent in the definition and use of the (interaction) connectors which are semantically poorer than in a traditional component-oriented approach, but more diversified. This diversity results simultaneously from the variety of types of information exchanged, but also and especially from the nature and structure of the problem: for example, if the elements of the problem are situated, the agents should perceive and act (and thus exchange information) in a situated environment.

5.3.3.3. *Decomposition and emergence*

This way of semantically coupling the elements of a system is accompanied by a change in the way the design is addressed: from a functional decomposition into subprograms, we move to a vision more integrated with the problem itself, where each agent has a local functionality that integrates the problem. The functionality of the system (the global behavior) then "emerges" from the interactions between the agents, which dictates how all the local functionalities are composed.

This is well illustrated by the application of manufacturing control (see section 5.2.4). A traditional approach consists of considering the question globally and dividing the search for the solution into several distinct tasks. For example, constraint solving relies on a generic algorithm that, sequentially, seeks valid values for the variables, checks the constraints and optimizes some criteria, and does that iteratively. When the problem changes, however, the solution process must be started again. In a MAS approach, however, we divide the problem among distinct participants, which collectively look for the best solution. By virtue of their local interactions and a social behavior unique to each element of the problem (e.g. to form allocations here two-by-two according to some local criteria), the global behavior of solving emerges, and the solution is continually adapted to the problem changes [KAD 11].

From an architectural point of view, this way of breaking down the system is thus even more interesting. In terms of agents and interactions, its architectural structure is not set but evolves at runtime: the agents play the role of guarantors of the validity of this structure with respect to the functional needs. We can consider the system as an architecture, reorganizing without stopping and thus adapting itself to the evolution of requirements it is answering. This is particularly true in the context of self-organizing MAS. The design of such MAS, based on emergence, is of course not simple, and this problem is the subject of many research works [DIM 11], and, amongst other things, to ensure the quality of the built software.

### 5.3.4. *Link with the requirements*

Aspect programming and the concept of software components were introduced to overcome some limitations of the object style. The concept of agents also contributes to this: although the concept of software components can be seen as an evolution of the concept of objects in order to better meet the requirements regarding decomposition, composition, reuse and administration, the concept of agents can be seen as a response regarding autonomy and sociality.

### 5.3.4.1. *Main requirements covered*

The MAS style meets different requirements relative to the realization of complex systems and enables a certain control of this complexity. At the "product" level, the main requirements that can be addressed are:

– integration of the application within physical and distributed social systems (this *de facto* distribution is generalized with the omnipresence of efficient communication networks and promotes decentralization of solutions and autonomy);

– the dynamicity and openness, and even the non-determinism, of these systems (constraints that MAS respond to with a constant dynamic adaptation and locality of processing);

– the capacity for evolution and learning, adaptability and "intelligence" in order to assist humans (tackled for example by self-organization and emergence);

– robustness, scalability and performance (which MAS responds to by its way of decomposing the system, multiplying the number of agents and the potential for parallelism).

MAS fully subscribe to the evolution of software engineering in the sense of a design in terms of units in interaction [FER 99]. Hence, concerning design and realization, the MAS style meets the following requirements:

– management of the complexity of problems and applications (e.g. problem solving or simulation) with the absence of a global solution model, which leads to the choice of a logical distribution as the foundation of the solution, accompanied by a local vision centered on the agents and their interactions rather than a global vision (additionally, the structural complexity of the solution increases linearly and not exponentially with the size of the problem because of their structural proximity);

– the expressiveness and abstraction level (see section 5.3.2.1) facilitate the development of such naturally concurrent systems, based on complex interactions between anthropomorphic entities that can be situated in an environment;

– the modifiability and modularity (multiplicity of agents' behaviors), in particular in the context of an incremental development, which is frequent in MAS practice.

### 5.3.4.2. *"Module" and "allocation" views*

The MAS style directly concerns the "component and connector" category of architectural views, as we discussed in section 5.3.1. Here, we discuss existing links with the "module" and "allocation" category of views [CLE 03].

It can be noted that the MAS paradigm indirectly meets requirements that concern the views of the "modules" category. On the one hand, the proximity between the problem and the solution (see section 5.3.2.1) naturally leads to the separation of concerns and the modularity of the solution. This concerns the system, but also agents for whom the separation between social concerns and decisional concerns is exploitable during development.

On the other hand, beyond the separation of concerns, the benefits of the MAS style for the "module" views are non-existent regarding code structuring (unlike objects with their class-based organization). Here, we touch on a major difficulty regarding the spreading of this technology: the question of organizing the development of MAS is still unanswered with little or no leads (in the previous section, we saw that the methods and tools essentially cover the upstream parts of the development). Thus, it is necessary to provide models, methods and tools in order to facilitate the design and implementation of MAS and, among other things, to promote reuse.

Let us note, moreover, that the modularity and separation of concerns also have an impact on the definition of the views of the "allocation" category. On the one hand, the allocation of tasks to development teams according to their skills is facilitated, which encourages the participation of experts from the application domain in the development. This is particularly true in the domain of multiagent simulation in which domain experts (called "thematicians") are stakeholders and participate in the design along computer science developers. On the other hand, MAS being strongly distributed by their nature, the allocation of physical resources to elements of the MAS is generally quite direct.

### 5.3.4.3. *Documentation*

In this section, we discuss the link between the MAS style and the requirements regarding documentation.

As we indicated in section 5.3.3, the interaction connectors do not have much significance in terms of the composition of functionality. In the context of software component or service-based architectures, the "component and connector" descriptions express how the system behaves at runtime: instances of connectors are associated with component interfaces with specific functional meanings and structurally embed a composition of functionalities. Conversely, the coupling between agents is mainly semantic: an interaction connector only describes how all agents communicate together inside their environment and the behavior of the MAS is not found in the structural connections between the agents but in the description of their social behaviors (interaction protocols and data exchanged, roles, etc.) and the environment dynamics, in particular when the latter is considered as a "software bus", mediator of interactions. By way of an illustration, let us consider a set of agents situated in a space, which communicate by sending messages over a limited (distance) range. It is the dynamics of the environment and the agents in it that explain, through their movements, how the system functions; more than the description of the structural links that exist between the agents.

It is thus not so much the nomenclature typically used by the "component and connector" views (elements, relations, interfaces) that enables a MAS architecture to be precisely and concisely documented, but rather the description of the elements themselves (behaviors, interaction protocols, the environment dynamics, etc.). Hence, as presented in section 5.2.5.2, documenting a MAS very often involves the use of models specific to an approach, rather than models such as those classically used in software architectures, such as the one used by Clements *et al.* [CLE 03]. On the other hand, as we will see in section 5.4, documenting the system in terms of agents and interactions is necessary but not sufficient to complete the development.

### 5.3.4.4. *Requirements not covered*

It should be noted that after around 20 years of research, principally undertaken by the "distributed artificial intelligence" community (much more than by the "software engineering" community), and despite all the advantages that we may hope for, MAS technologies have only marginally penetrated the software industry to date. It is essentially in academia that developments have been made. In this particular context, there are often few stakeholders and frequently, the client, developer and user are all the same person. As for the products developed, these are most often prototypes, not industrial software with a long lifespan. In this setting, the requirements can thus be quite different from those that we encounter in traditional software development.

Below, we list some limitations of MAS technologies that may explain how some requirements are badly covered, particularly regarding design and realization:

– software architects lack expertise on MAS technologies and development teams lack knowledge and training (and, for businesses, the return on investment in terms of productivity and quality remains uncertain);

– the technology still suffers from a lack of maturity and from its variety of approaches and models (and there cannot be a universal method or implementation support), which is likely to limit its ease of use;

– the tools are lacking, industrial ones in particular, all of which limits usefulness and productivity;

– the MAS technology poses problems regarding checking and validation (due, in particular, to the strong decomposition, distribution and semantic coupling), hence the importance of being able to at least organize the development with well-established methods.

### 5.3.5. A family of architectural styles

The MAS style covers a various set of properties and characteristics that we have discussed in this section. We have, however, seen that its use in the context of a development would require a number of refinements, depending on the approach chosen, business domain and design choices (for example types of agents and interaction mechanisms needed). These refinements lead to the definition of more concrete architecture styles, in practice used for a given problem. Rather than one style of architecture, it is more of a family of MAS architectural styles that exists.

This point is linked to another that we have already highlighted: there is a gap between the design and realization of MAS, which must be filled in such a way that the MAS can be produced in the context of reliable and efficient development processes. If not, there is extra work required from the developers in exchange of a lower quality of the produced software. This adds to the limitations discussed in the previous section. In the next section, we analyze the nature of this gap, then we outline a proposed solution in section 5.5.

## 5.4. The architectural gap

Figure 5.2 illustrates the sequence of activities during the development of a MAS. The design phase relies on a design method and produces an architecture of the solution using abstractions provided by an agent-based design model, the latter often being imposed by the design method. The implementation phase produces an implementation of the solution from the description of the MAS architecture.

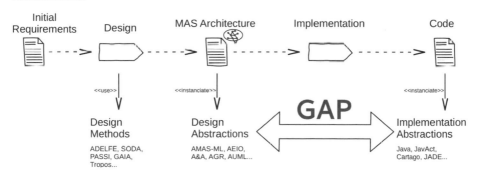

**Figure 5.2.** *The architectural gap in MAS*

However, as already mentioned, moving from design to implementation is not immediate: the distance between the abstractions that support the design and those available for implementation (i.e. those provided by the implementation support) creates a gap that must be filled. This problem has often been raised; it is presented, for example, in [BER 05]. For Molesini *et al.* [MOL 07], it resides in the fact that the MAS metamodels aims for the expression of agent-based solutions, whereas development support metamodels are generally inspired by concepts coming from the "object" style. For our part, in the previous section, we have underlined the high level of abstraction of the MAS style, the need for refinement of this style and the absence (in the general case) of an implementation support covering the real needs of the approach and the application.

The objective of this section is to highlight and discuss the nature of this architectural gap. The state of the practice is first described and then the question of the gap is analyzed from an architectural point of view.

### 5.4.1. *State of the practice*

An analysis of the practice shows that MAS development is most often based on one of the following sequences of tasks:

– choose a MAS approach, design the system, then choose an implementation support that suits the chosen approach and, finally, implement the system;

– choose an implementation support prior to design, then choose a compatible MAS approach, realize the design by taking into account constraints that result from these choices and, finally, implement the system;

– choose a MAS approach, design the system, and then implement it in an *ad hoc* way without relying on an adapted implementation support, which leads to the development parts of an implementation support to meet the needs of the chosen approach.

In the two first cases, efforts are demanded either to adapt the support to the design, i.e. to realize developments at the support level to modify the available abstractions, or add new ones, or either to adapt the design to the support, which leads to distort the design to make it correspond to the support and hence to take it away from the original intentions of the MAS designer. Generally, even if some design abstractions can be found directly in the implementation support (for example a way to program decisions using rules, or high-level interaction mechanisms such as message passing), the existing supports cannot respond specifically to all the needs resulting from the approach and design choices (at least, when the goal is to produce software of good quality and not simple prototypes).

The third case occurs for instance in the multi-agent simulation domain where the design is strongly constrained by the business domain and its specific abstractions: typically, real and complex interactions between individuals (agents) should be designed and implemented. This leads to the development *ad hoc* solutions, which is costly and rather unproductive.

### 5.4.2. *Analysis from an architectural point of view*

In this section, we study how the architectural gap appears when architectural requirements are handled and produced, as well as the links between the levels of architectural design and the skills of the designers.

#### 5.4.2.1. *"Macro" and "Micro-level" views*

For any software development, different requirements are expressed initially and then during the development. The initial requirements define the main characteristics and properties of the solution and its realization. By relying on an approach and a certain level of abstraction, MAS design initially responds to a subset of these requirements: usually, they are those concerning the system functionalities and the business domain, but also system qualities such as adaptation, extensibility and efficiency. More generally, they are those that the MAS style and the chosen approach naturally allow to answer (see section 5.3.4). Taking into account these requirements leads to architectural choices, which we call "macrolevel". Thus, the macrolevel architectural view of the solution defines the types of agents, their behaviors, the elements of the environment, the interactions, etc.

Nonetheless, architectural design is not finished at this stage. On the one hand, there are initial requirements that have yet to be taken into account. For example, they can be related to the interface with the user or the physical system, which the MAS is integrated into, or to the management of development activities (for example testability). On the other hand, the macrolevel design produces new requirements regarding its realization. For example, they may concern the needs for particular interaction means, the types of agents and their functioning, the environment dynamics, etc. These requirements relate to "operational" concerns. They originate from design choices and from the chosen approach or method. For example, some approaches impose a rule-based decision-making in agents or a particular organization model, and thus require support from the implementation to provide the adequate abstractions.

All these requirements must be considered after the macrolevel view has been made explicit. Since it is not possible, in the general case, to have an adequate development support available, taking into account these requirements leads to a new step of architectural design that we call "microlevel". Microlevel architectural design does not concern the MAS as a whole, but certain specific mechanisms that the MAS functioning relies on. It provides an operational semantics to the abstractions used at the macrolevel. The microlevel architectural view of the solution defines how some elements are refined, mainly the agents and thus their internal architecture and its connections with the other elements (for example the connections between agents and the environment). The design of such a microlevel architecture contributes to the development of a specialized support for the implementation of the targeted MAS, which can be implemented independently from the MAS itself.

The macro and microlevel categories of views reflect different points of view on the architecture, and the views result from taking into account requirements from different levels. This differentiation reflects the sequencing of design activities and the microlevel view can be considered as a kind of refinement of the macrolevel view. Figure 5.3 illustrates the development process, with the two architectural design levels previously described, the different categories of requirements specific to each of them, along with two particular activities as underlined in this section:

– requirement analysis to determine which of the initial requirements are to be taken into account at the macrolevel or at the microlevel;

– explicitation of new requirements resulting from the macrolevel design, which are to be taken into account at the microlevel.

Besides, note that the macro and microlevel views do not replace, but complement, the other architectural views traditionally present in software development.

5.4.2.2. *Separation of concerns and designer skills*

The separation between the macro- and microlevel views reflects the separation between MAS concerns and operational concerns.

Production of macro- and microlevel views calls for different skills. The macrolevel view is produced by the MAS designer, expert in MAS, approaches and development methods. The microlevel view is produced by a designer skilled in "operational" concerns: interaction protocols (communication and synchronization), scheduling, middleware, etc. Finally, the implementation must realize both the macro- and microarchitectures, but it is essential that the microlevel architectural choices are not relegated to the implementation phase.

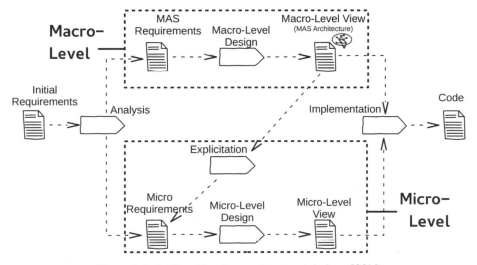

**Figure 5.3.** *Different levels in architectural design of MAS*

In practice, MAS development is frequently realized entirely by the same person, who takes on both design and implementation. This creates the risk of mixing the concerns related to the realization of the macrolevel (using an implementation support) and the microlevel (i.e. the support which the macrolevel relies on). In such a way, requirements are no longer taken into account following a well-defined order of priorities, which may damage the quality of the software. The limits of developers' skills can also cause a loss of quality of the software product. This situation is not unique to MAS development, but it is particularly significant in this context because of the plurality of concepts that the MAS paradigm provides, which is at the origin of the great diversity of tools presented in section 5.2.5.

### 5.4.3. *Assessment*

As a family of architectural styles, with common points as well as considerable differences, MAS development leads developers to refine the abstractions used in order to make them correspond to the approach and the problem. Therefore, they must work on the architecture, not of the system, but of the elements that support the abstractions that the macrolevel design relies on, i.e. the microlevel architecture. The main abstractions considered are the interaction connectors and the types of agents. In particular, types of agents serve as conceptual bridges between the macrolevel design, which uses them, and the microlevel design, which realizes them. Thus, the microlevel architectural design aims for the production of the architectural support that the macroarchitecture relies on, and, once implemented, supports the implementation of the macrolevel design.

For a better quality of MAS products, it is thus necessary to organize the development by separating the MAS development from the development of the specialized support used for its implementation. This enables us to better take into account the requirements, which are often implicit or taken into consideration too late in practice. This also highlights the existence of two separate roles in the development, which require different knowledge and skills.

### 5.5. How to fill the architectural gap

The objective of this section is to present the outline of a solution for MAS development, devised in order to achieve the objectives discussed in section 5.4.3. In addition, the objective is to facilitate reuse in a way that satisfies requirements regarding productivity and quality of the produced solution. But, the specialization of the implementation support seems to be opposite to its potential reuse. In this section, we will see that reuse may be favored in the context of an architectural design approach based on software components. For more details on this approach, readers can refer to [NOE 12].

### 5.5.1. *Limitations of existing solutions*

As presented in section 5.2.5, there are many responses to the question of the gap raised here, although this question has not actually been formulated in the terms used here. Essentially, there are agent-based supports, more or less flexible regarding the adaptation of the provided abstractions, used to implement the macrolevel design, and model-based approaches used to generate the implementation from a description of the macrolevel design. These proposals attempt to respond to the problem of the gap by proposing a unifying MAS style, i.e. using a particular refinement within the family of MAS styles. Unfortunately, as we have previously highlighted, there is such a variety of agent and environment types and interaction mechanisms that it is not possible to define abstractions suitable for every type of problem and macrolevel design.

When we are restricted to one approach, even to one domain, these solutions offer suitable abstractions, but from an architectural point of view, there are many requirements specific to the application to develop, whether they are initial requirements or requirements extracted from the design. These requirements impact the abstractions needed for implementation (e.g. runtime and connection to external systems or specific graphical interfaces), which leads to "tweaking" the implementation support to fully implement the application.

### 5.5.2. Realization of the microarchitecture

From the previous analysis, we deduce that filling the gap is an architectural question and not a question of implementation. Consequently, rather than attempting to adapt existing abstractions, we thus propose producing clean abstractions that meet the microlevel requirements and enable the macrolevel design to be implemented. From our point of view, it is the only way to address the problem satisfactorily.

This development must be supervised and must enable the design and reuse of recurrent solution elements, in particular interaction mechanisms, and the definition of elements specific to each application, in particular the types of agents. The agent itself is a software system (within a MAS) that must be the subject of a design concerning not only its functional aspects, but also its operational aspects.

As far as design is concerned, this proposal makes it possible to separate the role of the macrolevel view designer and the microlevel view designer. Also regarding implementation, the role of the MAS implementer is separated from the role of the implementer of the operational mechanisms.

### 5.5.2.1. *Challenges*

From our experience in MAS development, whether using generic implementation support (thus not directly adapted to the macrolevel design) or just a traditional programming language, and from the study of existing supports, we have identified the following challenges to best approach the design and implementation of the microlevel architecture:

– enabling the definition, implementation and reuse of mechanisms to interconnect the agents with their runtime platform during runtime[6];

– enabling the definition of types of agents, which use these mechanisms and have internal architectures;

– enabling the creation of instances of these types of agents during runtime and their dynamic connections to the platform.

The heart of the problem is in defining reusable and composable interconnection mechanisms (and not only for interaction: for example graphical interfaces and system scheduling) to define types of agents adapted to the application and usable for the macrolevel design.

### 5.5.2.2. *A component-based solution*

Existing implementation supports have an architecture in which the agents are connected to a runtime platform. To answer the challenges previously presented, it is needed to facilitate the realization of such support, adapted to the implementation of the targeted MAS application.

In practice, we suggest producing the microlevel architecture with the aid of abstractions similar to those available in component-oriented architectures and component-based programming. Our work has led us to define a new type of component, which enables us to build interconnection mechanisms composed of two parts: one linked to the platform and the other linked to the agents. Hence, types of agents are defined as a composition of the agent parts of these interconnection mechanisms and traditional components, whereas the runtime

---

6 While "environment" is a concept related to the macrolevel view, "runtime platform" relates to the microlevel view and realizes the environment as well as other operational aspects.

platform contains the other parts of interconnection mechanisms used by these types of agents (see Figure 5.4).

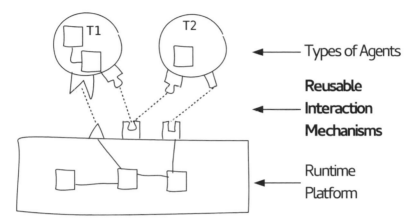

**Figure 5.4.** *The suggested abstractions for microlevel design*

These abstractions enable mechanisms specific to an application to be produced, such as graphical interfaces or environment displays, but also potentially reusable operational mechanisms, such as interaction or scheduling mechanisms and connection to the MAS environment. They also enable the instantiation of different parts of the agent, and their connection to the platform, to be automated, which simplifies development.

Hence, producing the microlevel architecture of a MAS can be reduced to:

– defining the runtime platform using components and interconnection mechanisms made available to the agents (specifically developed for the application or reused);

– defining the types of agents with components (specifically developed for the application or reused) and using the interconnection mechanisms of the platform.

All that remains then is to implement the components and interconnection mechanisms specific to the application, to define how to initialize the MAS (agent creation, in particular) and the macrolevel view can be implemented and then run, using these abstractions.

This solution was implemented in practice, and tested within the context of several research projects. In technical terms, it relies on a component model (species-based architectural design (SpeAD)), an architecture description language (species-based architectural description language (SpeADL)) and a design method (species to engineer architectures for agent frameworks (SpEArAF)), which facilitate and guide the design and implementation of MAS using these models [NOE 12]. A tool, MAY[7], which enables SpeADL to be used with Java, is made available to users in the form of an Eclipse *plugin*, as well as a collection of reusable components for various interconnection mechanisms and the internal architectures of agents and the environment.

## 5.6. Conclusion

The software systems that have to be produced are ever-growing in complexity. This complexity results from the size of problems to be resolved, from their heterogeneity and stability, and from the distribution and decentralization of the surrounding physical systems in which the software is integrated and embedded. Faced with this complexity, MAS is a style of software architecture (essentially concerning the "component and connector" category of views), more precisely a family of architectural styles, which meets certain major requirements such as complexity, distribution, scalability, dynamicity or adaptation. Choosing the MAS style implies a radical design paradigm shift. Then the main element is the agent, which is an autonomous, proactive and social entity capable of complex interactions. The unique features of this (these) style(s) are essentially the level of abstraction, the autonomy and decentralization, the nature of the coupling between the entities, and the means of composition and decomposition. Thus, MAS may provide a useful and efficient response to the architectural requirements of future computer systems.

Much work has been done in the field of AOSE but few have addressed MAS development from the viewpoint of software architectures. Now to enable true industrial use of MAS technologies, which today are still essentially confined to the academic world, it is necessary to offer solutions that reduce the effort needed for development and that increase productivity

---

7 www.irit.fr/MAY-en.

(efficient development tools, architectural patterns, methods for verification and validation, etc.), while guaranteeing a certain quality. These solutions must enable us to organize the development process by separating concerns and business skills. In addition, we consider that in order to prevent engineers facing a technological gap that is too large, solutions for MAS development must at the best integrate with more traditional approaches such as object-based or component-based approaches. Complementarily, software architects and developers should be trained.

Producing an application in the form of a MAS is an architectural design choice. However, by carrying out a state of practice and an analysis from an architectural point of view, we have observed an architectural gap between the design and the implementation of MAS. This gap can mainly be found in the distance between the concepts available for the design and those available for the implementation. In practice, it leads to the implementation of *ad hoc* and low-level constructions. Thus, a major challenge for MAS community is to propose generic and reusable solutions to fill this gap.

In the context of a recent work [NOE 12], we have suggested a solution to fill the architectural gap, which relies on the definition of two architectural views, the macrolevel view and the microlevel view, the latter supporting the realization of the former. In addition, we have proposed to build the microlevel architecture using abstractions that are similar to those available in the component-based software architecture and programming fields. These abstractions allow us to produce software units that are application specific or reusable, and facilitate the realization of the MAS and its deployment. Our proposal relies on a component model, an architecture description language, a method for the design and the implementation of MAS and a tool that allows the architecture description language to be used with Java.

## 5.7. Bibliography

[AGH 86] AGHA G., (ed.), *Actors: A Model of Concurrent Computation in Distributed Systems*, MIT Press, Cambridge, 1986.

[BER 04] BERGENTI F., GLEIZES M.-P., ZAMBONELLI F., (eds.), *Methodologies and Software Engineering for Agent Sytems*, Kluwer Academic Publishers, Dordrecht, 2004.

[BER 05] BERNON C., COSSENTINO M., PAVÓN J., "An overview of current trends in European AOSE research", *Informatica*, vol. 29, pp. 379–390, 2005.

[BRI 14]  BRIOT J.-P., "Composants et agents: évolution de la programmation et analyse comparative", *Technique et science informatiques*, Hermes-Lavoisier, vol. 33, no. 1–2, pp. 85–115, 2014.

[CLE 03]  CLEMENTS P., BACHMANN F., BASS L., *et al.*, *Documenting Software Architectures: Views and Beyond*, Addison-Wesley, Boston, 2nd edition, 2003.

[DEM 95]  DEMAZEAU Y., "From interactions to collective behaviour in agent-based systems", *Proceedings of the First European conference on cognitive science*, Saint-Malo, France, pp. 117–132, 1995.

[DIM 11]  DI MARZO SERUGENDO G., GLEIZES M.-P., KARAGEORGOS A., *Self-organising Software – From Natural to Artificial Adaptation*, Natural Computing Series, Springer, Berlin, 2011.

[FAV 04]  FAVRE J.-M., "Foundations of model (driven) (reverse) engineering: models – episode I: stories of the fidus papyrus and of the solarus", *Post-Proceedings of Dagsthul Seminar on Model Driven Reverse Engineering*, Dagstuhl, Germany, 2004.

[FER 99]  FERBER J., *Multi-agent systems: An introduction to distributed artificial intelligence*, Addison Wesley, London, 1999.

[FER 04]  FERBER J., GUTKNECHT O., MICHEL F., "From agents to organizations: an organizational view of multi-agent systems", GIORGINI P., MÜLLER J.P., ODELL J., (eds.), *Agent-Oriented Software Engineering IV, Proceedings of International Workshop AOSE 2003*, Lecture Notes in Computer Science, 2935, pp. 214–230, 2004.

[FIP 02]  FIPA, FIPA ACL Message Structure Specification, www.fipa.org/specs/fipa00061/SC00061G.html, 2002.

[FUG 98]  FUGGETTA A., PICCO G.P., VIGNA G., "Understanding code mobility", *IEEE Transactions on Software Engineering*, vol. 24, no. 5, pp. 342–361, 1998.

[GLE 08]  GLEIZES M.-P., BERNON C., MIGEON F., *et al.*, "Méthodes de développement de systèmes multi-agents", *Génie logiciel*, GL & IS, vol. 86, pp. 2–7, Septembre 2008.

[GRA 59]  GRASSÉ P.-P., "La reconstruction du nid et les coordinations interindividuelles chez Bellicositermes natalensis et Cubitermes sp. la théorie de la stigmergie: Essai d'interprétation du comportement des termites constructeurs", *Insectes sociaux*, vol. 6, no. 1, pp. 41–80, 1959.

[HEW 77]  HEWITT C., "Viewing control structures as patterns of passing messages", *Artificial Intelligence*, vol. 8, no. 3, pp. 323–364, 1977.

[KAD 11]  KADDOUM E., Optimization under constraints of distributed complex problems using cooperative self-organization, PhD thesis, Paul Sabatier University, Toulouse, 2011.

[MOL 07]  MOLESINI A., DENTI E., OMICINI A., "From AOSE methodologies to MAS infrastructures: the SODA case study", ARTIKIS A., O'HARE G., STATHIS K., VOUROS G., (eds.), *8th International Workshop "Engineering Societies in the Agents World" (ESAW'07)*, Athens, Greece, pp. 283–298, 2007.

[NOE 12]  NOEL V., Component-based software architectures and multi-agent systems: mutual and complementary contributions for supporting software development, PhD thesis, Paul Sabatier University, Toulouse, 2012.

[ODE 03]  ODELL J., VAN DYKE PARUNAK H., FLEISCHER M., "The role of roles", *Journal of Object Technology*, vol. 2, no. 1, pp. 39–51, 2003.

[OLU 07]  OLUYOMI A., KARUNASEKERA S., STERLING L., "A comprehensive view of agent-oriented patterns", *Autonomous Agents and Multi-Agent Systems*, vol. 15, pp. 337–377, Springer, 2007.

[PHA 07]  PHAN D., AMBLARD F., Eds., *Multi-agent Modelling and Simulation in the Social and Human Sciences*, Bardwell Press, http://www.bardwell-press.co.uk/, September 2007.

[PIC 09]  PICARD G., HUBNER J., BOISSIER O., *et al.*, "Reorganisation and self-organisation in multi-agent systems", *International Workshop on Organizational Modeling (ORGMOD)*, Paris, France, pp. 66–80, 2009.

[RAO 95]  RAO A.S., GEORGEFF M.P., "BDI-agents: from theory to practice", *Proceedings of the First International Conference on Multiagent Systems*, pp. 312–319, 1995.

[SHE 06]  SHEN W., HAO Q., YOON H.J., *et al.*, "Applications of agent-based systems in intelligent manufacturing: An updated review", *Advanced Engineering Informatics*, vol. 20, no. 4, pp. 415–431, 2006.

[WEI 99]  WEISS G., Ed., *Multiagent systems, a Modern Approach to Distributed Artificial Intelligence*, MIT Press, Cambridge, 1999.

[WEY 07]  WEYNS D., OMICINI A., ODELL J., "Environment as a first-class abstraction in multiagent systems", *Autonomous Agents and Multi-Agent Systems*, vol. 14, no. 1, pp. 5–30, 2007.

[WEY 10]  WEYNS D., Ed., *Architecture-Based Design of Multi-Agent Systems*, Springer, Berlin, 2010.

[WOO 09]  WOOLDRIDGE M., Ed., *An Introduction to Multiagent Systems*, John Wiley & Sons, Chichester, 2nd edition, 2009.

Chapter 6

# Software Architectures and Software Processes

Boehm [BOE 95] highlighted software product/software process duality regarding software architectures (SAs). Taking Osterweil's [OST 87] article "Software processes are software too" as a basis, he confirmed that if SAs are effective for software product reuse, they will be of real benefit for software process reuse. "If open architectures are good for software product reuse, then their process counterparts will be good for software process reuse". This chapter thus presents the evaluation of existing approaches for modeling and executing software processes based on SAs.

## 6.1. Introduction

In the software engineering field, it has long since been recognized that an application is a complex manufactured product, whose realization must be integrated within a methodological approach [COM 06]. The methodological approach is made explicit through the use of software process (SP) models.

An SP model is the description of activity sequences, resources and tools used, as well as the description of stakeholders for the realization and then the maintenance of a software product. The aim of the latter is control over the increasing complexity of software development projects.

Chapter written by Fadila AOUSSAT, Mourad Chabane OUSSALAH and Mohamed AHMED-NACER.

Software development is a complex, collective, creative and evolvable effort; consequently, the SP must provide sufficient support to be in charge of this reality of development. The quality of the SP model and the quality of its execution have a direct impact on the quality of the manufactured software product.

The richness of SPs field in terms of concepts, paradigms and languages, on the one hand, and experience and know-how [BOE 98], on the other hand, suggests the exploitation of reuse approaches for modeling SPs. The repetitiveness of tasks, significance of interactions and exploitation of recurrent structures all make up a part of the intrinsic characteristics of SPs. We mention the characteristics of SAs and are naturally oriented toward the exploration of SAs for SP modeling and reuse [AOU 10a].

SAs have contributed to the modeling of quality SPs. Indeed, the field of SAs has achieved a considerable degree of maturity and had a significant influence on the field of SPs. Hence, architectural concepts such as connectors, architectural styles and the use of languages (e.g. *Architecture Description Languages* (ADLs)) are major assets when modeling SA-based SPs.

In order to note the impact of SAs on SPs, in this chapter we present an initial contribution to the evaluation of SA-based SP modeling approaches. Hence, this chapter is organized as follows:

1) Section 6.2 is dedicated to the presentation of basic concepts from the field of SPs and summarizes the characteristics of SA-based modeling approaches studied.

2) In order to understand their reasoning and benefit from their experience in the field of SP reuse, these approaches must be evaluated and analyzed. From this perspective, we present our comparison framework in section 6.3, which offers support for the analysis and evaluation of SA-based SP modeling.

3) In section 6.4, we offer an analysis of the approaches studied, which we rely on to establish a summary and an assessment of the state of the field of SA-based SP reuse.

4) We end the chapter with a conclusion (section 6.5) summarizing the works presented and state the prospects for research.

## 6.2. Software process architectures

### 6.2.1. *Software process models: definition*

A model is an abstraction, a simplification of a system sufficient for understanding the system modeled [COM 08].

"A process model (PM) is an abstract description of an actual or proposed process that represents selected process elements that are considered important to the purpose of the model and can be enacted by a human or machine" [CUR 92].

Works on SPs are in agreement, for the most part, with the definition of the SP model. An SP model is the formalized representation of the SP; it makes the properties and variables governing the real world of development explicit.

The main objective of the SP model is to provide a more or less formal display for software development. It must deal with the expected and unexpected evolution [KAB 94] of the reality of the development, among other things.

Different SP models can describe software development from different perspectives [ACU 01]. Indeed, for the sake of clarity and precision, SP models can focus on a particular aspect of the development and relegate others to a position of secondary importance.

However, different SP modeling languages and different possible executions increase the number of existing SP models. Consequently, several SP classifications have been defined, and these classifications feature the following criteria:

    – the SP model's formalization level: non-formal, semi-formal, executable [SAN 05];

    – the SP model's central element: activity-centered, role-centered, artifact-centered, etc. [HUG 09];

    – the SP model orientation: configuration management-oriented, decision-oriented, strategy-oriented, etc. [HUG 09];

    – the type of SP modeling language used: object-oriented (OO), Petri net, rule-based languages, etc. [ACU 01, BEN 07b, ZAM 04];

– the execution type supported: distributed execution, simulation, etc. [ACU 01, BEN 07b, ZAM 01].

SP concept models vary according to their orientation; there are as many metamodels as there are SP orientations [HUG 09]. However, all these SPs are true to the same conceptual kernel (Figure 6.1: the SP is a sequence of activities, each activity needing "work product" input *(inputs)* to provide output products *(outputs)*. The SP being human-centered, an activity is under the responsibility of a role *(Role)*.

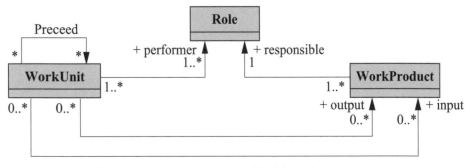

**Figure 6.1.** *The kernel meta-model of the software process*

Hence, the basic concepts of every SP model are:

– activity *(Activity)*: this represents a work unit undertaken. The successions and states of progress of activities can be described in a sequence of activities;

– work product *(Work Product)*: this represents the products manipulated. The transmissions, format, versions and storage of these products can also be processed;

– role *(Role)*: generally it describes the required or existing responsibilities and qualifications that an actor can, or must, have during the software development.

It is evident that other concepts such as strategy, organization and tool can be present in an SP metamodel. This will depend on the orientation and specialization of SP models that we want to describe.

### 6.2.2. *Modeling software architecture-based software processes*

Several SA-based SP modeling approaches have been proposed. Each approach brings a particular solution for addressing a particular concern (distribution, evolution, heterogeneity, simulation, dynamism, etc.). Nonetheless, all these approaches have a common point; they exploit architectural concepts as the basis of their solution.

In accordance with the architectural element that the approach focuses on, SA-based SP reuse approaches are classified into three categories:

– component-oriented approaches;

– connector-oriented approaches;

– configuration-oriented approaches.

The approaches studied are SP modeling and execution approaches which exploit architectural elements to promote SP reuse (Figure 6.2). In making an initial comparison, we note that these approaches are not uniform; each manipulates a number of concepts with the aim of handling specific problems. Table 6.1 summarizes these approaches and their objectives and strong points.

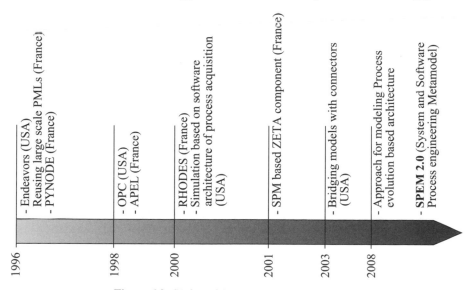

**Figure 6.2.** *SA-based SP reuse approaches studied*

According to Table 6.1, the majority of approaches do not offer a generic solution; the solutions proposed deal with particular problems and offer particular solutions, which limits the SP reuse. Nonetheless, we can make an initial classification. Indeed, we note that the oldest approaches were influenced by the industry community; hence, SP architectures are described using (OO) languages. On the other hand, the most recent approaches are instead influenced by the academic community; because of this, SP architectures are described by exploiting ADLs.

## 6.3. Comparison framework for SA-based SP model reuse solutions

As previously stated, putting a comparison framework in place is indispensable for being able to analyze SA-based SP reuse solutions. SA-based SP modeling solutions have the distinction of being at the intersection of two research fields: SP engineering and SA engineering.

Several comparison frameworks have been proposed in the SP field [ACU 01, AMB 97, BEN 07a, ZAM 01]. However, the introduction of new paradigms in the modeling and execution of SPs, such as multi-agent systems [AOU 05, WAN 02], SAs [CHO 01] and aspect-oriented programming [MIS 06], often leads to the introduction of new comparison criteria and, in some cases, imposes the definition of new comparison frameworks specific to these new paradigms.

In the confines of our work, the introduction of SAs as an SP modeling paradigm must be evaluated, hence the necessity of defining a suitable comparison framework.

The existing comparison frameworks introduce certain evaluation criteria, such as reuse or modularity [AMB 97], only, these criteria do not enable the architectural aspect of the SP to be evaluated effectively. Consequently, defining a new comparison framework is indispensable. SP architectures are above all SP models; because of this, they have the same characteristics and objectives as traditional SP models. Moreover, they are modeled by exploiting SA concepts (component, connector, configuration, etc.); they are considered SAs [AOU 11, AOU 11]; thus, they have the same characteristics and objectives as SAs.

| Approach | Objectives | Strong points | For. Mod. |
|---|---|---|---|
| Endeavors [HIT 97] | Process the *WorkFlow* processes specific to the distributed and dynamic work | Distribution via the *Web*, independent of execution platforms, graphic representation of the SP model | OO |
| PYNODE [AVR 96] | Dynamic reuse of heterogeneous components | Execution dynamic, heterogeneity of SP | OO fragments |
| SP-based configuration management [BEL 96] | Reuse of SP through versioning components | Reuse through versioning, consistency testing of the result | OO |
| OPC [GAR 98] | Dynamic reuse of heterogeneous components | Dynamic execution, heterogeneity of SP | OO fragments |
| APEL [DAM 98] | Distributed heterogeneous process execution | Distributed execution, independent of execution engines, heterogeneous SP models | OO |
| RHODES [COU 00] | Reuse of development knowledge, assistance with SP modeling | Assistance with modeling, checking of the consistency of the model | OO |
| Assembly of connector-based models [MED 03] | Definition of different connectors of models of data from development phases | Identification of rules, for moving from one data model to another, identification of common properties between the SP connectors | ADL |
| ADL ZETA for SP modeling [ALL 01] | Taking into account interactions of SP models | Definition of interaction models and interaction model types | ADL |
| SP acquisition architecture simulation [CHO 01] | Simulation, concurrency and distributed execution of acquisition models | Simulation of the execution of acquisition models (complex processes) | ADL |
| Evolution SP modeling [DAI 08] | Reuse of evolution components | Definition of a language for the description of SP architectures | ADL |
| SPEM [OMG 08] | Reuse of SP components | Metamodel definition for the reuse of SP-based components | OO |
| AoSP [AOU 10a] | Reuse of every SP-type independently of their language. | Definition of a standard SP architecture, definition of explicit connectors and SP styles | ADL |
| Abbreviations: Mod. For.: modeling formalism, App.: application | | | |

**Table 6.1.** *Summary of SA-based SP reuse approaches studied*

Our comparison framework must take into account these two axes at least: the SP axis and the SA axis. These two axes define the technical aspect of SA-based SP reuse solutions and they focus on the quantitative side of the SP architecture (Figure 6.3).

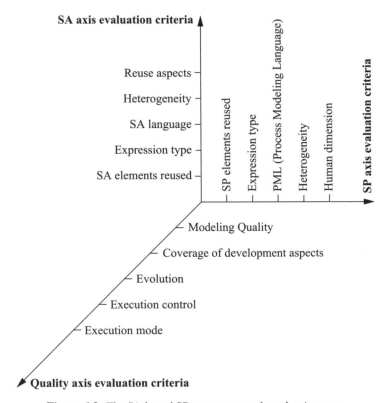

**Figure 6.3.** *The SA-based SP reuse approach evaluation axes*

The qualitative aspect must also be evaluated; hence, the third axis of our comparison framework will concern the quality aspect of the SP architecture. We define one axis for the evaluation of SP architecture quality resulting from reuse approaches, as we evaluate the SP architecture as one single entity with a certain number of quality criteria. Furthermore, most of the qualitative criteria from two domains (SA and SP) overlap and are similar.

Hence, we define the evaluation criteria according to the following axes:

– the SP axis evaluation criteria: these criteria enable the evaluation of SP concepts and languages used to describe the SP independent of the architecture vision;

– the SA axis evaluation criteria: unlike the previous characteristics, these criteria enable the evaluation of concepts and languages exploited to describe the abstract structure of the SP architecture independent of the process aspect;

– the qualitative evaluation criteria: these criteria enable the evaluation of the quality of SA-based SP models.

We detail these criteria in the following sections.

### 6.3.1. *The software process axis evaluation criteria*

These criteria define the characteristics of SP models independent of the SA vision. SA-based SPs arc first and foremost SPs; it is valid to take into account classifications and comparison frameworks already established in this field.

Table 6.2 summarizes the criteria selected to evaluate the technical aspect of reuse solutions according to the SP axis. These criteria are inspired by the classifications of Longchamps [LON 93], Accuna *et al.* [ACU 01], Conradi *et al.* [FUG 00] and Zamli [ZAM 01, ZAM 04]; hence, we evaluate them.

| |
|---|
| SP elements reused<br>- Basis (activity, role and product)<br>- Secondary (resource, actor, etc.) |
| Expression types<br>- Non-formal<br>- Semi-formal<br>- Formal |
| *Process Modeling Language* (PML)<br>- Object oriented<br>- Petri net<br>- Rule-based<br>- Functional |
| Heterogeneity<br>- Syntactic<br>- Semantic<br>- Execution platform |
| Human dimension<br>- Assistance during execution<br>- Control of human interaction |

**Table 6.2.** *SP axis evaluation criteria*

#### 6.3.1.1. *The SP elements reused*

As mentioned previously, the conceptual kernel of the SP is constituted of activity (work unit), work product and role concepts. Other elements said to be secondary can be used to describe other facets of the SP. Hence, we regroup the SP elements reused into two groups:

– basic: the "activity", "role" and "product" elements are considered basic concepts in SPs. These concepts remain the basic elements for SA-based SPs;

– secondary: these elements describe the concerns and objectives specific to certain SP model. SPs can be dedicated to configuration management, time management or development resources [GAL 00]. Additional concepts can be integrated to take into account these concerns; the "resources", "tools" and "strategy" or "guidance" concepts are some examples of secondary SP concepts.

By defining this criterion, our aim is not to identify the exact concepts manipulated by the approaches studied, but to check if SA-based modeling requires additional or specific concepts to deal with the architectural aspect.

### 6.3.1.2. *The expression type*

This criterion enables the degree of abstraction of formalisms used during SA-based SP modeling to be specified. As for SPs, according to the objective and complexity of the SP model, we distinguish several expression types. In our comparison framework, we classify SP models according to three types of formalisms:

– non-formal: SP models are described without using a strict formalism, but rather natural language-based formalisms (the objective is understanding of the SP);

– semi-formal: SP models are described graphically (the objective is structuring of the SP);

– formal: the languages used are languages with a rigorous syntax and semantic (the objective is enabling effective exploitation of the SP model by execution).

### 6.3.1.3. *The Process Modeling Language*

The *Process Modeling Language* (PML) is a language which allows SPs to be modeled. A considerable number of PMLs have been defined, exploiting different paradigms [ZAM 01]. For comparison of SP models based on architectural concepts, we use different categories of formalisms defined in the classification of Ambriola *et al.* [FUG 00]. They are as follows:

– object-oriented PML, where the PML is based on object-oriented concepts and mechanisms;

– Petri net, where the PML uses Petri nets [ZAM 01];

– rule-based, where the PML uses planning techniques based on rule-based languages;

– programming language, where the PML defines the SP model as a program by exploiting known programming languages.

### 6.3.1.4. *Heterogeneity*

Heterogeneity can be evaluated principally in distributed SP models. Indeed, the different fragments of the SP model can be heterogeneous in accordance with three levels:

– syntactic: the fragments of SP models are modeled by exploiting different PMLs;

– semantic: the fragments of SP models do not work with the same metamodel,

– execution platform: the SP fragments can be run on different execution platforms.

### 6.3.1.5. *The human dimension*

SPs are human-oriented; the tasks of reflection, analysis and creation are typically human development tasks. The influence of social and cultural practices, which are human and non-technical, on SP modeling and execution has already been highlighted [SOM 96]. Taking this dimension into account during SP architecture modeling is fundamentally important. For this, we define two criteria:

– assistance during execution: the approach must enable the identification of typically human tasks and offer suitable assistance to the producer of this task during the the SP model execution;

– control of human interaction: human interaction can determine the success of the SP model. This criterion enables evaluation of the importance given to the control of human interactions.

### 6.3.2. *The software architecture axis evaluation criteria*

In their *Framework*, Ambriola *et al.* [FUG 00] have dedicated a category "reuse" for the description of SP models; they consider reusability to be an important criterion making up part of the quality criteria of an SP.

In this chapter, we deal with SA-based SPs. These SP models exploit reusable concepts such as the component, connector or configuration. Reusability is the very essence of SAs and, by transition, the essence of SA-based SPs. Consequently, the presence of reusability in SA-based SP models is not questioned, but rather detailed. Hence, in this section, we identify the criteria which enable the type and degree of reusability of SA-based SP models to be evaluated.

In the same way as for the identification of the SP axis evaluation criteria, to identify the SA axis evaluation criteria, we draw inspiration from the *Frameworks* [BAB 04, MED 97, MEH 00] put in place in the SA field.

Table 6.3 summarizes the SA axis evaluation criteria adopted for the SP reuse approaches.

#### 6.3.2.1. *SA elements reused*

As previously defined, an SA describes the system as a set of components (calculation or storage units) that communicate with each other through the intermediary of connectors (interaction units). Most of the existing works consider "component", "connector" and "configuration" as basic concepts for SA. This assessment remains valid for SA-based SP models.

The importance of these concepts varies from one SP reuse approach to another. This variation depends on the interpretation that the author may give to the reusable entities.

In this chapter, we evaluate the use and interpretation of basic architectural elements, i.e. component, connector and configuration. Nonetheless, we introduce the "style" concept as we think it very important for SP reuse. Our objective is to evaluate the importance given to this concept in SA-based SP reuse approaches.

Even if the architectural concepts evaluated are specific to SPs, they keep the same definitions adopted by the SA community; hence:

– component: this is an entity that provides calculation and storage functionalities specific to the SPs, the component interacts with the other components to realize one or more objectives of the SP architecture;

– connector: this is an architectural construction block used to model the interactions between the SP components and to specify the rules governing these interactions;

– configuration: this displays a graph of components and connectors and defines the way in which they are related to each other;

– style: this enables capturing of the characteristics of recurrent structures and behaviors of SPs.

| |
|---|
| SA elements reused<br>- Component<br>- Connector<br>- Configuration<br>- Style |
| Expression type<br>- Implicit<br>- Predefined<br>- Explicit |
| SA languages<br>- OO language<br>- ADL specific to the SP<br>- Other ADL |
| Heterogeneity<br>- Homogeneous<br>- Heterogeneous (component, connector, configuration) |
| Reuse aspect<br>- Reuse mechanisms<br>- Storage space adopted<br>- Scope for reuse : internal or external to the system<br>- Deployment and code generation |

**Table 6.3.** *The SA axis evaluation criteria*

### 6.3.2.2. *Expression type*

The expression type of reused elements can have different forms:

– implicit: exploited but in a non-formal way, without using the modeling language, or else without having its own existence;

– predefined: the instances of predefined elements are known structures and functionalities, stored and reused;

– explicit: the instances of elements have a rigorous syntax and semantic, instances can be modified and other instances can be added.

### 6.3.2.3. *Software architecture languages*

ADLs are formalisms specific to SAs and are used to describe the structure of a system as an assembly of software elements. We hope to identify the types of languages used for the modeling of architectural concepts of SP models. For this, we use three categories:

– the OO languages: some architectures are described through the use of OO languages and exploit object mechanisms such as instancing, aggregation and heritage;

– ADLs specific to SPs: these are ADLs but specific to the description of SP architectures;

– the ADL standards: these are the languages intended for describing SA but not intended for the SP field.

### 6.3.2.4. *Heterogeneity*

SA-based SP models can be:

– heterogeneous: the SP architecture components or connectors can be heterogeneous syntactically or semantically;

– homogeneous: the SA-based SP model exploits the same concepts and language during modeling.

### 6.3.2.5. *Reuse aspects*

This criterion enables some aspects that we deem important to be evaluated to facilitate the SP reuse. Hence, we evaluate:

– the mechanisms used for effective reuse: e.g. composition and object-oriented mechanisms such as heritage and instancing;

– the storage space and storage strategies adopted: the storage spaces can be databases, files, ontologies, etc.;

– the scope for reuse [OUS 05]: we identify two levels - internal scope for reuse, where blocks are reused only by the system which has created them, and external scope for reuse, where blocks (components, connectors) can be exported and reused by other systems [OUS 05];

– the deployment and generation of the SP model: this criterion enables evaluation of the mechanisms put in place to enable generation of the final SP model.

### 6.3.3. *The quality axis evaluation criteria*

Reuse solutions must enable modeling of SA-based SPs with a certain quality.

In order to evaluate the quality of SA-based SPs modeled, we identify a number of quality criteria. Most quality criteria are common to SP models and SA. Indeed, the modeling facility, understanding and evolution are the characteristics attributable to SPs, as to SA. The possible execution modes for SP architectures are also inventoried and are inspired by the execution modes of the two fields. Nonetheless, we add the "execution control" criterion as an evaluation criterion which is specific to SPs. Table 6.4 summarizes the quality criteria adopted in order to evaluate the SA-based SP.

| Modeling qualities<br>- Modeling facility<br>- Understanding<br>- Consistency and persistence |
| --- |
| Execution mode<br>- Simulation<br>- Distributed<br>- Heterogeneous<br>- Dynamic<br>- Incremental<br>- Iterative<br>- Standard |
| Execution control |
| Evolution<br>- Static<br>- Dynamic |

**Table 6.4.** *The quality axis evaluation criteria*

### 6.3.3.1. *Modeling quality*

This criterion enables the modeling quality to be specified. This quality can be evaluated through:

– modeling facility: modeling must be easy and independent of the SP modeling language used; tools for assistance and guidance must be integrated to facilitate SP modeling;

– understanding: the modeling result must be easily understandable;

– consistency and persistence of the result: the reuse solution must allow checking of the modeling result. This option is indispensable for all the SPs and the SP architectures particularly, as SA-based SP modeling takes into account two aspects: the structure aspect and the content aspect.

### 6.3.3.2. *Execution mode*

This criterion enables the possible execution modes for an SP architecture to be specified.

We note that most execution modes for the two fields (SA and SPs) are similar. Also, in order to take into account the execution modes of agile processes, we introduce the iterative and incremental execution modes, which are considered as particular types of dynamic execution. The execution modes identified are summarized as follows:

– simulation: SP model execution simulation is a virtual execution of the SP model. The objective of simulation is to study the behavior of certain types of SP models, whose real execution is confronted with difficulties such as their complexity, feasibility, cost or execution time;

– distributed: execution occurs on distributed platforms or work environments, and enables developers to work as a team on geographically distant locations;

– heterogeneous: heterogeneous execution is often associated with distributed execution, which means that the SP models are run on heterogeneous platforms or execution engines;

– dynamic: the characteristics of this execution are that it is possible to make modifications without interrupting the SP model execution;

– incremental: considered to be a particular type of dynamic execution, the SP is modeled first and then run partially (incrementally); the initial part of the SP model concerns the activities to follow to implement the kernel functionalities. SP model layers are added, enabling other functionalities to be implemented. The objective of this execution type is to have an operational result as soon as possible in the development cycle;

– iterative: also considered to be a particular type of dynamic execution where some SP model sequences are restarted and rerun;

– standard: execution is launched once it is standard and does not belong to any of the previous categories.

### 6.3.3.3. *Execution control*

Execution control is an important aspect in the SP model. The proposed solution must enable execution control of the SP model and manage the adaptations made.

### 6.3.3.4. *Evolution*

As mentioned in the previous sections, SPs, like SA, are evolvable by nature. Hence, this criterion enables evaluation of the mechanisms put in place to promote the different types of SP evolution.

In general, two types of evolution are possible:

– static: where evolution occurs when the SP model is not run;

– dynamic: where evolution occurs during the SP model execution.

## 6.4. Evaluation of SA-based SP modeling and execution approaches

### 6.4.1. *SP axis evaluation of SA-based SP reuse approaches*

Table 6.5 summarizes the characteristics of the SP axis evaluation of SA-based SP reuse approaches studied.

By analyzing the information collected from reuse solutions studied, we make the following observations:

– The SP model concepts modeled are generally basic and limited, for the most part, to the "activity" and "product" concepts. We also noticed that the approaches studied have not exploited additional concepts in order to introduce the architectural concepts, except the approach of Belkhatir *et al.* [BEL 96], which exploits "versioning" in the reuse of its components.

| Approach | SP elements reused | | T.E. | PML | Hetero | Human dimension | |
|---|---|---|---|---|---|---|---|
| | Basic | Additional | | | geneity | Assistance | I.T. |
| Endeavors | Activity, product | Resource | Formal, semi-formal | ObjV, Lisp (OO) | Execution platform | R.G. | - |
| PYNODE | Activity, product, role | - | Formal, semi-formal | Any | Syntactic | R.G. | - |
| SP-based conf. man. | Activity, product | Version | Formal, semi-formal | Depends on the model | Heterogeneous | Checking the consistency | - |
| OPC | Activity, product, role | - | Formal, semi-formal | Any | Syntactic | R.G. | - |
| APEL | Activity, Product | Agent | Formal, semi-formal | Depends on the model | Syntactic, semantic | R. G. | - |
| RHODES | Activity, product, role | Strategy | Formal, semi-formal | PBOOL+ (OO) | Homogeneous | R.G., detection of inconsistencies | - |
| Simulation of acquisition processes | Depends on the model | | | | | R. G. | - |
| Assembly of connector-based models | Activity, product | Phase | Non formal | - | - | - | - |
| ADL ZETA-based SP interactions | Activity, product | - | Formal | Depends on the model | Syntactic, semantic | R.G. | - |
| Evolution SP modeling | Activity, product | - | Semi-formal | Petri net | Homogeneous | R.G. | - |
| SPEM | Activity, product, role | Depends on the environment working with SPEM | | | | | |
| AoSP | Activity, Product | - - | Formal Semi-formal | Depends on the deployment of the SP architecture | | R. G., connectors human-centered | |
| *Abbreviations*: E.T.: expression type, conf. man.: configuration management, I.T.: interaction control, G.R.: graphic representation. | | | | | | | |

**Table 6.5.** *SP axis evaluation of SA-based SP reuse approaches*

– Most approaches offer solutions that model formal SPs: the objective is often to provide executable SP models. These formal models are often combined with semi-formal models, translated as graphic representations of the SP model. The objective of the graphic representations is to provide assistance for developers and SP model users.

– Analyzing the SP modeling languages exploited, we noticed that there are no particular trends and no language is mentioned as a language facilitating the SP model reuse, except the PBOOL+ language of the RHODES environment [COU 00], which integrates the notion of component procedure and SP reuse. It should also be noted that in some solutions, the SP modeling language has no influence and the components are black boxes, as in Alloui and Oquendo's approach [ALL 01] and the approach of Medvidovic *et al.* [MED 03], and in some cases the SP modeling language is not the same as mentioned in Choi and Scatcchi's approach [CHO 01].

– Regarding human interaction, no particular assistance is provided; human interaction occurs implicitly and is not controlled by any specific mechanism, which can be considered a disadvantage particularly for SP models with strong human interaction, except for the RHODES environment which provides assistance in the form of "sketches" and "textual guidance" [CRE 97]. The AoSP approach offers a more substantial solution, as it offers explicitly human-centered connectors for human interaction management. These human-centered connectors capture and suggest the best behaviors to adopt when faced with situations which may present themselves during the SP model execution. These connectors enable not only the reuse of human know-how, but also facilitate this reuse by being explicit and independent of the SP modeling language. AoSP also offers the use of an SP ontology [AOU 10b, AOU 12a] and several optimal solution search algorithms to assist developers of new SPs.

– Analyzing the SPEM approach, we noticed that its unique feature of being a standard meta-model potentially allows it to cover the modeling of a large range of SPs. Hence, additional concepts and expression types, and the value of other criteria, will depend on the environment working with the SPEM metamodel, giving it the ability to model every type of SP. The AoSP approach also has this unique feature; its SP models work with the SPEM metamodel, giving them a certain standardization.

| Approach | SA elements reused | | | | Language | Reuse aspects | |
|---|---|---|---|---|---|---|---|
| | Com. | Conn. | Conf. | Style | SA | Mechanisms | Storage space |
| Endeavors | Exp. | Imp. | Imp. | - | Object-oriented | Instancing, composition, multiple heritage | ASCII files |
| PYNODE | Exp. | Imp. | Imp. | - | Object-oriented | Instancing, dynamic composition, heritage | Component BD |
| SP-based conf. management | Exp. | Imp. | Imp. | - | PIL (object-oriented) | Instancing, composition, heritage, versioning | DBMS component database |
| OPC | Exp. | Imp. | Imp. | - | Object-oriented | Instancing, composition, dynamic, heritage | Component-based |
| APEL | Exp. | Imp. | Imp. | - | Object-oriented | - | No component storage |
| RHODES | Exp. | Imp. | Imp. | - | PBOOL+ (object-oriented) | Instancing, composition, modular heritage, subtyping | Based on components managed by the SGBD OO jasmin |
| Simulation of acquisition processes | Exp. | Exp. | Exp. | - | HLA (ADL) | Composition | Library of acquisition models |
| Assembly of connector-based models | Imp. | Pre. | Imp. | - | - | - | - |
| ADL ZETA-based SP interactions | Exp. | Exp. | Exp. | I.T. | ZETA (ADL) | Instancing | No storage |
| Evolution SP modeling | Exp. | pre. | Exp. | - | EPCDL (ADL for SP) | Composition | component-based |
| SPEM | Exp. | Imp. | Imp. | - | Object-oriented | Composition, instancing | - |
| AoSP | Explicit | | | | ADL ACME | Composition, instancing | Domain ontology |
| Abbreviations: Com.: Component, Conn.: Connector, Conf.: Configuration, Imp.: Implicit, Exp.: explicit, Pre.: predefined, I.T.: *interaction type*, PIL: *process interconnection language* HLA: *high level architecture*, EPCDL: *evolution process component description language*. | | | | | | | |

**Table 6.6.** *SA axis evaluation of SA-based SP reuse approaches*

### 6.4.2. *SA axis evaluation of SA-based SP reuse approaches*

Analyzing the characteristics of reuse solutions studied from the SA axis, we found the following:

– The basic brick for SP reuse is the component. Most approaches studied define the SP component as a unit of work, or a series of units of work. Hence, the SP component can be an SP fragment or an SP model [AOU 09]. The SP component is explicit in most cases, except in the approach of Medvidovic *et al.* [MED 03], which focuses on the connectors and has not made its components explicit. Also, even if details regarding the components of the approaches of Alloui and Oquendo [ALL 01] and Choi and Scacchi [CHO 01] are not provided, they are explicit.

– Regarding the connector concept, we noted that it is implicit in less recent approaches; it is considered a data transmission or execution flow. These transmissions have not received much attention; their management is integrated in the SP and depends on the language and nature of the SP. However, the most recent solutions give more importance to the connectors, which are either predefined or explicit. However, it must be noted that the definitions adopted regarding these connectors cannot be generalized. Indeed, depending on the SP modeling language and author's interpretation, these connectors remain specific and the scope for reuse remains limited to the originating environment.

– Also, in most solutions, the notion of configuration is implicit. In the former approaches, the implicit configuration results from the exploitation of the graphic representation of the SP model, but without processing or analysis in particular at the structural level. The configuration becomes explicit with the use of ADLs, which enable its elements to be described and the assembly constraints governing it to be specified.

– The notion of architectural style is not exploited in the approaches studied, except Alloui and Oquendo's [ALL 01] approach, which defined connector types *(interaction type)* and configuration types *(container type)* which are basic elements of an architectural style. Nonetheless, according to this approach, the component has no type as it is considered a black box. Description of these element types is possible thankfully due to the use of the ADL ZETA, which is a tool of SA engineering.

– Unlike the previous approaches, the architectural elements of the AoSP approach are all explicit, including the style. Indeed, different styles specific to SP architectures have been identified, increasing reuse of SP architectures. Hence, different SP architecture styles have been defined, the most important contribution being the definition of two categories of styles: structural styles, inspired by software lifecycles and recurrent sequences, and the execution styles capturing the recurrent execution strategies adopted by the heads of software projects [AOU 12b].

– Analyzing the SA languages column, we found that these languages are generally OO languages; reuse is realized by exploiting operations offered by the object paradigm (instancing, heritage, multiple heritage, composition, etc.). Use of ADL has only made an appearance in the most recent approaches, which has allowed these approaches to make all the architectural elements explicit.

– Although most of the solutions offer component stores (component-based, libraries, etc.) to allow SP component reuse, the detail of the organization or classification of SP components is not presented. What we take from this is that most approaches have not explored the possibility of exploiting a domain ontology; this choice is justified by the orientation adopted by the solutions proposed. Indeed, for SP reuse, the approaches studied exploit the architectural concepts, the exploitation of a domain ontology requires another vision and other mechanisms for reuse (knowledge procedure, inference, reasoning, etc.). This is not the objective of these solutions, except for the AoSP approach, which proposed a domain ontology, "SPEMontology", and was able to combine the two visions: the SP architecture vision and the SP knowledge vision. Indeed, the ontology is exploited to infer and extract SP knowledge; this knowledge is exploited to deploy the SP architecture and then generate the final SP model.

– During modeling of the SA-based SP, the approaches studied implement homogeneous SA; in other words, they use the same language for all the components and connectors, except for in the approach of Medvidovic et al. [MED 03], where the connectors can be described in natural language or in programming language.

– The scope for reuse of all the approaches studied is limited to internal reuse; the solutions proposed process internal concerns and do not focus on the genericity and portability of architectural elements. The AoSP approach is an exception, as the SP architecture is modeled in ADL ACME, which makes it independent of SP modeling languages. Furthermore, according to the deployment program, the SP architecture can be deployed using different SP modeling languages.

– The approaches studied do not propose the deployment of SA; indeed, most solutions are based on the component concept; the configuration concept is implicit, which does not allow an architecture deployment to be proposed, except for the AoSP approach, which offers several deployment modes [AOU 12b]. It even offers deployments specific to SPs, such as iterative deployment and incremental deployment.

### 6.4.2.1. *Other interpretations of architectural concept terms*

Some approaches use the terms "architecture", "connector", "component", "configuration" and "family" (which are used to designate a style in the ACME studio environment) but not to describe the architectural elements; their interpretations depend on the solutions proposed:

– *Component:* in APEL [DAM 98], the component is a product component and not a procedure component. It displays a part of the SP modeling and execution environment; the objective is to have the models and distributed executions of several local SP models.

– *Connector:* APEL [DAM 98] uses the term "connector" to describe the links (*data flow* and *control flow*) between the SP activities, while the SP description is not component-oriented.

– *Architecture:* Borsoi *et al.* [BOR 08] use the term "architecture" to describe the general structure of the SP not in terms of components, but in terms of "phase" and "activity", which will be refined during a modeling process defined in its SP modeling solution.

– *Family:* Belkhatir *et al.* [BEL 96] define the *family* concept (which can imply architectural styles) to describe a *process unit* (a component) and its versions.

– *Configuration:* SPEM [OMG 08] uses the term "configuration" to describe the elements – not necessarily architectural elements – enabling an SP to be described.

### 6.4.3. *Quality axis evaluation of SA-based SP reuse approaches*

Table 6.7 summarizes the qualitative characteristics of approaches studied. Analyzing this information, we found the following:

– The proposed solutions focus on the modeling of executable SPs. Furthermore, the use of SA-based modeling has made it possible to put in place distributed, heterogeneous SP models and to offer dynamic execution options. The characteristics of distribution, heterogeneity and evolution are considered indispensable for quality SPs. These characteristics were able to be provided by exploiting the SA concepts.

– The solutions studied do not offer incremental or iterative execution, except for the AoSP approach, which allows the deployment and generation of iterative and incremental SP models.

– Execution control is the responsibility of the SP administrator. Apart from the graphic representations used during execution control, no mechanism specific to human-centered execution is made explicit, which increases the dependence of execution quality on human abilities. As mentioned before, the AoSP approach retained processing particular to the interactions and human execution; hence, human-centered connectors were defined in order to guide and facilitate human interactions.

– SAs contribute to improve the understanding of SP models and increasing the modeling facility. Indeed, the formalization and then the use of the abstract structure of the SP model, in addition to the separation between interactions and processing, improve the readability and, consequently, the understanding and modeling facility of the SP. These two criteria (understanding and modeling facility) have not been evaluated in detail, as we think that the contribution of SAs to their improvement is the same for all the approaches studied. On the other hand, these two criteria are subject to other influences such as the type of SP modeling language used.

– Regarding the criterion of coverage of development aspects, the SA does not influence this criterion as the latter depends exclusively on the SP modeling language used.

– Most of the approaches studied, which model formal SPs, implement evolution mechanisms (dynamic or static). However, these mechanisms are varied, and vary from one approach to another. Furthermore, the evolutions offered are all situated at the content level and not at the structural level, whereas it is possible to exploit the evolution of the SP model at the structural level (architectural vision of the SP model).

| Approach | Modeling quality | Execution mode | Execution test. | Evolution | |
|---|---|---|---|---|---|
| | | | | Static | Dynamic |
| Endeavors | - | Dynamic, heterogeneous, distributed | - | Flexible integration mechanisms for incremental evolution of the support | Dynamic declarations, modifications to fields, states, variables and object interfaces |
| PYNODE | Dynamic composition protocol | Dynamic, heterogeneous, distributed | - | - | - |
| SP-based configuration management | Compatibility control, consistency during component selection | Distributed | - | Versioning | - |
| OPC | - | Dynamic, heterogeneous, distributed | State diag. transition | - | Dynamic composition, change in the state diag. transitions |
| APEL | - | Dynamic, distributed | - | - | - |
| RHODES | Detect inconsistencies, manage indeterminism | Standard | - | Polymorphism and subtyping mechanism | - |
| Simulation of acquisition SP | - | Simulation | - | - | - |
| Assembly of connector-based models | - | - | - | - | - |
| ADL ZETA-based Interactions SP | - | Standard | Interaction models | - | - |
| Evolution SP modeling | - | Standard | Petri net | - | Component evolutions |
| SPEM | - | Non defined | Object-oriented | Class *variability* | - |
| AoSP | Use of configurations, styles and connectors | Dynamic, heterogeneous, distributed | Explicit connectors | Component search mechanism | Partial deployment mechanisms, incremental or iterative |

**Table 6.7.** *Quality axis evaluation of SA-based SP reuse approaches*

### 6.4.4. *Assessment and discussions*

From the study of these approaches from the SP axis, we found that there is no particular trend in the field of SA-based SP reuse: the concepts manipulated are often kernel concepts of the SP, and in most cases, there are no concepts specific to SP reuse. Also, the SP modeling languages are known languages in the field of SP engineering and not specific to SP reuse.

However, we noted that one of the basic specificities of SPs, i.e. the human dimension, has not had much attention. Assistance for developers and the control of human interactions in particular have not been effectively managed.

Also, from the study of these approaches from the SP axis, we noted that the architectural concepts as defined in the SA field are not well exploited for SP reuse. The connector, configuration and style concepts are badly exploited or, in some cases, they are not used at all. Interpretation of the connectors remains linked to the SP modeling language used, which does not allow for strongly reusable connectors. Exploitation of the configuration concept remains implicit, when using graphic representations without reflection or reasoning at this level during the modeling phase.

SP architectural styles have not yet made their appearance. The solutions proposed remain intuitive and are based on the need for reuse of a certain type of SP rather than on the definition of a relevant methodology for global SP reuse. The novelty of this field (SP architectures) is one justification for these deficiencies; the solutions proposed are often component-based modeling solutions, which explain the weakness of the connector, configuration and style concepts in these approaches.

On the other hand, from the qualitative side, the benefit of SAs for SP modeling is considerable. The exploitation of SAs for SP modeling contributes to the understanding and facilitation of the SP modeling. Also, SAs offer mechanisms that enable easier modeling of distributed SPs, either heterogeneous or dynamic.

The most relevant approach, offering a solution which can generally be adapted to every SP type, is the AoSP approach. Modeling SPs as SA and explicitly taking into account most SA concepts have made it possible to improve the quality of SPs modeled. Indeed, AoSP has made it possible to increase the understanding and the modeling facility of SPs through exploitation of the SP configuration and SP style during the modeling phase. It has also enabled agility (required by agile methods) and execution control (required by traditional methods) to be combined, by retaining processing particular to interactions, and this, by defining explicit connectors independent of all SP modeling languages. Unlike other approaches, the AoSP approach has dealt with human interactions by defining explicit human-centered connectors; the latter ensure suitable processing in order to facilitate decision-making and ensure the progress of the SP model execution.

Finally, AoSP is the only approach that offers SP architectural styles. These SP styles have allowed the specificities of recurrent structures and assemblies to be capitalized on, have enabled the specificities of execution strategies to be captured and adopted by the heads of software projects and are often the result of know-how acquired through long experience in the field of SP executions.

## 6.5. Conclusion

The modeling and improvement of SPs is a current research subject; technological and commercial competition between software developers, the pressures of the software market (fast, high-quality and low-cost production), as well as the technological advances that must continually be taken into account, all drive the improvement of SP models.

Exploiting the advances in the field of SAs for the benefit of the SP field is the solution studied in this chapter. Hence, we have addressed the evaluation of SA-based SP reuse approaches. Initially, we summarized the most significant approaches, which have brought solutions as varied as they are interesting. In order to understand the characteristics of these approaches, we have defined our own comparison framework. Our comparison framework is inspired by the comparison frameworks established both in the SP field and the SA field.

Our comparison framework was organized as follows:

– an axis describing the technical aspects of reuse solutions according to the SP view;

– an axis describing the technical aspects of reuse solutions according to the SA view;

– an axis describing the qualitative aspect of reuse solutions.

Hence, based on the criteria of this comparison framework, we studied a set of works emerging from the SA-based SP reuse field. We have concluded this study by giving our own evaluation of these reuse approaches.

Based on our comparison framework, we can suggest a summary assessment. What we essentially take from this assessment is that the exploitation of SA is considered a very promising solution for the quality modeling of SP. It enables not only the reusability of SP models, but also other quality criteria, to be increased (e.g. understanding and the modeling facility). Also, this approach (SA-based SP modeling) can be applied to different SPs using different concepts or modeling languages, which increases its effectiveness as a reuse solution. Nonetheless, it should be noted that in the approaches studied, exploitation of architectural concepts was not optimal. Some concepts, such as the architectural styles, are not exploited; solutions using all the architectural elements at once are rare. AoSP is the only approach to offer a full SA-based reuse solution and to optimally exploit the advantages and concepts of SAs.

Integration of SA as an SP modeling paradigm in its own right has made it possible to give an unedited and innovative vision not only for modeling SPs, but also for their execution. After the study and recognition of the potential of SA, it is clear that exploiting SA constitutes a promising solution to current concerns in the field of SPs, and opens the door for original and innovative proposals.

## 6.6. Bibliography

[ACU 01] ACUÑA S.T., FERRÉ X., *Multi-Conference on Systemics, Cybernetics and Informatics (ISAS-SCI)*, IIIS, pp. 237–242, 2001.

[ALL 01] ALLOUI I., OQUENDO F., "Supporting decentralised software-intensive processes using ZETA component-based architecture description language", *International Conference on Enterprise Information Systems*, pp. 207–215, 2001.

[AMB 97] AMBRIOLA V., CONRADI R., FUGGETTA A., "Assessing process-centered software engineering environments", *ACM Transactions on Software Engineering Methodology*, vol. 6, no. 3, pp. 283–328, 1997.

[AOU 11] AOUSSAT F., OUSSALAH M., AHMED-NACER M., "Méta modélisation architecturale des procédés logiciels", *5ème Conférence francophone sur les architectures logicielles (CAL '11)*, Lille, France, 2011.

[AOU 05]  AOUSSAT F., AHMED-NACER M., "Modeling and executing software processes based on intelligent agents", *International Conference on Enterprise Information Systems*, Miami, FL, pp. 441–444, 2005.

[AOU 09]  AOUSSAT F., AHMED-NACER M., "Reusing heterogeneous software process models", *IEEE Symposium on Computers and Communications (ISCC '09)*, Sousse, Tunisia, pp. 291–294, 2009.

[AOU 10a]  AOUSSAT F., AHMED-NACER M., OUSSALAH M., "Reusing approach for software processes based on software architectures", *International Conference on Enterprise Information Systems*, Funchal, Madeira, Portugal, pp. 366–369, 2010.

[AOU 10b]  AOUSSAT F., OUSSALAH M., AHMED-NACER M., "Approach for software processes models reusing based software architecture", *The 15th World Multi-Conference on Systemics, Cybernetics and Informatics (WMSCI '10)*, Orlando, FL, pp. 291–294, 2010.

[AOU 11]  AOUSSAT F., OUSSALAH M., AHMED-NACER M., "SPEM extension with software process architectural concepts", *IEEE International Computer Software and Applications Conference*, Munich, Germany, pp. 215–223, 2011.

[AOU 12a]  AOUSSAT F., OUSSALAH M., AHMED-NACER M., "Domain ontology for software process description", *7th International Conference on Evaluation of Novel Software Approaches to Software Engineering*, Wroclaw, Poland, pp. 366–369, 2012.

[AOU 12b]  AOUSSAT F., OUSSALAH M., AHMED-NACER M., "SPEMOntology for software process reusing", *Computing and Informatics Journal*, vol. 33–1, pp. 343–354, 2012. Available at: www.cai.sk/ojs/index.php/cai.

[AVR 96]  AVRILIONIS D., BELKHATIR N., CUNIN P Y., "A unified framework for software process enactment and improvement", *4th International Conference on the Software Process*, Washington, WA, IEEE Computer Society, p. 102, 1996.

[BAB 04]  BABAR M.A., ZHU L., JEFFERY R., "A framework for classifying and comparing software architecture evaluation methods", *Proceedings of the 2004 Australian Software Engineering Conference*, Washington, WA, IEEE Computer Society, p. 309, 2004.

[BEL 96]  BELKHATIR N., ESTUBLIER J., "Supporting reuse and configuration for large scale software process models", *10th International Software Process Workshop*, Washington, WA, IEEE Computer Society, p. 35, 1996.

[BEN 07a]  BENDRAOU R., GERVAIS M.P., "A framework for classifying and comparing process technology domains", *Proceedings of the International Conference on Software Engineering Advances (ICSEA '07)*, Washington, WA, IEEE Computer Society, p. 5, 2007.

[BEN 07b]  BENDRAOU R., SADOVYKH A., GERVAIS M.P., *et al.*, "Software process modeling and execution: the UML4SPM to WS-BPEL approach", *EUROMICRO-SEAA*, pp. 314–321, 2007.

[BOE 95]  BOEHM B., "Software process architectures", *Software Architecture Workshop, 17th International Conference on Software Engineering*, pp. 351–365, 1995.

[BOE 98]  BOEHM B., EGYED A., KWAN J., *et al.*, "Using the WinWin spiral model: a case study", *Computer*, vol. 31, pp. 33–44, July 1998.

[BOR 08] BORSOI B.T., BECERRA J.L.R., "A method to define an object oriented software process architecture.", *Australian Software Engineering Conference*, IEEE Computer Society, pp. 650–655, 2008.

[CHO 01] CHOI S.J., SCACCHI W., "Modeling and simulating software acquisition process architectures", *Journal of Systems and Software*, vol. 59, no. 3, pp. 343–354, 2001.

[COM 06] COMBEMALE B., CRÉGUT X., CAPLAIN A., *et al.*, "Modélisation rigoureuse en SPEM de procédé de développement", *Langages et Modèles à Objets (LMO)*, Nêmes, France, pp. 135–150, 2006.

[COM 08] COMBEMALE B., Approche de métamodélisation pour la simulation et la vérification de modèle: application à l'ingénierie des procédés, PhD Thesis, National Polytechnic Institute of Toulouse, France, 2008.

[COU 00] COULETTE B., THU T.D., CRÉGUT X., *et al.*, "RHODES, a process component centered software engineering environment", *International Conference on Enterprise Information Systems*, pp. 253–260, 2000.

[CRE 97] CREGUT X., COULETTE B., "PBOOL: an object-oriented language for definition and reuse of enactable processes", *Software – Concepts and Tools*, vol. 18, no. 2, pp. 47–62, 1997.

[CUR 92] CURTIS B., KELLNER M.I., OVER J., "Process modeling", *Communications of the ACM*, vol. 35, no. 9, pp. 75–90, 1992.

[DAI 08] DAI F., LI T., ZHAO N., *et al.*, "Evolution process component composition based on process architecture", *International Symposium on Intelligent Information Technology Application Workshops*, Washington, WA, IEEE Computer Society, pp. 1097–1100, 2008.

[DAM 98] DAMI S., ESTUBLIER J., AMIOUR M., "Apel: a graphical yet executable formalism for process modeling.", *Automated Software Engineering*, vol. 5, no. 1, pp. 61–96, 1998.

[FUG 00] FUGGETTA A., "Software process: a roadmap", *Proceedings of the Conference on the Future of Software Engineering*, New York, NY, pp. 25–34, 2000.

[GAL 00] GALLARDO L., Une approche à base de composants pour la modélisation des procédés logiciels, PhD Thesis, University of Grenoble, France, 2000.

[GAR 98] GARY K., LINDQUIST T.E., KOEHNEMANN H., *et al.*, "Component-based software process support", *Automated Software Engineering*, vol. 8, pp. 196–199, 1998.

[HIT 97] HITOMI A.S., BOLCER G.A., TAYLOR R.N., "Endeavors: a process system infrastructure", *19th international Conference on Software Engineering*, New York, NY, pp. 598–599, 1997.

[HUG 09] HUG C., Méthode, modèles et outil pour la méta-modélisation des processus d'ingénierie de systèmes d'information, PhD Thesis, Joseph Fourier University, Grenoble I, France, 2009.

[KAB 94] KABA A., TANKOANO J., DERNIAME J., "Une approche incrémentale d'évolution des modèles de procédés de développement de logiciels", *Actes du deuxième colloque africain sur la recherche en informatique*, pp. 35–365, Paris, France, 1994.

[LON 93] LONCHAMP J., "A structured conceptual and terminological framework for software process engineering", *International Conference on Software Process*, Berlin, Germany, pp. 41–53, 1993.

[MED 97] MEDVIDOVIC N., TAYLOR R.N., "A framework for classifying and comparing architecture description languages", *ACM SIGSOFT Software Engineering Notes*, vol. 22, no. 6, pp. 60–76, 1997.

[MED 03] MEDVIDOVIC N., GRÜNBACHER P., EGYED A., *et al.*, "Bridging models across the software lifecycle", *Journal of System and Software*, vol. 68, pp. 199–215, December 2003.

[MEH 00] MEHTA N.R., MEDVIDOVIC N., PHADKE S., "Towards a taxonomy of software connectors", *22nd International Conference on Software Engineering*, Limerick, Ireland, pp. 178–187, 2000.

[MIS 06] MISHALI O., KATZ S., "Using aspects to support the software process: XP over Eclipse", *5th International Conference on Aspect-Oriented Software Development*, Bonn, Germany, pp. 169–179, 2006.

[OMG 08] OMG, OBJECT MANAGEMENT GROUP, "Software & Systems Process Engineering Metamodel, v2.0", 2008. Available at http://www.omg.org/spec/SPEM/2.0/PDF/.

[OST 87] OSTERWEIL L., "Software processes are software too", *9th International Conference on Software Engineering*, Monterey, CA, pp. 2–13, 1987.

[OUS 05] OUSSALAH M., *Ingénierie des composants logiciels, Principes et fondements*, Genie Logiciel, Vuibert, 2005.

[SAN 05] SANLAVILLE S.D., Environnement de procédé extensible pour l'orchestration. Application aux services web, PhD Thesis, Joseph Fourier University, Grenoble, France, 2005.

[SOM 96] SOMMERVILLE I., RODDEN T., "Human, social and organisational influences on the software process", *Software Process*, vol. 4, pp. 194–199, 1996.

[WAN 02] WANG A.I., "A process centred environment for cooperative software engineering", *14th International Conference on Software Engineering and Knowledge Engineering*, Ischia, Italy, pp. 469–472, 2002.

[ZAM 01] ZAMLI K.Z., LEE P.A., "Taxonomy of process modeling languages", *IEEE International Conference on Computer Systems and Applications*, pp. 435–437, 2001.

[ZAM 04] ZAMLI K.Z., "A survey and analysis of process modeling languages", *Malaysian Journal of Computer Science*, vol. 17, no. 2, pp. 68–89, 2004.

# List of Authors

Mathieu ACHER
INRIA/IRISA
Rennes
France

Mohamed AHMED-NACER
USTHB
Alger
Algeria

Fadila AOUSSAT
LINA
University of Nantes
France

Jean-Paul ARCANGELI
IRIT
Paul Sabatier University
Toulouse
France

Philippe COLLET
I3S
Nice Sophia Antipolis
France

Philippe LAHIRE
I3S
Nice Sophia Antipolis
France

Nicole LÉVY
CEDRIC
CNAM
Paris
France

Francisca LOSAVIO
MoST
Central University of Venezuela
Caracas
Venezuela

Frédéric MIGEON
IRIT
Paul Sabatier University
Toulouse
France

Victor NOËL
IRIT
Paul Sabatier University
Toulouse
France

Mourad Chabane OUSSALAH
LINA
University of Nantes
France

Yann POLLET
CEDRIC
CNAM
Paris
France

Adel SMEDA
University of Tripoli
Libya

Chouki TIBERMACINE
LIRMM
Montpellier
France

# Index